The State of Strategy

THE STATE OF STRATEGY

A Harvard Business Review Paperback

Harvard Business Review paperback No. 90082

ISBN 0-87584-271-2

P03046

The *Harvard Business Review* articles in this collection are
available individually. Discounts apply to quantity purchases.
For information and ordering contact Operations Department,
Harvard Business School Publishing Division, Boston, MA
02163. Telephone: (617) 495-6192, 9 a.m. to 5 p.m. EST. Fax:
(617) 495-6985, 24 hours a day.

Editor's Note: Some articles in this book may have been written before authors and editors began to take into consideration the role of women in management. We hope the archaic
usage representing all managers as male does not detract from
the usefulness of the collection.

Contents

Gaining Strategic Advantage

The Core Competence of the Corporation
C.K. Prahalad and Gary Hamel
3

A company that remains organized around strategic business units jeopardizes its ability to compete. Today, competitiveness derives from a company's ability to identify and nurture its core competencies.

Strategic Intent
Gary Hamel and C.K. Prahalad
17

Current models of strategy lead to a pathology of surrender, say the authors. They offer a new model based on a simple principle.

Time—The Next Source of Competitive Advantage
George Stalk, Jr.
31

As a strategic weapon, time is the equivalent of money, productivity, quality—even innovation.

Strategic Choices for Newly Opened Markets
Joel A. Bleeke
43

The author offers strategies for survival *and* success in new markets, based on the competitive dynamics of deregulated industries.

How An Industry Builds Political Advantage
David B. Yoffie
51

Companies can strengthen their competitive advantage by forging closer ties to government. Indeed, in many industries a business strategy that doesn't include a political strategy is doomed.

From Competitive Advantage to Corporate Strategy
Michael E. Porter
59

The renowned strategist delineates the four basic types of corporate strategy and how to choose one.

Getting Back to Strategy
Kenichi Ohmae
77

Meeting and beating the competition is an unambiguous way of defining the goal of strategy. It's also the wrong way.

Must Finance and Strategy Clash?
Patrick Barwise, Paul R. Marsh, and Robin Wensley
85

Marketing and finance often reach different conclusions about long-term strategic investments. When each analysis is done correctly, however, the results should be complementary, not contradictory.

vi

Planning Corporate Strategy

**Putting Strategy into
Shareholder Value Analysis**
George S. Day and Liam Fahey
93

Value analysis is a useful planning tool—when rigorous strategy analysis goes with it.

**Matrix Management:
Not a Structure, a Frame of Mind**
*Christopher A. Bartlett
and Sumantra Ghoshal*
101

In many corporations, strategic thinking has outdistanced organizational capability. Here's how to keep a company light on its feet.

Crafting Strategy
Henry Mintzberg
109

Strategy emerges less from rational control and systematic analysis than from intimacy and harmony with the materials at hand—in short, through craft rather than linear planning.

Strategic Planning—Forward In Reverse?
Robert H. Hayes
119

Planning is better grounded if it proceeds from means to ends rather than from the conventional ends to means.

Planning as Learning
Arie P. de Geus
129

If the planning process doesn't result in institutional learning, it isn't worth the trouble.

Many Best Ways to Make Strategy
Michael Goold and Andrew Campbell
135

The strategy planning process in large diversified companies can successfully be organized in radically different ways, depending upon the nature of the company.

Uses and Misuses of Strategic Planning
Daniel H. Gray
143

Contrary to popular belief, there's nothing wrong with formal strategic planning. Rather, problems arise because of faulty preparation and implementation.

Gaining
Strategic Advantage

HBR

The Core Competence of the Corporation

by C.K. Prahalad and Gary Hamel

The most powerful way to prevail in global competition is still invisible to many companies. During the 1980s, top executives were judged on their ability to restructure, declutter, and delayer their corporations. In the 1990s, they'll be judged on their ability to identify, cultivate, and exploit the core competencies that make growth possible – indeed, they'll have to rethink the concept of the corporation itself.

Consider the last ten years of GTE and NEC. In the early 1980s, GTE was well positioned to become a major player in the evolving information technology industry. It was active in telecommunications. Its operations spanned a variety of businesses including telephones, switching and transmission systems, digital PABX, semiconductors, packet switching, satellites, defense systems, and lighting products. And GTE's Entertainment Products Group, which pro-

C.K. Prahalad is professor of corporate strategy and international business at the University of Michigan. Gary Hamel is lecturer in business policy and management at the London Business School. Their most recent HBR article, "Strategic Intent" (May-June 1989), won the 1989 McKinsey Award for excellence. This article is based on research funded by the Gatsby Charitable Foundation.

duced Sylvania color TVs, had a position in related display technologies. In 1980, GTE's sales were $9.98 billion, and net cash flow was $1.73 billion. NEC, in contrast, was much smaller, at $3.8 billion in sales. It had a comparable technological base and computer businesses, but it had no experience as an operating telecommunications company.

Yet look at the positions of GTE and NEC in 1988. GTE's 1988 sales were $16.46 billion, and NEC's sales were considerably higher at $21.89 billion. GTE has, in effect, become a telephone operating company with a position in defense and lighting products. GTE's other businesses are small in global terms. GTE has divested Sylvania TV and Telenet, put switching, transmission, and digital PABX into joint ventures, and closed down semiconductors. As a result, the international position of GTE has eroded. Non-U.S. revenue as a percent of total revenue dropped from 20% to 15% between 1980 and 1988.

NEC has emerged as the world leader in semiconductors and as a first-tier player in telecommunications products and computers. It has consolidated its position in mainframe computers. It has moved beyond public switching and transmission to include such lifestyle products as mobile telephones, facsimile machines, and laptop computers – bridging the gap between telecommunications and office automation. NEC is the only company in the world to be in the top five in revenue in telecommunications, semiconductors, and mainframes. Why did these two companies, starting with comparable business portfolios, perform so differently? Largely because NEC conceived of itself in terms of "core competencies," and GTE did not.

Rethinking the Corporation

Once, the diversified corporation could simply point its business units at particular end product markets and admonish them to become world leaders. But with market boundaries changing ever more quickly, targets are elusive and capture is at best temporary. A few companies have proven themselves adept at inventing new markets, quickly entering emerging markets, and dramatically shifting patterns of customer choice in established markets. These are the ones to emulate. The critical task for management is to create an organization capable of infusing products with irresistible functionality or, better yet, creating products that customers need but have not yet even imagined.

This is a deceptively difficult task. Ultimately, it requires radical change in the management of major companies. It means, first of all, that top managements of Western companies must assume responsibility for competitive decline. Everyone knows about high interest rates, Japanese protectionism, outdated antitrust laws, obstreperous unions, and impatient investors. What is harder to see, or harder to acknowledge, is how little added momentum companies actually get from political or macroeconomic "relief." Both the theory and practice of Western management have created a drag on our forward motion. It is the principles of management that are in need of reform.

NEC versus GTE, again, is instructive and only one of many such comparative cases we analyzed to understand the changing basis for global leadership. Early in the 1970s, NEC articulated a strategic intent to exploit the convergence of computing and communications, what it called "C&C."[1] Success, top management reckoned, would hinge on acquiring *competencies*, particularly in semiconductors. Management adopted an appropriate "strategic architecture," summarized by C&C, and then communicated its intent to the whole organization and the outside world during the mid-1970s.

NEC constituted a "C&C Committee" of top managers to oversee the development of core products and core competencies. NEC put in place coordination groups and committees that cut across the interests of individual businesses. Consistent with its strategic architecture, NEC shifted enormous resources to strengthen its position in components and central processors. By using collaborative arrangements to multiply internal resources, NEC was able to accumulate a broad array of core competencies.

NEC carefully identified three interrelated streams of technological and market evolution. Top management determined that computing would evolve from large mainframes to distributed processing, components from simple ICs to VLSI, and communications from mechanical cross-bar exchange to complex digital systems we now call ISDN. As things evolved further, NEC reasoned, the computing, communications, and components businesses would so overlap that it would be very hard to distinguish among them, and that there would be enormous opportunities for any company that had built the competencies needed to serve all three markets.

NEC top management determined that semiconductors would be the company's most important

> ## Why did NEC enter myriad alliances between 1980 and 1988? To learn and absorb other companies' skills.

"core product." It entered into myriad strategic alliances – over 100 as of 1987 – aimed at building competencies rapidly and at low cost. In mainframe computers, its most noted relationship was with Honeywell and Bull. Almost all the collaborative arrangements in the semiconductor-component field were oriented toward technology access. As they entered collaborative arrangements, NEC's operating managers understood the rationale for these alliances and the goal of internalizing partner skills. NEC's director of research summed up its competence acquisition during the 1970s and 1980s this way: "From an investment standpoint, it was much quicker and cheaper to use foreign technology. There wasn't a need for us to develop new ideas."

No such clarity of strategic intent and strategic architecture appeared to exist at GTE. Although senior executives discussed the implications of the evolving information technology industry, no commonly accepted view of which competencies would be re-

---

1. For a fuller discussion, see our article, "Strategic Intent" HBR May-June 1989, p. 63.

quired to compete in that industry were communicated widely. While significant staff work was done to identify key technologies, senior line managers continued to act as if they were managing independent business units. Decentralization made it difficult to focus on core competencies. Instead, individual businesses became increasingly dependent on outsiders for critical skills, and collaboration became a route to staged exits. Today, with a new management team in place, GTE has repositioned itself to apply its competencies to emerging markets in telecommunications services.

The Roots of Competitive Advantage

The distinction we observed in the way NEC and GTE conceived of themselves – a portfolio of competencies versus a portfolio of businesses – was repeated across many industries. From 1980 to 1988, Canon grew by 264%, Honda by 200%. Compare that with Xerox and Chrysler. And if Western managers were once anxious about the low cost and high quality of Japanese imports, they are now overwhelmed by the pace at which Japanese rivals are inventing new markets, creating new products, and enhancing them. Canon has given us personal copiers; Honda has moved from motorcycles to four-wheel off-road buggies. Sony developed the 8mm camcorder, Yamaha, the digital piano. Komatsu developed an underwater remote-controlled bulldozer, while Casio's latest gambit is a small-screen color LCD television. Who would have anticipated the evolution of these vanguard markets?

In more established markets, the Japanese challenge has been just as disquieting. Japanese companies are generating a blizzard of features and functional enhancements that bring technological sophistication to everyday products. Japanese car producers have been pioneering four-wheel steering, four-valve-per-cylinder engines, in-car navigation systems, and sophisticated electronic engine-management

systems. On the strength of its product features, Canon is now a player in facsimile transmission machines, desktop laser printers, even semiconductor manufacturing equipment.

In the short run, a company's competitiveness derives from the price/performance attributes of current products. But the survivors of the first wave of global competition, Western and Japanese alike, are all converging on similar and formidable standards for product cost and quality – minimum hurdles for continued competition, but less and less important as sources of differential advantage. In the long run, competitiveness derives from an ability to build, at lower cost and more speedily than competitors, the core competencies that spawn unanticipated products. The real sources of advantage are to be found in management's ability to consolidate corporatewide technologies and production skills into competencies that empower individual businesses to adapt quickly to changing opportunities.

Senior executives who claim that they cannot build core competencies either because they feel the autonomy of business units is sacrosanct or because

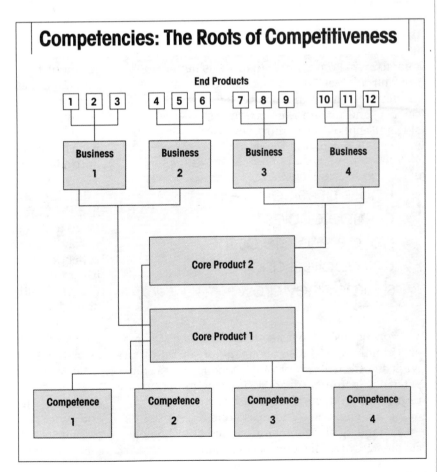

Competencies: The Roots of Competitiveness

End Products

| 1 | 2 | 3 | | 4 | 5 | 6 | | 7 | 8 | 9 | | 10 | 11 | 12 |

Business 1   Business 2   Business 3   Business 4

Core Product 2

Core Product 1

Competence 1   Competence 2   Competence 3   Competence 4

The corporation, like a tree, grows from its roots. Core products are nourished by competencies and engender business units, whose fruit are end products.

their feet are held to the quarterly budget fire should think again. The problem in many Western companies is not that their senior executives are any less capable than those in Japan nor that Japanese companies possess greater technical capabilities. Instead, it is their adherence to a concept of the corporation that unnecessarily limits the ability of individual businesses to fully exploit the deep reservoir of technological capability that many American and European companies possess.

The diversified corporation is a large tree. The trunk and major limbs are core products, the smaller branches are business units; the leaves, flowers, and fruit are end products. The root system that provides nourishment, sustenance, and stability is the core competence. You can miss the strength of competitors by looking only at their end products, in the same way you miss the strength of a tree if you look only at its leaves. (See the chart "Competencies: The Roots of Competitiveness.")

Core competencies are the collective learning in the organization, especially how to coordinate diverse production skills and integrate multiple streams of technologies. Consider Sony's capacity to miniaturize or Philips's optical-media expertise. The theoretical knowledge to put a radio on a chip does not in itself assure a company the skill to produce a miniature radio no bigger than a business card. To bring off this feat, Casio must harmonize know-how in miniaturization, microprocessor design, material science, and ultrathin precision casing—the same skills it applies in its miniature card calculators, pocket TVs, and digital watches.

> ## Unlike physical assets, competencies do not deteriorate as they are applied and shared. They grow.

If core competence is about harmonizing streams of technology, it is also about the organization of work and the delivery of value. Among Sony's competencies is miniaturization. To bring miniaturization to its products, Sony must ensure that technologists, engineers, and marketers have a shared understanding of customer needs and of technological possibilities. The force of core competence is felt as decisively in services as in manufacturing. Citicorp was ahead of others investing in an operating system that allowed it to participate in world mar-

kets 24 hours a day. Its competence in systems has provided the company the means to differentiate itself from many financial service institutions.

Core competence is communication, involvement, and a deep commitment to working across organizational boundaries. It involves many levels of people and all functions. World-class research in, for example, lasers or ceramics can take place in corporate laboratories without having an impact on any of the businesses of the company. The skills that together constitute core competence must coalesce around individuals whose efforts are not so narrowly focused that they cannot recognize the opportunities for blending their functional expertise with those of others in new and interesting ways.

Core competence does not diminish with use. Unlike physical assets, which do deteriorate over time, competencies are enhanced as they are applied and shared. But competencies still need to be nurtured and protected; knowledge fades if it is not used. Competencies are the glue that binds existing businesses. They are also the engine for new business development. Patterns of diversification and market entry may be guided by them, not just by the attractiveness of markets.

Consider 3M's competence with sticky tape. In dreaming up businesses as diverse as "Post-it" notes, magnetic tape, photographic film, pressure-sensitive tapes, and coated abrasives, the company has brought to bear widely shared competencies in substrates, coatings, and adhesives and devised various ways to combine them. Indeed, 3M has invested consistently in them. What seems to be an extremely diversified portfolio of businesses belies a few shared core competencies.

In contrast, there are major companies that have had the potential to build core competencies but failed to do so because top management was unable to conceive of the company as anything other than a collection of discrete businesses. GE sold much of its consumer electronics business to Thomson of France, arguing that it was becoming increasingly difficult to maintain its competitiveness in this sector. That was undoubtedly so, but it is ironic that it sold several key businesses to competitors who were already competence leaders—Black & Decker in small electrical motors, and Thomson, which was eager to build its competence in microelectronics and had learned from the Japanese that a position in consumer electronics was vital to this challenge.

Management trapped in the strategic business unit (SBU) mind-set almost inevitably finds its individual businesses dependent on external sources for critical components, such as motors or compressors. But these are not just components. They are core products that contribute to the competitiveness of a wide range of end products. They are the physical embodiments of core competencies.

How Not to Think of Competence

Since companies are in a race to build the competencies that determine global leadership, successful companies have stopped imagining themselves as bundles of businesses making products. Canon, Honda, Casio, or NEC may seem to preside over portfolios of businesses unrelated in terms of customers, distribution channels, and merchandising strategy. Indeed, they have portfolios that may seem idiosyncratic at times: NEC is the only global company to be among leaders in computing, telecommunications, and semiconductors *and* to have a thriving consumer electronics business.

But looks are deceiving. In NEC, digital technology, especially VLSI and systems integration skills, is fundamental. In the core competencies underlying them, disparate businesses become coherent. It is Honda's core competence in engines and power trains that gives it a distinctive advantage in car, motorcycle, lawn mower, and generator businesses. Canon's core competencies in optics, imaging, and

> Cultivating core competence does *not* mean outspending rivals on R&D or getting businesses to become more vertically integrated.

microprocessor controls have enabled it to enter, even dominate, markets as seemingly diverse as copiers, laser printers, cameras, and image scanners. Philips worked for more than 15 years to perfect its optical-media (laser disc) competence, as did JVC in building a leading position in video recording. Other examples of core competencies might include mechantronics (the ability to marry mechanical and electronic engineering), video displays, bioengineering, and microelectronics. In the early stages of its competence building, Philips could not have imagined all the products that would be spawned by its optical-media competence, nor could JVC have anticipated miniature camcorders when it first began exploring videotape technologies.

Unlike the battle for global brand dominance, which is visible in the world's broadcast and print media and is aimed at building global "share of mind," the battle to build world-class competencies is invisible to people who aren't deliberately looking for it. Top management often tracks the cost and quality of competitors' products, yet how many managers untangle the web of alliances their Japanese competitors have constructed to acquire competencies at low cost? In how many Western boardrooms is there an explicit, shared understanding of the competencies the company must build for world leadership? Indeed, how many senior executives discuss the crucial distinction between competitive strategy at the level of a business and competitive strategy at the level of an entire company?

Let us be clear. Cultivating core competence does *not* mean outspending rivals on research and development. In 1983, when Canon surpassed Xerox in worldwide unit market share in the copier business, its R&D budget in reprographics was but a small fraction of Xerox's. Over the past 20 years, NEC has spent less on R&D as a percentage of sales than almost all of its American and European competitors.

Nor does core competence mean shared costs, as when two or more SBUs use a common facility—a plant, service facility, or sales force—or share a common component. The gains of sharing may be substantial, but the search for shared costs is typically a post hoc effort to rationalize production across existing businesses, not a premeditated effort to build the competencies out of which the businesses themselves grow.

Building core competencies is more ambitious and different than integrating vertically, moreover. Managers deciding whether to make or buy will start with end products and look upstream to the efficiencies of the supply chain and downstream toward distribution and customers. They do not take inventory of skills and look forward to applying them in nontraditional ways. (Of course, decisions about competencies *do* provide a logic for vertical integration. Canon is not particularly integrated in its copier business, except in those aspects of the vertical chain that support the competencies it regards as critical.)

Identifying Core Competencies—And Losing Them

At least three tests can be applied to identify core competencies in a company. First, a core competence provides potential access to a wide variety of markets. Competence in display systems, for example, enables a company to participate in such diverse businesses as calculators, miniature TV sets, monitors for laptop computers, and automotive dashboards—which is why Casio's entry into the handheld TV market was predictable. Second, a core competence should make a significant contribution to the perceived customer benefits of the end product. Clearly, Honda's engine expertise fills this bill.

Finally, a core competence should be difficult for competitors to imitate. And it *will* be difficult if it is a complex harmonization of individual technologies and production skills. A rival might acquire some of the technologies that comprise the core competence, but it will find it more difficult to duplicate the more or less comprehensive pattern of internal coordination and learning. JVC's decision in the early 1960s to pursue the development of a videotape competence passed the three tests outlined here. RCA's decision in the late 1970s to develop a stylus-based video turntable system did not.

Few companies are likely to build world leadership in more than five or six fundamental competencies. A company that compiles a list of 20 to 30 capabilities has probably not produced a list of core competencies. Still, it is probably a good discipline to generate a list of this sort and to see aggregate capabilities as building blocks. This tends to prompt the search for licensing deals and alliances through which the company may acquire, at low cost, the missing pieces.

Most Western companies hardly think about competitiveness in these terms at all. It is time to take a tough-minded look at the risks they are running. Companies that judge competitiveness, their own and their competitors', primarily in terms of the price/performance of end products are courting the erosion of core competencies—or making too little effort to enhance them. The embedded skills that give rise to the next generation of competitive products cannot be "rented in" by outsourcing and OEM-supply relationships. In our view, too many compa-

> ## Unlike Chrysler, Honda would never yield manufacturing responsibility for its engines— much less design of them.

nies have unwittingly surrendered core competencies when they cut internal investment in what they mistakenly thought were just "cost centers" in favor of outside suppliers.

Consider Chrysler. Unlike Honda, it has tended to view engines and power trains as simply one more component. Chrysler is becoming increasingly dependent on Mitsubishi and Hyundai: between 1985

and 1987, the number of outsourced engines went from 252,000 to 382,000. It is difficult to imagine Honda yielding manufacturing responsibility, much less design, of so critical a part of a car's function to an outside company—which is why Honda has made such an enormous commitment to Formula One auto racing. Honda has been able to pool its engine-related technologies; it has parlayed these into a corporatewide competency from which it develops world-beating products, despite R&D budgets smaller than those of GM and Toyota.

Of course, it is perfectly possible for a company to have a competitive product line up but be a laggard in developing core competencies—at least for a while. If a company wanted to enter the copier business today, it would find a dozen Japanese companies more than willing to supply copiers on the basis of an OEM private label. But when fundamental technologies changed or if its supplier decided to enter the market directly and become a competitor, that company's product line, along with all of its investments in marketing and distribution, could be vulnerable. Outsourcing can provide a shortcut to a more competitive product, but it typically contributes little to building the people-embodied skills that are needed to sustain product leadership.

Nor is it possible for a company to have an intelligent alliance or sourcing strategy if it has not made a choice about where it will build competence leadership. Clearly, Japanese companies have benefited from alliances. They've used them to learn from Western partners who were not fully committed to preserving core competencies of their own. As we've argued in these pages before, learning within an alliance takes a positive commitment of resources—travel, a pool of dedicated people, test-bed facilities, time to internalize and test what has been learned.[2] A company may not make this effort if it doesn't have clear goals for competence building.

Another way of losing is forgoing opportunities to establish competencies that are evolving in existing businesses. In the 1970s and 1980s, many American and European companies—like GE, Motorola, GTE, Thorn, and GEC—chose to exit the color television business, which they regarded as mature. If by "mature" they meant that they had run out of new product ideas at precisely the moment global rivals had targeted the TV business for entry, then yes, the industry was mature. But it certainly wasn't mature in the sense that all opportunities to enhance and apply video-based competencies had been exhausted.

In ridding themselves of their television businesses, these companies failed to distinguish be-

---

2. "Collaborate with Your Competitors and Win," HBR January-February 1989, p. 133, with Yves L. Doz.

tween divesting the business and destroying their video media-based competencies. They not only got out of the TV business but they also closed the door on a whole stream of future opportunities reliant on video-based competencies. The television industry, considered by many U.S. companies in the 1970s to be unattractive, is today the focus of a fierce public policy debate about the inability of U.S. corporations to benefit from the $20-billion-a-year opportunity that HDTV will represent in the mid- to late 1990s. Ironically, the U.S. government is being asked to fund a massive research project—in effect, to compensate U.S. companies for their failure to preserve critical core competencies when they had the chance.

In contrast, one can see a company like Sony reducing its emphasis on VCRs (where it has not been very successful and where Korean companies now threaten), without reducing its commitment to video-related competencies. Sony's Betamax led to a debacle. But it emerged with its videotape recording competencies intact and is currently challenging Matsushita in the 8mm camcorder market.

There are two clear lessons here. First, the costs of losing a core competence can be only partly calculated in advance. The baby may be thrown out with the bath water in divestment decisions. Second, since core competencies are built through a process of continuous improvement and enhancement that may span a decade or longer, a company that has failed to invest in core competence building will find it very difficult to enter an emerging market, unless, of course, it will be content simply to serve as a distribution channel.

American semiconductor companies like Motorola learned this painful lesson when they elected to forgo direct participation in the 256k generation of DRAM chips. Having skipped this round, Motorola, like most of its American competitors, needed a large infusion of technical help from Japanese partners to rejoin the battle in the 1-megabyte generation. When it comes to core competencies, it is difficult to get off the train, walk to the next station, and then reboard.

From Core Competencies to Core Products

The tangible link between identified core competencies and end products is what we call the core products—the physical embodiments of one or more core competencies. Honda's engines, for example, are core products, linchpins between design and development skills that ultimately lead to a proliferation of end products. Core products are the components or subassemblies that actually contribute to the value of the end products. Thinking in terms of core products forces a company to distinguish between the brand share it achieves in end product markets (for example, 40% of the U.S. refrigerator market) and the manufacturing share it achieves in any particular core product (for example, 5% of the world share of compressor output).

Canon is reputed to have an 84% world manufacturing share in desktop laser printer "engines," even though its brand share in the laser printer business is minuscule. Similarly, Matsushita has a world manufacturing share of about 45% in key VCR components, far in excess of its brand share (Panasonic, JVC, and others) of 20%. And Matsushita has a commanding core product share in compressors worldwide, estimated at 40%, even though its brand share in both the air-conditioning and refrigerator businesses is quite small.

> **Maintain world manufacturing dominance in core products, and you reserve the power to shape the evolution of end products.**

It is essential to make this distinction between core competencies, core products, and end products because global competition is played out by different rules and for different stakes at each level. To build or defend leadership over the long term, a corporation will probably be a winner at each level. At the level of core competence, the goal is to build world leadership in the design and development of a particular class of product functionality—be it compact data storage and retrieval, as with Philips's optical-media competence, or compactness and ease of use, as with Sony's micromotors and microprocessor controls.

To sustain leadership in their chosen core competence areas, these companies *seek to maximize their world manufacturing share in core products*. The manufacture of core products for a wide variety of external (and internal) customers yields the revenue and market feedback that, at least partly, determines the pace at which core competencies can be enhanced and extended. This thinking was behind JVC's decision in the mid-1970s to establish VCR supply relationships with leading national consumer electronics companies in Europe and the United States. In supplying Thomson, Thorn, and Telefunken (all independent companies at that time) as well as U.S. partners, JVC was able to gain the cash and the diversity of market experience that ultimately enabled it to outpace Philips and Sony. (Philips developed videotape competencies in parallel with JVC, but it failed to build a worldwide network of OEM relationships that would have allowed it to accelerate the refinement of its videotape competence through the sale of core products.)

JVC's success has not been lost on Korean companies like Goldstar, Sam Sung, Kia, and Daewoo, who are building core product leadership in areas as diverse as displays, semiconductors, and automotive engines through their OEM-supply contracts with Western companies. Their avowed goal is to capture investment initiative away from potential competitors, often U.S. companies. In doing so, they accelerate their competence-building efforts while "hollowing out" their competitors. By focusing on competence and embedding it in core products, Asian competitors have built up advantages in component markets first and have then leveraged off their superior products to move downstream to build brand share. And they are not likely to remain the low-cost suppliers forever. As their reputation for brand leadership is consolidated, they may well gain price leadership. Honda has proven this with its Acura line, and other Japanese car makers are following suit.

Control over core products is critical for other reasons. A dominant position in core products allows a company to shape the evolution of applications and end markets. Such compact audio disc-related core products as data drives and lasers have enabled Sony and Philips to influence the evolution of the computer-peripheral business in optical-media storage. As a company multiplies the number of application arenas for its core products, it can consistently reduce the cost, time, and risk in new product development. In short, well-targeted core products can lead to economies of scale *and* scope.

The Tyranny of the SBU

The new terms of competitive engagement cannot be understood using analytical tools devised to manage the diversified corporation of 20 years ago, when competition was primarily domestic (GE versus Westinghouse, General Motors versus Ford) and all the key players were speaking the language of the same business schools and consultancies. Old prescriptions have potentially toxic side effects. The need for new principles is most obvious in companies organized exclusively according to the logic of SBUs. The implications of the two alternate concepts of the corporation are summarized in "Two Concepts of the Corporation: SBU or Core Competence."

Obviously, diversified corporations have a portfolio of products and a portfolio of businesses. But we believe in a view of the company as a portfolio of competencies as well. U.S. companies do not lack the technical resources to build competencies, but their top management often lacks the vision to build them and the administrative means for assembling resources spread across multiple businesses. A shift in commitment will inevitably influence patterns of diversification, skill deployment, resource allocation priorities, and approaches to alliances and outsourcing.

We have described the three different planes on which battles for global leadership are waged: core competence, core products, and end products. A corporation has

Two Concepts of the Corporation: SBU or Core Competence

	SBU	Core Competence
Basis for competition	Competitiveness of today's products	Interfirm competition to build competencies
Corporate structure	Portfolio of businesses related in product-market terms	Portfolio of competencies, core products, and businesses
Status of the business unit	Autonomy is sacrosanct; the SBU "owns" all resources other than cash	SBU is a potential reservoir of core competencies
Resource allocation	Discrete businesses are the unit of analysis; capital is allocated business by business	Businesses and competencies are the unit of analysis: top management allocates capital and talent
Value added of top management	Optimizing corporate returns through capital allocation trade-offs among businesses	Enunciating strategic architecture and building competencies to secure the future

to know whether it is winning or losing on each plane. By sheer weight of investment, a company might be able to beat its rivals to blue-sky technologies yet still lose the race to build core competence leadership. If a company is winning the race to build core competencies (as opposed to building leadership in a few technologies), it will almost certainly outpace rivals in new business development. If a company is winning the race to capture world manufacturing share in core products, it will probably outpace rivals in improving product features and the price/performance ratio.

Determining whether one is winning or losing end product battles is more difficult because measures of product market share do not necessarily reflect various companies' underlying competitiveness. Indeed, companies that attempt to build market share by relying on the competitiveness of others, rather than investing in core competencies and world coreproduct leadership, may be treading on quicksand. In the race for global brand dominance, companies like 3M, Black & Decker, Canon, Honda, NEC, and Citicorp have built global brand umbrellas by proliferating products out of their core competencies. This has allowed their individual businesses to build image, customer loyalty, and access to distribution channels.

When you think about this reconceptualization of the corporation, the primacy of the SBU—an organizational dogma for a generation—is now clearly an anachronism. Where the SBU is an article of faith, resistance to the seductions of decentralization can seem heretical. In many companies, the SBU prism means that only one plane of the global competitive battle, the battle to put competitive products on the shelf *today*, is visible to top management. What are the costs of this distortion?

Underinvestment in Developing Core Competencies and Core Products. When the organization is conceived of as a multiplicity of SBUs, no single business may feel responsible for maintaining a viable position in core products nor be able to justify the investment required to build world leadership in some core competence. In the absence of a more comprehensive view imposed by corporate management, SBU managers will tend to underinvest. Recently, companies such as Kodak and Philips have recognized this as a potential problem and have begun searching for new organizational forms that will allow them to develop and manufacture core products for both internal and external customers.

SBU managers have traditionally conceived of competitors in the same way they've seen themselves. On the whole, they've failed to note the emphasis Asian competitors were placing on building leadership in core products or to understand the criti-cal linkage between world manufacturing leadership and the ability to sustain development pace in core competence. They've failed to pursue OEM-supply opportunities or to look across their various product divisions in an attempt to identify opportunities for coordinated initiatives.

Imprisoned Resources. As an SBU evolves, it often develops unique competencies. Typically, the people who embody this competence are seen as the sole property of the business in which they grew up. The manager of another SBU who asks to borrow talented people is likely to get a cold rebuff. SBU managers are not only unwilling to lend their competence carriers but they may actually hide talent to prevent its redeployment in the pursuit of new opportunites. This may be compared to residents of an underdeveloped country hiding most of their cash under their mattresses. The benefits of competencies, like the benefits of the money supply, depend on the velocity of their circulation as well as on the size of the stock the company holds.

Western companies have traditionally had an advantage in the stock of skills they possess. But have they been able to reconfigure them quickly to re-

> How strange that SBU managers should be made to compete for corporate cash but never for key people.

spond to new opportunities? Canon, NEC, and Honda have had a lesser stock of the people and technologies that compose core competencies but could move them much quicker from one business unit to another. Corporate R&D spending at Canon is not fully indicative of the size of Canon's core competence stock and tells the casual observer nothing about the velocity with which Canon is able to move core competencies to exploit opportunities.

When competencies become imprisoned, the people who carry the competencies do not get assigned to the most exciting opportunities, and their skills begin to atrophy. Only by fully leveraging core competencies can small companies like Canon afford to compete with industry giants like Xerox. How strange that SBU managers, who are perfectly willing to compete for cash in the capital budgeting process, are unwilling to compete for people—the company's most precious asset. We find it ironic that top management devotes so much attention to the capital budgeting process yet typically has no comparable mechanism for allocating the human skills that embody core competencies. Top managers are sel-

Vickers Learns the Value of Strategic Architecture

The idea that top management should develop a corporate strategy for acquiring and deploying core competencies is relatively new in most U.S. companies. There are a few exceptions. An early convert was Trinova (previously Libbey Owens Ford), a Toledo-based corporation, which enjoys a worldwide position in power and motion controls and engineered plastics. One of its major divisions is Vickers, a premier supplier of hydraulics components like valves, pumps, actuators, and filtration devices to aerospace, marine, defense, automotive, earth-moving, and industrial markets.

Vickers saw the potential for a transformation of its traditional business with the application of electronics disciplines in combination with its traditional technologies. The goal was "to ensure that change in technology does not displace Vickers from its customers." This, to be sure, was initially a defensive move: Vickers recognized that unless it acquired new skills, it could not protect existing markets or capitalize on new growth opportunities. Managers at Vickers attempted to conceptualize the likely evolution of (a) technologies relevant to the power and motion control business, (b) functionalities that would satisfy emerging customer needs, and (c) new competencies needed to creatively manage the marriage of technology and customer needs.

Despite pressure for short-term earnings, top management looked to a 10- to 15-year time horizon in developing a map of emerging customer needs, changing technologies, and the core competencies that would be necessary to bridge the gap between the two. Its slogan was "Into the 21st Century." (A simplified version of the overall architecture developed is shown here.)

Vickers is currently in fluid-power components. The architecture identifies two additional competencies, electric-power components and electronic controls. A systems integration capability that would unite hardware, software, and service was also targeted for development.

The strategic architecture, as illustrated by the Vickers example, is not a forecast of specific products or specific technologies but a broad map of the evolving linkages between customer functionality requirements, potential technologies, and core competencies. It assumes that products and systems cannot be defined with certainty for the future but that preempting competitors in the development of new markets requires an early start to building core competencies. The strategic architecture developed by Vickers, while describing the future in competence terms, also provides the basis for making "here and now" decisions about product priorities, acquisitions, alliances, and recruitment.

Since 1986, Vickers has made more than ten clearly targeted acquisitions, each one focused on a specific component or technology gap identified in the overall architecture. The architecture is also the basis for internal development of new competencies. Vickers has undertaken, in parallel, a reorganization to enable the integration of electronics and electrical capabilities with mechanical-based competencies. We believe that it will take another two to three years before Vickers reaps the total benefits from developing the strategic architecture, communicating it widely to all its employees, customers, and investors, and building administrative systems consistent with the architecture.

Vickers Map of Competencies

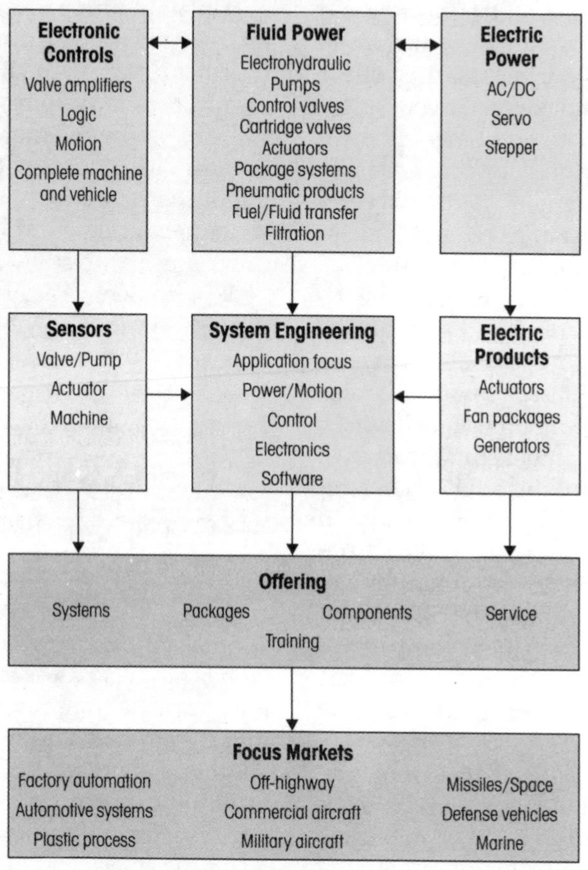

Electronic Controls
Valve amplifiers
Logic
Motion
Complete machine and vehicle

Fluid Power
Electrohydraulic Pumps
Control valves
Cartridge valves
Actuators
Package systems
Pneumatic products
Fuel/Fluid transfer
Filtration

Electric Power
AC/DC
Servo
Stepper

Sensors
Valve/Pump
Actuator
Machine

System Engineering
Application focus
Power/Motion
Control
Electronics
Software

Electric Products
Actuators
Fan packages
Generators

Offering
Systems   Packages   Components   Service
Training

Focus Markets
Factory automation   Off-highway   Missiles/Space
Automotive systems   Commercial aircraft   Defense vehicles
Plastic process   Military aircraft   Marine

dom able to look four or five levels down into the organization, identify the people who embody critical competencies, and move them across organizational boundaries.

Bounded Innovation. If core competencies are not recognized, individual SBUs will pursue only those innovation opportunities that are close at hand—marginal product-line extensions or geographic expansions. Hybrid opportunities like fax machines, laptop computers, hand-held televisions, or portable music keyboards will emerge only when managers take off their SBU blinkers. Remember, Canon appeared to be in the camera business at the time it was preparing to become a world leader in copiers. Conceiving of the corporation in terms of core competencies widens the domain of innovation.

Developing Strategic Architecture

The fragmentation of core competencies becomes inevitable when a diversified company's information systems, patterns of communication, career paths, managerial rewards, and processes of strategy development do not transcend SBU lines. We believe that senior management should spend a significant amount of its time developing a corporatewide strategic architecture that establishes objectives for competence building. A strategic architecture is a road map of the future that identifies which core competencies to build and their constituent technologies.

By providing an impetus for learning from alliances and a focus for internal development efforts, a strategic architecture like NEC's C&C can dramatically reduce the investment needed to secure future market leadership. How can a company make partnerships intelligently without a clear understanding of the core competencies it is trying to build and those it is attempting to prevent from being unintentionally transferred?

Of course, all of this begs the question of what a strategic architecture should look like. The answer will be different for every company. But it is helpful to think again of that tree, of the corporation organized around core products and, ultimately, core competencies. To sink sufficiently strong roots, a company must answer some fundamental questions: How long could we preserve our competitiveness in this business if we did not control this particular core competence? How central is this core competence to perceived customer benefits? What future opportunities would be foreclosed if we were to lose this particular competence?

The architecture provides a logic for product and market diversification, moreover. An SBU manager would be asked: Does the new market opportunity add to the overall goal of becoming the best player in the world? Does it exploit or add to the core competence? At Vickers, for example, diversification options have been judged in the context of becoming the best power and motion control company in the world (see the insert "Vickers Learns the Value of Strategic Architecture").

The strategic architecture should make resource allocation priorities transparent to the entire organization. It provides a template for allocation decisions by top management. It helps lower level managers understand the logic of allocation priorities and disciplines senior management to maintain consistency. In short, it yields a definition of the company and the markets it serves. 3M, Vickers, NEC, Canon, and Honda all qualify on this score. Honda *knew* it was exploiting what it had learned from motorcycles—how to make high-revving, smooth-running, lightweight engines—when it entered the car business. The task of creating a strategic architecture forces the organization to identify and commit to the technical and production linkages across SBUs that will provide a distinct competitive advantage.

It is consistency of resource allocation and the development of an administrative infrastructure appropriate to it that breathes life into a strategic architecture and creates a managerial culture, teamwork, a capacity to change, and a willingness to share resources, to protect proprietary skills, and to think long term. That is also the reason the specific architecture cannot be copied easily or overnight by competitors. Strategic architecture is a tool for communicating with customers and other external constituents. It reveals the broad direction without giving away every step.

Redeploying to Exploit Competencies

If the company's core competencies are its critical resource and if top management must ensure that competence carriers are not held hostage by some particular business, then it follows that SBUs should bid for core competencies in the same way they bid for capital. We've made this point glancingly. It is important enough to consider more deeply.

Once top management (with the help of divisional and SBU managers) has identified overarching competencies, it must ask businesses to identify the projects and people closely connected with them. Corporate officers should direct an audit of the location, number, and quality of the people who embody competence.

This sends an important signal to middle managers: core competencies are *corporate* resources and may be reallocated by corporate management. An in-

> Send a message to your middle managers: the people critical to core competencies are *corporate* assets to be deployed by corporate management.

dividual business doesn't own anybody. SBUs are entitled to the services of individual employees so long as SBU management can demonstrate that the opportunity it is pursuing yields the highest possible pay-off on the investment in their skills. This message is further underlined if each year in the strategic planning or budgeting process, unit managers must justify their hold on the people who carry the company's core competencies.

Elements of Canon's core competence in optics are spread across businesses as diverse as cameras, copiers, and semiconductor lithographic equipment and are shown in "Core Competencies at Canon." When Canon identified an opportunity in digital laser printers, it gave SBU managers the right to raid other SBUs to pull together the required pool of talent. When Canon's reprographics products division undertook to develop microprocessor-controlled copiers, it turned to the photo products group, which had developed the world's first microprocessor-controlled camera.

Also, reward systems that focus only on product-line results and career paths that seldom cross SBU boundaries engender patterns of behavior among unit managers that are destructively competitive. At NEC, divisional managers come together to iden-

tify next-generation competencies. Together they decide how much investment needs to be made to build up each future competency and the contribution in capital and staff support that each division will need to make. There is also a sense of equitable exchange. One division may make a disproportionate contribution or may benefit less from the progress made, but such short-term inequalities will balance out over the long term.

Incidentally, the positive contribution of the SBU manager should be made visible across the company. An SBU manager is unlikely to surrender key people if only the other business (or the general manager of that business who may be a competitor for promotion) is going to benefit from the redeployment. Cooperative SBU managers should be celebrated as team players. Where priorities are clear, transfers are less likely to be seen as idiosyncratic and politically motivated.

Core Competencies at Canon

	Precision Mechanics	Fine Optics	Micro-electronics
Basic camera	■	■	
Compact fashion camera	■	■	
Electronic camera	■	■	
EOS autofocus camera	■	■	■
Video still camera	■	■	■
Laser beam printer	■	■	■
Color video printer	■		■
Bubble jet printer	■		■
Basic fax	■		■
Laser fax	■		■
Calculator			■
Plain paper copier	■	■	■
Battery PPC	■	■	■
Color copier	■	■	■
Laser copier	■	■	■
Color laser copier	■	■	■
NAVI	■	■	■
Still video system	■	■	■
Laser imager	■	■	■
Cell analyzer	■	■	■
Mask aligners	■		■
Stepper aligners	■		■
Excimer laser aligners	■	■	■

Every Canon product is the result of at least one core competency.

Transfers for the sake of building core competence must be recorded and appreciated in the corporate memory. It is reasonable to expect a business that has surrendered core skills on behalf of corporate opportunities in other areas to lose, for a time, some of its competitiveness. If these losses in performance bring immediate censure, SBUs will be unlikely to assent to skills transfers next time.

> ## Top management's real responsibility is a strategic architecture that guides competence building.

Finally, there are ways to wean key employees off the idea that they belong in perpetuity to any particular business. Early in their careers, people may be exposed to a variety of businesses through a carefully planned rotation program. At Canon, critical people move regularly between the camera business and the copier business and between the copier business and the professional optical-products business. In mid-career, periodic assignments to cross-divisional project teams may be necessary, both for diffusing core competencies and for loosening the bonds that might tie an individual to one business even when brighter opportunities beckon elsewhere. Those who embody critical core competencies should know that their careers are tracked and guided by corporate human resource professionals. In the early 1980s at Canon, all engineers under 30 were invited to apply for membership on a seven-person committee that was to spend two years plotting Canon's future direction, including its strategic architecture.

Competence carriers should be regularly brought together from across the corporation to trade notes and ideas. The goal is to build a strong feeling of community among these people. To a great extent, their loyalty should be to the integrity of the core competence area they represent and not just to particular businesses. In traveling regularly, talking frequently to customers, and meeting with peers, competence carriers may be encouraged to discover new market opportunities.

Core competencies are the wellspring of new business development. They should constitute the focus for strategy at the corporate level. Managers have to win manufacturing leadership in core products and capture global share through brand-building programs aimed at exploiting economies of scope. Only if the company is conceived of as a hierarchy of core competencies, core products, and market-focused business units will it be fit to fight.

Nor can top management be just another layer of accounting consolidation, which it often is in a regime of radical decentralization. Top management must add value by enunciating the strategic architecture that guides the competence acquisition process. We believe an obsession with competence building will characterize the global winners of the 1990s. With the decade underway, the time for rethinking the concept of the corporation is already overdue. ⊟

Reprint 90311

To revitalize corporate performance,
we need a whole new model of strategy.

STRATEGIC INTENT

by Gary Hamel and C.K. Prahalad

Today managers in many industries are working hard to match the competitive advantages of their new global rivals. They are moving manufacturing offshore in search of lower labor costs, rationalizing product lines to capture global scale economies, instituting quality circles and just-in-time production, and adopting Japanese human resource practices. When competitiveness still seems out of reach, they form strategic alliances – often with the very companies that upset the competitive balance in the first place.

Important as these initiatives are, few of them go beyond mere imitation. Too many companies are expending enormous energy simply to reproduce the cost and quality advantages their global competitors already enjoy. Imitation may be the sincerest form of flattery, but it will not lead to competitive revitalization. Strategies based on imitation are transparent to competitors who have already mastered them. Moreover, successful competitors rarely stand still. So it is not surprising that many executives feel trapped in a seemingly endless game of catch-up – regularly surprised by the new accomplishments of their rivals.

For these executives and their companies, regaining competitiveness will mean rethinking many of

the basic concepts of strategy.[1] As "strategy" has blossomed, the competitiveness of Western companies has withered. This may be coincidence, but we think not. We believe that the application of concepts such as "strategic fit" (between resources and opportunities), "generic strategies" (low cost vs. differentiation vs. focus), and the "strategy hierarchy" (goals, strategies, and tactics) have often abetted the process of competitive decline. The new global competitors approach strategy from a perspective that is funda-

> **A company's strategic orthodoxies are more dangerous than its well-financed rivals.**

mentally different from that which underpins Western management thought. Against such competitors, marginal adjustments to current orthodoxies are no more likely to produce competitive revitalization than are marginal improvements in operat-

Gary Hamel is lecturer in business policy and management at the London Business School. C.K. Prahalad is professor of corporate strategy and international business at the University of Michigan. Their most recent HBR article is "Collaborate with Your Competitors – and Win" (January-February 1989), with Yves L. Doz.

1. Among the first to apply the concept of strategy to management were H. Igor Ansoff in *Corporate Strategy: An Analytic Approach to Business Policy for Growth and Expansion* (New York: McGraw-Hill, 1965) and Kenneth R. Andrews in *The Concept of Corporate Strategy* (Homewood, Ill.: Dow Jones-Irwin, 1971).

ing efficiency. (The insert, "Remaking Strategy," describes our research and summarizes the two contrasting approaches to strategy we see in large, multinational companies.)

Few Western companies have an enviable track record anticipating the moves of new global competitors. Why? The explanation begins with the way most companies have approached competitor analysis. Typically, competitor analysis focuses on the existing resources (human, technical, and financial) of present competitors. The only companies seen as a threat are those with the resources to erode margins and market share in the next planning period. Resourcefulness, the pace at which new competitive advantages are being built, rarely enters in.

In this respect, traditional competitor analysis is like a snapshot of a moving car. By itself, the photograph yields little information about the car's speed or direction – whether the driver is out for a quiet Sunday drive or warming up for the Grand Prix. Yet many managers have learned through painful experience that a business's initial resource endowment (whether bountiful or meager) is an unreliable predictor of future global success.

Think back. In 1970, few Japanese companies possessed the resource base, manufacturing volume, or technical prowess of U.S. and European industry leaders. Komatsu was less than 35% as large as Caterpillar (measured by sales), was scarcely represented outside Japan, and relied on just one product line – small bulldozers – for most of its revenue. Honda was smaller than American Motors and had not yet begun to export cars to the United States. Canon's first

---

■ **Traditional competitor analysis is like a snapshot of a moving car.**

---

halting steps in the reprographics business looked pitifully small compared with the $4 billion Xerox powerhouse.

If Western managers had extended their competitor analysis to include these companies, it would merely have underlined how dramatic the resource discrepancies between them were. Yet by 1985, Komatsu was a $2.8 billion company with a product scope encompassing a broad range of earth-moving equipment, industrial robots, and semiconductors. Honda manufactured almost as many cars worldwide in 1987 as Chrysler. Canon had matched Xerox's global unit market share.

The lesson is clear: assessing the current tactical advantages of known competitors will not help you understand the resolution, stamina, and inventiveness of potential competitors. Sun-tzu, a Chinese military strategist, made the point 3,000 years ago: "All men can see the tactics whereby I conquer," he wrote, "but what none can see is the strategy out of which great victory is evolved."

Companies that have risen to global leadership over the past 20 years invariably began with ambitions that were out of all proportion to their resources and capabilities. But they created an obsession with winning at all levels of the organization and then sustained that obsession over the 10- to 20-year quest for global leadership. We term this obsession "strategic intent."

On the one hand, strategic intent envisions a desired leadership position and establishes the criterion the organization will use to chart its progress. Komatsu set out to "Encircle Caterpillar." Canon sought to "Beat Xerox." Honda strove to become a second Ford – an automotive pioneer. All are expressions of strategic intent.

At the same time, strategic intent is more than simply unfettered ambition. (Many companies possess an ambitious strategic intent yet fall short of their goals.) The concept also encompasses an active management process that includes: focusing the organization's attention on the essence of winning; motivating people by communicating the value of the target; leaving room for individual and team contributions; sustaining enthusiasm by providing new operational definitions as circumstances change; and using intent consistently to guide resource allocations.

Strategic intent captures the essence of winning. The Apollo program – landing a man on the moon ahead of the Soviets – was as competitively focused as Komatsu's drive against Caterpillar. The space program became the scorecard for America's technology race with the USSR. In the turbulent information technology industry, it was hard to pick a single competitor as a target, so NEC's strategic intent, set in the early 1970s, was to acquire the technologies that would put it in the best position to exploit the convergence of computing and telecommunications. Other industry observers foresaw this convergence, but only NEC made convergence the guiding theme for subsequent strategic decisions by adopting "computing and communications" as its intent. For Coca-Cola, strategic intent has been to put a Coke within "arm's reach" of every consumer in the world.

Strategic intent is stable over time. In battles for global leadership, one of the most critical tasks is to

Remaking Strategy

Over the last ten years, our research on global competition, international alliances, and multinational management has brought us into close contact with senior managers in America, Europe, and Japan. As we tried to unravel the reasons for success and surrender in global markets, we became more and more suspicious that executives in Western and Far Eastern companies often operated with very different conceptions of competitive strategy. Understanding these differences, we thought, might help explain the conduct and outcome of competitive battles as well as supplement traditional explanations for Japan's ascendance and the West's decline.

We began by mapping the implicit strategy models of managers who had participated in our research. Then we built detailed histories of selected competitive battles. We searched for evidence of divergent views of strategy, competitive advantage, and the role of top management.

Two contrasting models of strategy emerged. One, which most Western managers will recognize, centers on the problem of maintaining strategic fit. The other centers on the problem of leveraging resources. The two are not mutually exclusive, but they represent a significant difference in emphasis—an emphasis that deeply affects how competitive battles get played out over time.

Both models recognize the problem of competing in a hostile environment with limited resources. But while the emphasis in the first is on trimming ambitions to match available resources, the emphasis in the second is on leveraging resources to reach seemingly unattainable goals.

Both models recognize that relative competitive advantage determines relative profitability. The first emphasizes the search for advantages that are inherently sustainable, the second emphasizes the need to accelerate organizational learning to outpace competitors in building new advantages.

Both models recognize the difficulty of competing against larger competitors. But while the first leads to a search for niches (or simply dissuades the company from challenging an entrenched competitor), the second produces a quest for new rules that can devalue the incumbent's advantages.

Both models recognize that balance in the scope of an organization's activities reduces risk. The first seeks to reduce financial risk by building a balanced portfolio of cash-generating and cash-consuming businesses. The second seeks to reduce competitive risk by ensuring a well-balanced and sufficiently broad portfolio of advantages.

Both models recognize the need to disaggregate the organization in a way that allows top management to differentiate among the investment needs of various planning units. In the first model, resources are allocated to product-market units in which relatedness is defined by common products, channels, and customers. Each business is assumed to own all the critical skills it needs to execute its strategy successfully. In the second, investments are made in core competences (microprocessor controls or electronic imaging, for example) as well as in product-market units. By tracking these investments across businesses, top management works to assure that the plans of individual strategic units don't undermine future developments by default.

Both models recognize the need for consistency in action across organizational levels. In the first, consistency between corporate and business levels is largely a matter of conforming to financial objectives. Consistency between business and functional levels comes by tightly restricting the means the business uses to achieve its strategy—establishing standard operating procedures, defining the served market, adhering to accepted industry practices. In the second model, business-corporate consistency comes from allegiance to a particular strategic intent. Business-functional consistency comes from allegiance to intermediate-term goals, or challenges, with lower level employees encouraged to invent how those goals will be achieved.

lengthen the organization's attention span. Strategic intent provides consistency to short-term action, while leaving room for reinterpretation as new opportunities emerge. At Komatsu, encircling Caterpillar encompassed a succession of medium-term programs aimed at exploiting specific weaknesses in Caterpillar or building particular competitive advantages. When Caterpillar threatened Komatsu in Japan, for example, Komatsu responded by first improving quality, then driving down costs, then cultivating export markets, and then underwriting new product development.

Strategic intent sets a target that deserves personal effort and commitment. Ask the chairmen of many American corporations how they measure their contributions to their companies' success and you're likely to get an answer expressed in terms of shareholder wealth. In a company that possesses a strategic intent, top management is more likely to talk in terms of global market leadership. Market share leadership typically yields shareholder wealth, to be sure. But the two goals do not have the same motivational impact. It is hard to imagine middle managers, let alone blue-collar employees, waking up each day with the sole thought of creating more shareholder wealth. But mightn't they feel different given the challenge to "Beat Benz"—the rallying cry at one Japanese auto producer? Strategic intent gives employees the only goal that is worthy of commitment: to unseat the best or remain the best, worldwide.

Many companies are more familiar with strategic planning than they are with strategic intent. The planning process typically acts as a "feasibility sieve." Strategies are accepted or rejected on the basis of whether managers can be precise about the "how" as well as the "what" of their plans. Are the milestones clear? Do we have the necessary skills and resources? How will competitors react? Has the market been thoroughly researched? In one form or another, the admonition "Be realistic!" is given to line managers at almost every turn.

But can you *plan* for global leadership? Did Komatsu, Canon, and Honda have detailed, 20-year "strategies" for attacking Western markets? Are Japanese and Korean managers better planners than their Western counterparts? No. As valuable as strategic planning is, global leadership is an objective that lies outside the range of planning. We know of few companies with highly developed planning systems that have managed to set a strategic intent. As tests of strategic fit become more stringent, goals that cannot be planned for fall by the wayside. Yet companies that are afraid to commit to goals that lie outside the range of planning are unlikely to become global leaders.

Although strategic planning is billed as a way of becoming more future oriented, most managers, when pressed, will admit that their strategic plans reveal more about today's problems than tomorrow's opportunities. With a fresh set of problems confronting managers at the beginning of every planning cycle, focus often shifts dramatically from year to year. And with the pace of change accelerating in most industries, the predictive horizon is becoming shorter and shorter. So plans do little more than project the present forward incrementally. The goal of strategic intent is to fold the future back into the present. The important question is not "How will next year be different from this year?" but "What must we do differently next year to get closer to our strategic intent?" Only with a carefully articulated and adhered to strategic intent will a succession of year-on-year plans sum up to global leadership.

Just as you cannot plan a 10- to 20-year quest for global leadership, the chance of falling into a leadership position by accident is also remote. We don't believe that global leadership comes from an undirected process of intrapreneurship. Nor is it the product of a skunkworks or other techniques for internal venturing. Behind such programs lies a nihilistic assumption: the organization is so hidebound, so orthodox ridden that the only way to innovate is to put a few bright people in a dark room, pour in some money, and hope that something wonderful will happen. In this "Silicon Valley" approach to innovation, the only role for top managers is to retrofit their corporate strategy to the entrepreneurial successes that emerge from below. Here the value added of top management is low indeed.

Sadly, this view of innovation may be consistent with the reality in many large companies.[2] On the one hand, top management lacks any particular point of view about desirable ends beyond satisfying shareholders and keeping raiders at bay. On the other, the planning format, reward criteria, definition of served market, and belief in accepted industry practice all

> **Planners ask "How will next year be different?" Winners ask "What must we do differently?"**

work together to tightly constrain the range of available means. As a result, innovation is necessarily an isolated activity. Growth depends more on the inventive capacity of individuals and small teams than on the ability of top management to aggregate the efforts of multiple teams towards an ambitious strategic intent.

In companies that overcame resource constraints to build leadership positions, we see a different relationship between means and ends. While strategic intent is clear about ends, it is flexible as to means—it

2. Robert A. Burgelman, "A Process Model of Internal Corporate Venturing in the Diversified Major Firm," *Administrative Science Quarterly*, June 1983.

leaves room for improvisation. Achieving strategic intent requires enormous creativity with respect to means: witness Fujitsu's use of strategic alliances in Europe to attack IBM. But this creativity comes in the service of a clearly prescribed end. Creativity is unbridled, but not uncorralled, because top management establishes the criterion against which employees can pretest the logic of their initiatives. Middle managers must do more than deliver on promised financial targets; they must also deliver on the broad direction implicit in their organization's strategic intent.

Strategic intent implies a sizable stretch for an organization. Current capabilities and resources will not suffice. This forces the organization to be more inventive, to make the most of limited resources. Whereas the traditional view of strategy focuses on the degree of fit between existing resources and current opportunities, strategic intent creates an extreme misfit between resources and ambitions. Top management then challenges the organization to close the gap by systematically building new advantages. For Canon this meant first understanding Xerox's patents, then licensing technology to create a product that would yield early market experience, then gearing up internal R&D efforts, then licensing its own technology to other manufacturers to fund further R&D, then entering market segments in Japan and Europe where Xerox was weak, and so on.

In this respect, strategic intent is like a marathon run in 400-meter sprints. No one knows what the terrain will look like at mile 26, so the role of top management is to focus the organization's attention on the ground to be covered in the next 400 meters. In several companies, management did this by presenting the organization with a series of corporate challenges, each specifying the next hill in the race to achieve strategic intent. One year the challenge might be quality, the next total customer care, the next entry into new markets, the next a rejuvenated product line. As this example indicates, corporate challenges are a way to stage the acquisition of new competitive advantages, a way to identify the focal point for employees' efforts in the near to medium term. As with strategic intent, top management is specific about the ends (reducing product development times by 75%, for example) but less prescriptive about the means.

Like strategic intent, challenges stretch the organization. To preempt Xerox in the personal copier business, Canon set its engineers a target price of $1,000 for a home copier. At the time, Canon's least expensive copier sold for several thousand dollars. Trying to reduce the cost of existing models would not have given Canon the radical price-performance improvement it needed to delay or deter Xerox's entry into personal copiers. Instead, Canon engineers were challenged to reinvent the copier–a challenge they met by substituting a disposable cartridge for the complex image-transfer mechanism used in other copiers.

Corporate challenges come from analyzing competitors as well as from the foreseeable pattern of industry evolution. Together these reveal potential competitive openings and identify the new skills the organization will need to take the initiative away from better positioned players. The exhibit, "Building Competitive Advantage at Komatsu," illustrates the way challenges helped that company achieve its intent.

For a challenge to be effective, individuals and teams throughout the organization must understand it and see its implications for their own jobs. Companies that set corporate challenges to create new competitive advantages (as Ford and IBM did with quality improvement) quickly discover that engaging the entire organization requires top management to:

Create a sense of urgency, or quasi crisis, by amplifying weak signals in the environment that point up the need to improve, instead of allowing inaction

> The "Silicon Valley" approach to innovation: put a few bright people in a dark room, pour in money, and hope.

to precipitate a real crisis. (Komatsu, for example, budgeted on the basis of worst case exchange rates that overvalued the yen.)

Develop a competitor focus at every level through widespread use of competitive intelligence. Every employee should be able to benchmark his or her efforts against best-in-class competitors so that the challenge becomes personal. (For example, Ford showed production-line workers videotapes of operations at Mazda's most efficient plant.)

Provide employees with the skills they need to work effectively–training in statistical tools, problem solving, value engineering, and team building, for example.

Give the organization time to digest one challenge before launching another. When competing initiatives overload the organization, middle managers often try to protect their people from the whipsaw of shifting priorities. But this "wait and see if they're serious this time" attitude ultimately destroys the credibility of corporate challenges.

Building Competitive Advantage At Komatsu

Corporate Challenge	Protect Komatsu's home market against Caterpillar		Reduce costs while maintaining quality		Make Komatsu an International enterprise and build export markets		Respond to external shocks that threaten markets		Create new products and markets	
Programs	early 1960s	Licensing deals with Cummins Engine, International Harvester, and Bucyrus-Erie to acquire technology and establish benchmarks	1965	C D (Cost Down) program	early 1960s	Develop Eastern bloc countries	1975	V-10 program to reduce costs by 10% while maintaining quality; reduce parts by 20%; rationalize manufacturing system	late 1970s	Accelerate product development to expand line
	1961	Project A (for Ace) to advance the product quality of Komatsu's small- and medium-sized bulldozers above Caterpillar's	1966	Total C D program	1967	Komatsu Europe marketing subsidiary established	1977	¥ 180 program to budget companywide for 180 yen to the dollar when exchange rate was 240	1979	Future and Frontiers program to identify new businesses based on society's needs and company's know-how
	1962	Quality Circles companywide to provide training for all employees			1970	Komatsu America established	1979	Project E to establish teams to redouble cost and quality efforts in response to oil crisis	1981	EPOCHS program to reconcile greater product variety with improved production efficiencies
					1972	Project B to improve the durability and reliability and to reduce costs of large bulldozers				
					1972	Project C to improve payloaders				
					1972	Project D to improve hydraulic excavators				
					1974	Establish presales and service department to assist newly industrializing countries in construction projects				

Establish clear milestones and review mechanisms to track progress and ensure that internal recognition and rewards reinforce desired behavior. The goal is to make the challenge inescapable for everyone in the company.

It is important to distinguish between the process of managing corporate challenges and the advantages that the process creates. Whatever the actual challenge may be—quality, cost, value engineering, or something else—there is the same need to engage employees intellectually and emotionally in the development of new skills. In each case, the challenge will take root only if senior executives and lower level employees feel a reciprocal responsibility for competitiveness.

We believe workers in many companies have been asked to take a disproportionate share of the blame for competitive failure. In one U.S. company, for example, management had sought a 40% wage-package concession from hourly employees to bring labor costs into line with Far Eastern competitors. The result was a long strike and, ultimately, a 10% wage concession from employees on the line. However, direct labor costs in manufacturing accounted for less

than 15% of total value added. The company thus succeeded in demoralizing its entire blue-collar work force for the sake of a 1.5% reduction in total costs. Ironically, further analysis showed that their competitors' most significant cost savings came not from lower hourly wages but from better work methods invented by employees. You can imagine how eager the U.S. workers were to make similar contributions after the strike and concessions. Contrast this situation with what happened at Nissan when the yen strengthened: top management took a big pay cut and then asked middle managers and line employees to sacrifice relatively less.

Reciprocal responsibility means shared gain and shared pain. In too many companies, the pain of revitalization falls almost exclusively on the employees least responsible for the enterprise's decline. Too often, workers are asked to commit to corporate goals without any matching commitment from top management—be it employment security, gain sharing, or an ability to influence the direction of the business. This one-sided approach to regaining competi-

3. For example, see Michael E. Porter, *Competitive Strategy* (New York: Free Press, 1980).

tiveness keeps many companies from harnessing the intellectual horsepower of their employees.

Creating a sense of reciprocal responsibility is crucial because competitiveness ultimately depends on the pace at which a company embeds new advantages deep within its organization, not on its stock of advantages at any given time. Thus we need to expand the concept of competitive advantage beyond the scorecard many managers now use: Are my costs lower? Will my product command a price premium?

Few competitive advantages are long lasting. Uncovering a new competitive advantage is a bit like getting a hot tip on a stock: the first person to act on the insight makes more money than the last. When the experience curve was young, a company that built capacity ahead of competitors, dropped prices to fill plants, and reduced costs as volume rose went to the bank. The first mover traded on the fact that competitors undervalued market share – they didn't price to capture additional share because they didn't understand how market share leadership could be translated into lower costs and better margins. But there is no more undervalued market share when each of 20 semiconductor companies builds enough capacity to serve 10% of the world market.

Keeping score of existing advantages is not the same as building new advantages. The essence of strategy lies in creating tomorrow's competitive advantages faster than competitors mimic the ones you possess today. In the 1960s, Japanese producers relied on labor and capital cost advantages. As Western manufacturers began to move production offshore, Japanese companies accelerated their investment in process technology and created scale and quality advantages. Then as their U.S. and European competitors rationalized manufacturing, they added another string to their bow by accelerating the rate of product development. Then they built global brands. Then they deskilled competitors through alliances and outsourcing deals. The moral? An organization's capacity to improve existing skills and learn new ones is the most defensible competitive advantage of all.

To achieve a strategic intent, a company must usually take on larger, better financed competitors. That means carefully managing competitive engagements so that scarce resources are conserved. Managers cannot do that simply by playing the same game better – making marginal improvements to competitors' technology and business practices. Instead, they must fundamentally change the game in ways that disadvantage incumbents – devising novel approaches to market entry, advantage building, and competitive warfare. For smart competitors, the goal is not competitive imitation but competitive innovation, the art of containing competitive risks within manageable proportions.

Four approaches to competitive innovation are evident in the global expansion of Japanese companies. These are: building layers of advantage, searching for loose bricks, changing the terms of engagement, and competing through collaboration.

The wider a company's portfolio of advantages, the less risk it faces in competitive battles. New global competitors have built such portfolios by steadily expanding their arsenals of competitive weapons. They have moved inexorably from less defensible advantages such as low wage costs to more defensible advantages like global brands. The Japanese color television industry illustrates this layering process.

By 1967, Japan had become the largest producer of black-and-white television sets. By 1970, it was closing the gap in color televisions. Japanese manufacturers used their competitive advantage – at that time, primarily, low labor costs – to build a base in the private-label business, then moved quickly to estab-

---

To keep the pressure on, Komatsu set its budgets on the basis of an even stronger yen.

---

lish world-scale plants. This investment gave them additional layers of advantage – quality and reliability – as well as further cost reductions from process improvements. At the same time, they recognized that these cost-based advantages were vulnerable to changes in labor costs, process and product technology, exchange rates, and trade policy. So throughout the 1970s, they also invested heavily in building channels and brands, thus creating another layer of advantage, a global franchise. In the late 1970s, they enlarged the scope of their products and businesses to amortize these grand investments, and by 1980 all the major players – Matsushita, Sharp, Toshiba, Hitachi, Sanyo – had established related sets of businesses that could support global marketing investments. More recently, they have been investing in regional manufacturing and design centers to tailor their products more closely to national markets.

These manufacturers thought of the various sources of competitive advantage as mutually desirable layers, not mutually exclusive choices. What some call competitive suicide – pursuing both cost and differentiation – is exactly what many competitors strive for.[3] Using flexible manufacturing technologies and better marketing intelligence, they are moving away from standardized "world products" to products like Mazda's mini-van, developed in California expressly for the U.S. market.

Another approach to competitive innovation—searching for loose bricks—exploits the benefits of surprise, which is just as useful in business battles as it is in war. Particularly in the early stages of a war for global markets, successful new competitors work to stay below the response threshold of their larger, more powerful rivals. Staking out underdefended territory is one way to do this.

To find loose bricks, managers must have few orthodoxies about how to break into a market or challenge a competitor. For example, in one large U.S. multinational, we asked several country managers to describe what a Japanese competitor was doing in the local market. The first executive said, "They're coming at us in the low end. Japanese companies always come in at the bottom." The second speaker found the comment interesting but disagreed: "They don't offer any low-end products in my market, but they have some exciting stuff at the top end. We really should reverse engineer that thing." Another colleague told still another story. "They haven't taken any business away from me," he said, "but they've just made me a great offer to supply components." In each country, their Japanese competitor had found a different loose brick.

The search for loose bricks begins with a careful analysis of the competitor's conventional wisdom: How does the company define its "served market"? What activities are most profitable? Which geographic markets are too troublesome to enter? The objective is not to find a corner of the industry (or niche) where larger competitors seldom tread but to build a base of attack just outside the market terri-

---

> Honda was building a core competence in engines. Its U.S. rivals saw only 50 cc motorcycles.

---

tory that industry leaders currently occupy. The goal is an uncontested profit sanctuary, which could be a particular product segment (the "low end" in motorcycles), a slice of the value chain (components in the computer industry), or a particular geographic market (Eastern Europe).

When Honda took on leaders in the motorcycle industry, for example, it began with products that were just outside the conventional definition of the leaders' product-market domains. As a result, it could build a base of operations in underdefended territory and then use that base to launch an expanded attack. What many competitors failed to see was Honda's strategic intent and its growing competence in engines and power trains. Yet even as Honda was selling 50cc motorcycles in the United States, it was already racing larger bikes in Europe—assembling the design skills and technology it would need for a systematic expansion across the entire spectrum of motor-related businesses.

Honda's progress in creating a core competence in engines should have warned competitors that it might enter a series of seemingly unrelated industries—automobiles, lawn mowers, marine engines, generators. But with each company fixated on its own market, the threat of Honda's horizontal diversification went unnoticed. Today companies like Matsushita and Toshiba are similarly poised to move in unexpected ways across industry boundaries. In protecting loose bricks, companies must extend their peripheral vision by tracking and anticipating the migration of global competitors across product segments, businesses, national markets, value-added stages, and distribution channels.

Changing the terms of engagement—refusing to accept the front runner's definition of industry and segment boundaries—represents still another form of competitive innovation. Canon's entry into the copier business illustrates this approach.

During the 1970s, both Kodak and IBM tried to match Xerox's business system in terms of segmentation, products, distribution, service, and pricing. As a result, Xerox had no trouble decoding the new entrants' intentions and developing countermoves. IBM eventually withdrew from the copier business, while Kodak remains a distant second in the large copier market that Xerox still dominates.

Canon, on the other hand, changed the terms of competitive engagement. While Xerox built a wide range of copiers, Canon standardized machines and components to reduce costs. Canon chose to distribute through office-product dealers rather than try to match Xerox's huge direct sales force. It also avoided the need to create a national service network by designing reliability and serviceability into its product and then delegating service responsibility to the dealers. Canon copiers were sold rather than leased, freeing Canon from the burden of financing the lease base. Finally, instead of selling to the heads of corporate duplicating departments, Canon appealed to secretaries and department managers who wanted distributed copying. At each stage, Canon neatly sidestepped a potential barrier to entry.

Canon's experience suggests that there is an important distinction between barriers to entry and barriers to imitation. Competitors that tried to match Xerox's business system had to pay the same entry costs – the barriers to imitation were high. But Canon dramatically reduced the barriers to entry by changing the rules of the game.

Changing the rules also short-circuited Xerox's ability to retaliate quickly against its new rival. Confronted with the need to rethink its business strategy and organization, Xerox was paralyzed for a time. Xerox managers realized that the faster they downsized the product line, developed new channels, and improved reliability, the faster they would erode the company's traditional profit base. What might have been seen as critical success factors – Xerox's national sales force and service network, its large installed base of leased machines, and its reliance on service revenues – instead became barriers to retaliation. In this sense, competitive innovation is like judo: the goal is to use a larger competitor's weight against it. And that happens not by matching the leader's capabilities but by developing contrasting capabilities of one's own.

Competitive innovation works on the premise that a successful competitor is likely to be wedded to a "recipe" for success. That's why the most effective weapon new competitors possess is probably a clean sheet of paper. And why an incumbent's greatest vulnerability is its belief in accepted practice.

Through licensing, outsourcing agreements, and joint ventures, it is sometimes possible to win without fighting. For example, Fujitsu's alliances in Europe with Siemens and STC (Britain's largest computer maker) and in the United States with Amdahl yield manufacturing volume and access to Western markets. In the early 1980s, Matsushita established a joint venture with Thorn (in the United Kingdom), Telefunken (in Germany), and Thomson (in France), which allowed it to quickly multiply the forces arrayed against Philips in the battle for leadership in the European VCR business. In fighting larger global rivals by proxy, Japanese companies have adopted a maxim as old as human conflict itself: my enemy's enemy is my friend.

Hijacking the development efforts of potential rivals is another goal of competitive collaboration. In the consumer electronics war, Japanese competitors attacked traditional businesses like TVs and hi-fis

while volunteering to manufacture "next generation" products like VCRs, camcorders, and compact disc players for Western rivals. They hoped their rivals would ratchet down development spending, and in most cases that is precisely what happened. But companies that abandoned their own development efforts seldom reemerged as serious competitors in subsequent new product battles.

Collaboration can also be used to calibrate competitors' strengths and weaknesses. Toyota's joint venture with GM, and Mazda's with Ford, give these automakers an invaluable vantage point for assessing the progress their U.S. rivals have made in cost reduction, quality, and technology. They can also

> **Competitive innovation is like judo: upset your rivals by using their size against them.**

learn how GM and Ford compete – when they will fight and when they won't. Of course, the reverse is also true: Ford and GM have an equal opportunity to learn from their partner-competitors.

The route to competitive revitalization we have been mapping implies a new view of strategy. Strategic intent assures consistency in resource allocation over the long term. Clearly articulated corporate challenges focus the efforts of individuals in the medium term. Finally, competitive innovation helps reduce competitive risk in the short term. This consistency in the long term, focus in the medium term, and inventiveness and involvement in the short term provide the key to leveraging limited resources in pursuit of ambitious goals. But just as there is a process of winning, so there is a process of surrender. Revitalization requires understanding that process too.

Given their technological leadership and access to large regional markets, how did U.S. and European companies lose their apparent birthright to dominate global industries? There is no simple answer. Few companies recognize the value of documenting failure. Fewer still search their own managerial orthodoxies for the seeds for competitive surrender. But we believe there is a pathology of surrender (summarized in "The Process of Surrender") that gives some important clues.

It is not very comforting to think that the essence of Western strategic thought can be reduced to eight rules for excellence, seven S's, five competitive forces, four product life-cycle stages, three generic strategies, and innumerable two-by-two matrices.[4]

4. Strategic frameworks for resource allocation in diversified companies are summarized in Charles W. Hofer and Dan E. Schendel, *Strategy Formulation: Analytical Concepts* (St. Paul, Minn.: West Publishing, 1978).

The Process of Surrender

In the battles for global leadership that have taken place during the last two decades, we have seen a pattern of competitive attack and retrenchment that was remarkably similar across industries. We call this the process of surrender.

The process started with unseen intent. Not possessing long-term, competitor-focused goals themselves, Western companies did not ascribe such intentions to their rivals. They also calculated the threat posed by potential competitors in terms of their existing resources rather than their resourcefulness. This led to systematic underestimation of smaller rivals who were fast gaining technology through licensing arrangements, acquiring market understanding from downstream OEM partners, and improving product quality and manufacturing productivity through companywide employee involvement programs. Oblivious of the strategic intent and intangible advantages of their rivals, American and European businesses were caught off guard.

Adding to the competitive surprise was the fact that the new entrants typically attacked the periphery of a market (Honda in small motorcycles, Yamaha in grand pianos, Toshiba in small black-and-white televisions) before going head-to-head with incumbents. Incumbents often misread these attacks, seeing them as part of a niche strategy and not as a search for "loose bricks." Unconventional market entry strategies (minority holdings in less developed countries, use of nontraditional channels, extensive corporate advertising) were ignored or dismissed as quirky. For example, managers we spoke with said Japanese companies' position in the European computer industry was nonexistent. In terms of brand share that's nearly true, but the Japanese control as much as one-third of the manufacturing value added in the hardware sales of European-based computer businesses. Similarly, German auto producers claimed to feel unconcerned over the proclivity of Japanese producers to move upmarket. But with its low-end models under tremendous pressure from Japanese producers, Porsche has now announced that it will no longer make "entry level" cars.

Western managers often misinterpreted their rivals' tactics. They believed that Japanese and Korean companies were competing solely on the basis of cost and quality. This typically produced a partial response to those competitors' initiatives: moving manufacturing offshore, outsourcing, or instituting a quality program. Seldom was the full extent of the

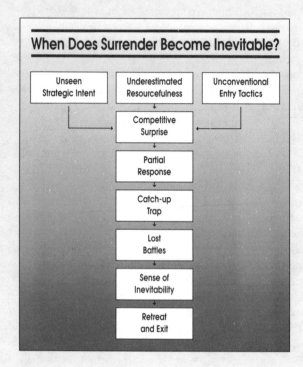

When Does Surrender Become Inevitable?

competitive threat appreciated—the multiple layers of advantage, the expansion across related product segments, the development of global brand positions. Imitating the currently visible tactics of rivals put Western businesses into a perpetual catch-up trap. One by one, companies lost battles and came to see surrender as inevitable. Surrender was not inevitable, of course, but the attack was staged in a way that disguised ultimate intentions and sidestepped direct confrontation.

Yet for the past 20 years, "advances" in strategy have taken the form of ever more typologies, heuristics, and laundry lists, often with dubious empirical bases. Moreover, even reasonable concepts like the product life cycle, experience curve, product portfolios, and generic strategies often have toxic side effects: They reduce the number of strategic options management is willing to consider. They create a preference for selling businesses rather than defending them. They yield predictable strategies that rivals easily decode.

Strategy "recipes" limit opportunities for competitive innovation. A company may have 40 businesses and only four strategies—invest, hold, harvest, or divest. Too often strategy is seen as a positioning exercise in which options are tested by how they fit the existing industry structure. But current industry structure reflects the strengths of the industry leader; and playing by the leader's rules is usually competitive suicide.

Armed with concepts like segmentation, the value chain, competitor benchmarking, strategic groups, and mobility barriers, many managers have become better and better at drawing industry maps. But while they have been busy map making, their competitors have been moving entire continents. The strategist's goal is not to find a niche within the existing industry space but to create new space that is uniquely suited to the company's own strengths, space that is off the map.

This is particularly true now that industry boundaries are becoming more and more unstable. In industries such as financial services and communica-

Playing by the industry leader's rules is competitive suicide.

tions, rapidly changing technology, deregulation, and globalization have undermined the value of traditional industry analysis. Map-making skills are worth little in the epicenter of an earthquake. But an industry in upheaval presents opportunities for ambitious companies to redraw the map in their favor, so long as they can think outside traditional industry boundaries.

Concepts like "mature" and "declining" are largely definitional. What most executives mean when they label a business mature is that sales growth has stagnated in their current geographic markets for existing products sold through existing channels. In such cases, it's not the industry that is mature, but the executives' conception of the industry. Asked if the piano business was mature, a senior executive in Yamaha replied, "Only if we can't take any market share from anybody anywhere in the world and still make money. And anyway, we're not in the 'piano' business, we're in the 'keyboard' business." Year after year, Sony has revitalized its radio and tape recorder businesses, despite the fact that other manufacturers long ago abandoned these businesses as mature.

A narrow concept of maturity can foreclose a company from a broad stream of future opportunities. In the 1970s, several U.S. companies thought that consumer electronics had become a mature industry. What could possibly top the color TV? they asked themselves. RCA and GE, distracted by opportunities in more "attractive" industries like mainframe computers, left Japanese producers with a virtual monopoly in VCRs, camcorders, and compact disc players. Ironically, the TV business, once thought mature, is on the verge of a dramatic renaissance. A $20 billion-a-year business will be created when high-definition television is launched in the United States. But the pioneers of television may capture only a small part of this bonanza.

Most of the tools of strategic analysis are focused domestically. Few force managers to consider global opportunities and threats. For example, portfolio planning portrays top management's investment options as an array of businesses rather than as an array of geographic markets. The result is predictable: as businesses come under attack from foreign competitors, the company attempts to abandon them and enter others in which the forces of global competition are not yet so strong. In the short term, this may be an appropriate response to waning competitiveness, but there are fewer and fewer businesses in which a domestic-oriented company can find refuge. We seldom hear such companies asking: Can we move into emerging markets overseas ahead of our global rivals and prolong the profitability of this business? Can we counterattack in our global competitors' home markets and slow the pace of their expansion? A senior executive in one successful global company made a telling comment: "We're glad to find a competitor managing by the portfolio concept—we can almost predict how much share we'll have to take away to put the business on the CEO's 'sell list.'"

Companies can also be overcommitted to organizational recipes, such as strategic business units and the decentralization an SBU structure implies. Decentralization is seductive because it places the responsibility for success or failure squarely on the shoulders of line managers. Each business is assumed to have all the resources it needs to execute its strategies successfully, and in this no-excuses environment, it is hard for top management to fail. But desirable as clear lines of responsibility and accountability are, competitive revitalization requires positive value added from top management.

Few companies with a strong SBU orientation have built successful global distribution and brand positions. Investments in a global brand franchise typically transcend the resources and risk propensity of a single business. While some Western companies have had global brand positions for 30 or 40 years or more (Heinz, Siemens, IBM, Ford, and Kodak, for example), it is hard to identify any American or European company that has created a new global brand franchise in the last 10 to 15 years. Yet Japanese companies have created a score or more—NEC, Fujitsu,

Panasonic (Matsushita), Toshiba, Sony, Seiko, Epson, Canon, Minolta, and Honda, among them.

General Electric's situation is typical. In many of its businesses, this American giant has been almost unknown in Europe and Asia. GE made no coordinated effort to build a global corporate franchise. Any GE business with international ambitions had to bear the burden of establishing its credibility and credentials in the new market alone. Not surprisingly, some once-strong GE businesses opted out of the difficult task of building a global brand position. In contrast, smaller Korean companies like Samsung, Daewoo, and Lucky Gold Star are busy building global-brand umbrellas that will ease market entry

Can you name one global brand developed by a U.S. company in the last ten years?

for a whole range of businesses. The underlying principle is simple: economies of scope may be as important as economies of scale in entering global markets. But capturing economies of scope demands interbusiness coordination that only top management can provide.

We believe that inflexible SBU-type organizations have also contributed to the deskilling of some companies. For a single SBU, incapable of sustaining investment in a core competence such as semiconductors, optical media, or combustion engines, the only way to remain competitive is to purchase key components from potential (often Japanese or Korean) competitors. For an SBU defined in product-market terms, competitiveness means offering an end product that is competitive in price and performance. But that gives an SBU manager little incentive to distinguish between external sourcing that achieves "product embodied" competitiveness and internal development that yields deeply embedded organizational competences that can be exploited across multiple businesses. Where upstream component manufacturing activities are seen as cost centers with cost-plus transfer pricing, additional investment in the core activity may seem a less profitable use of capital than investment in downstream activities. To make matters worse, internal accounting data may not reflect the competitive value of retaining control over core competence.

Together a shared global corporate brand franchise and shared core competence act as mortar in many Japanese companies. Lacking this mortar, a company's businesses are truly loose bricks – easily knocked out by global competitors that steadily invest in core competences. Such competitors can co-opt domestically oriented companies into long-term sourcing dependence and capture the economies of scope of global brand investment through interbusiness coordination.

Last in decentralization's list of dangers is the standard of managerial performance typically used in SBU organizations. In many companies, business unit managers are rewarded solely on the basis of their performance against return on investment targets. Unfortunately, that often leads to denominator management because executives soon discover that reductions in investment and head count – the denominator – "improve" the financial ratios by which they are measured more easily than growth in the numerator – revenues. It also fosters a hair-trigger sensitivity to industry downturns that can be very costly. Managers who are quick to reduce investment and dismiss workers find it takes much longer to regain lost skills and catch up on investment when the industry turns upward again. As a result, they lose market share in every business cycle. Particularly in industries where there is fierce competition for the best people and where competitors invest relentlessly, denominator management creates a retrenchment ratchet.

The concept of the general manager as a movable peg reinforces the problem of denominator management. Business schools are guilty here because they have perpetuated the notion that a manager with net present value calculations in one hand and portfolio planning in the other can manage any business anywhere.

In many diversified companies, top management evaluates line managers on numbers alone because no other basis for dialogue exists. Managers move so many times as part of their "career development" that they often do not understand the nuances of the businesses they are managing. At GE, for example, one fast-track manager heading an important new venture had moved across five businesses in five years. His series of quick successes finally came to an end when he confronted a Japanese competitor whose managers had been plodding along in the same business for more than a decade.

Regardless of ability and effort, fast-track managers are unlikely to develop the deep business knowledge they need to discuss technology options, competitors' strategies, and global opportunities substantively. Invariably, therefore, discussions gravitate to "the numbers," while the value added of managers is limited to the financial and planning savvy they carry from job to job. Knowledge of the company's internal planning and accounting systems substitutes for substantive knowledge of the business, making competitive innovation unlikely.

When managers know that their assignments have a two- to three-year time frame, they feel great pressure to create a good track record fast. This pressure often takes one of two forms. Either the manager does not commit to goals whose time line extends beyond his or her expected tenure. Or ambitious goals are adopted and squeezed into an unrealistically short time frame. Aiming to be number one in a business is the essence of strategic intent; but imposing a three- to four-year horizon on the effort simply invites disaster. Acquisitions are made with little attention to the problems of integration. The organization becomes overloaded with initiatives. Collaborative ventures are formed without adequate attention to competitive consequences.

Almost every strategic management theory and nearly every corporate planning system is premised on a strategy hierarchy in which corporate goals guide business unit strategies and business unit strategies guide functional tactics.[5] In this hierarchy, senior management makes strategy and lower levels execute it. The dichotomy between formulation and implementation is familiar and widely accepted. But the strategy hierarchy undermines competitiveness by fostering an elitist view of management that tends to disenfranchise most of the organization. Employees fail to identify with corporate goals or involve themselves deeply in the work of becoming more competitive.

The strategy hierarchy isn't the only explanation for an elitist view of management, of course. The myths that grow up around successful top managers – "Lee Iacocca saved Chrysler," "De Benedetti rescued Olivetti," "John Sculley turned Apple around" – perpetuate it. So does the turbulent business environment. Middle managers buffeted by circumstances that seem to be beyond their control desperately want to believe that top management has all the answers. And top management, in turn, hesitates to admit it does not for fear of demoralizing lower level employees.

The result of all this is often a code of silence in which the full extent of a company's competitiveness problem is not widely shared. We interviewed business unit managers in one company, for example, who were extremely anxious because top management wasn't talking openly about the competitive challenges the company faced. They assumed the lack of communication indicated a lack of awareness

on their senior managers' part. But when asked whether they were open with their own employees, these same managers replied that while they could face up to the problems, the people below them could not. Indeed, the only time the work force heard about the company's competitiveness problems was during wage negotiations when problems were used to extract concessions.

Unfortunately, a threat that everyone perceives but no one talks about creates more anxiety than a threat that has been clearly identified and made the focal point for the problem-solving efforts of the entire company. That is one reason honesty and humility on the part of top management may be the first prerequisite of revitalization. Another reason is the need to make participation more than a buzzword.

Programs such as quality circles and total customer service often fall short of expectations because management does not recognize that successful implementation requires more than administrative structures. Difficulties in embedding new capabilities are typically put down to "communication" problems, with the unstated assumption that if only downward communication were more effective – "if only middle management would get the message straight" – the new program would quickly take root. The need for upward communication is often ignored, or assumed to mean nothing more than feedback. In contrast, Japanese companies win, not because they have smarter managers, but because they have developed ways to harness the "wisdom of the anthill." They realize that top managers are a bit

> **Top managers are like astronauts – to perform well, they need the intelligence that's back on the ground.**

like the astronauts who circle the earth in the space shuttle. It may be the astronauts who get all the glory, but everyone knows that the real intelligence behind the mission is located firmly on the ground.

Where strategy formulation is an elitist activity it is also difficult to produce truly creative strategies. For one thing, there are not enough heads and points of view in divisional or corporate planning departments to challenge conventional wisdom. For another, creative strategies seldom emerge from the annual planning ritual. The starting point for next year's strategy is almost always this year's strategy. Improvements are incremental. The company sticks to the seg-

---

5. For example, see Peter Lorange and Richard F. Vancil, *Strategic Planning Systems* (Englewood Cliffs, N.J.: Prentice-Hall, 1977).

ments and territories it knows, even though the real opportunities may be elsewhere. The impetus for Canon's pioneering entry into the personal copier business came from an overseas sales subsidiary – not from planners in Japan.

The goal of the strategy hierarchy remains valid – to ensure consistency up and down the organization. But this consistency is better derived from a clearly

Investors aren't hopelessly short-term. They're justifiably skeptical of top management.

articulated strategic intent than from inflexibly applied top-down plans. In the 1990s, the challenge will be to enfranchise employees to invent the means to accomplish ambitious ends.

We seldom found cautious administrators among the top managements of companies that came from behind to challenge incumbents for global leadership. But in studying organizations that had surrendered, we invariably found senior managers who, for whatever reason, lacked the courage to commit their companies to heroic goals – goals that lay beyond the reach of planning and existing resources. The conservative goals they set failed to generate pressure and enthusiasm for competitive innovation or give the organization much useful guidance. Financial targets and vague mission statements just cannot provide

the consistent direction that is a prerequisite for winning a global competitive war.

This kind of conservatism is usually blamed on the financial markets. But we believe that in most cases investors' so-called short-term orientation simply reflects their lack of confidence in the ability of senior managers to conceive and deliver stretch goals. The chairman of one company complained bitterly that even after improving return on capital employed to over 40% (by ruthlessly divesting lackluster businesses and downsizing others), the stock market held the company to an 8:1 price/earnings ratio. Of course the market's message was clear: "We don't trust you. You've shown no ability to achieve profitable growth. Just cut out the slack, manage the denominators, and perhaps you'll be taken over by a company that can use your resources more creatively." Very little in the track record of most large Western companies warrants the confidence of the stock market. Investors aren't hopelessly short-term, they're justifiably skeptical.

We believe that top management's caution reflects a lack of confidence in its own ability to involve the entire organization in revitalization – as opposed to simply raising financial targets. Developing faith in the organization's ability to deliver on tough goals, motivating it to do so, focusing its attention long enough to internalize new capabilities – this is the real challenge for top management. Only by rising to this challenge will senior managers gain the courage they need to commit themselves and their companies to global leadership.

Reprint 89308

"It's either a shift away from Reaganomics, a shift in moral values, or an earthquake!"

As a strategic weapon, time is the equivalent of money, productivity, quality, even innovation.

Time—The Next Source of Competitive Advantage

by GEORGE STALK, JR.

Like competition itself, competitive advantage is a constantly moving target. For any company in any industry, the key is not to get stuck with a single simple notion of its source of advantage. The best competitors, the most successful ones, know how to keep moving and always stay on the cutting edge.

Today, *time* is on the cutting edge. The ways leading companies manage time—in production, in new product development and introduction, in sales and distribution—represent the most powerful new sources of competitive advantage. Though certain Western companies are pursuing these advantages, Japanese experience and practice provide the most instructive examples—not because they are necessarily unique but because they best illustrate the evolutionary stages through which leading companies have advanced.

In the period immediately following World War II, Japanese companies used their low labor costs to gain entry to various industries. As wage rates rose and technology became more significant, the Japanese shifted first to scale-based strategies and then to focused factories to achieve advantage. The advent of just-in-time production brought with it a move to

George Stalk is vice president of the Boston Consulting Group, where he specializes in time-based competition. With James C. Abbeglen, he wrote Kaisha, the Japanese Corporation: The New Competitors in World Business *(Basic Books, 1985).*

flexible factories, as leading Japanese companies sought both low cost and great variety in the market. Cutting-edge Japanese companies today are capitalizing on time as a critical source of competitive advantage: shortening the planning loop in the product development cycle and trimming process time in the factory—managing time the way most companies manage costs, quality, or inventory.

In fact, as a strategic weapon, time is the equivalent of money, productivity, quality, even innovation. Managing time has enabled top Japanese companies not only to reduce their costs but also to offer broad product lines, cover more market segments, and upgrade the technological sophistication of their products. These companies are time-based competitors.

From Low Wages to Variety Wars

Since 1945, Japanese competitors have shifted their strategic focus at least four times. These early adaptations were straightforward; the shift to time-based competitive advantage is not nearly so obvious. It does, however, represent a logical evolution from the earlier stages.

In the immediate aftermath of World War II, with their economy devastated and the world around them in a shambles, the Japanese concentrated on achieving competitive advantage through low labor costs. Since Japan's workers were still productive and the yen was devalued by 98.8% against the dollar, its labor costs were extraordinarily competitive with those of the West's developed economies.

Hungry for foreign exchange, the Japanese government encouraged companies to make the most of their one edge by targeting industries with high labor content: textiles, shipbuilding, and steel—businesses where the low labor rates more than offset low productivity rates. As a result, Japanese companies took market share from their Western competition.

But this situation did not last long. Rising wages, caused by high inflation, combined with fixed exchange rates to erode the advantage. In many industries, manufacturers could not improve their productivity fast enough to offset escalating labor costs. By the early 1960s, for instance, the textile companies—comprising Japan's largest industry—were hard-pressed. Having lost their competitive edge in world markets, they spiraled downward, first losing share, then volume, then profits, and finally position and prestige. While the problem was most severe for the textile business, the rest of Japanese industry suffered as well.

The only course was adaptation: in the early 1960s, the Japanese shifted their strategy, using capital investment to boost work-force productivity. They inaugurated the era of scale-based strategies, achieving high productivity and low costs by building the largest and most capital-intensive facilities that were

Using focused factories, the Japanese achieved high productivity and low costs.

technologically feasible. Japanese shipbuilders, for example, revolutionized the industry in their effort to raise labor productivity. Adapting fabrication techniques from mass production processes and using automatic and semiautomatic equipment, they constructed vessels in modules. The approach produced two advantages for the Japanese. It drove up their own productivity and simultaneously erected a high capital-investment barrier to others looking to compete in the business.

The search for ways to achieve even higher productivity and lower costs continued, however. And in the mid-1960s, it led top Japanese companies to a new source of competitive advantage—the focused factory. Focused competitors manufactured products either made nowhere else in the world or located in the high-volume segment of a market, often in the

heart of their Western competitors' product lines. Focusing of production allowed the Japanese to remain smaller than established broad-line producers, while still achieving higher productivity and lower costs—giving them great competitive power.

Factory costs are very sensitive to the variety of goods a plant produces. Reduction of the product-line

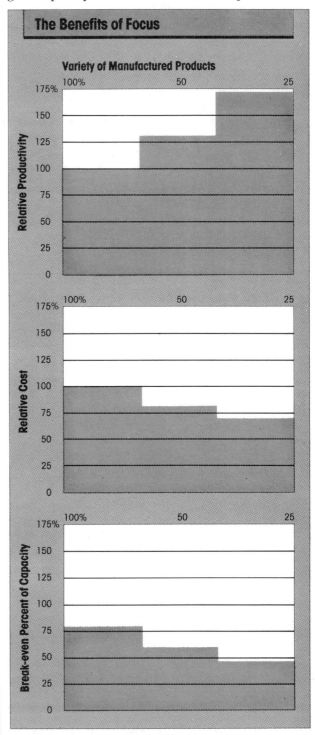

Cutting variety yields higher productivity, lower costs, and reduced break-even points.

variety by half, for example, raises productivity by 30%, cuts costs 17%, and substantially lowers the break-even point. Cutting the product line in half again boosts productivity by 75%, slashes costs 30%, and diminishes the break-even point to below 50%. (See "The Benefits of Focus.")

In industries like bearings, where competition was fierce in the late 1960s, the Japanese fielded product lines with one-half to one-quarter the variety of their Western competitors. Targeting the high-volume segments of the bearing business—bearings for automobile applications was one—the Japanese used the low costs of their highly productive focused factories to undercut the prices of Western competitors.

SKF was one victim. With factories scattered throughout Europe, each geared to a broad product line for the local market, the Swedish company was a big target for the Japanese. SKF reacted by trying to avoid direct competition with the Japanese: it added higher margin products to serve specialized applications. But SKF did not simultaneously drop any low-margin products, thereby complicating its plant operations and adding to production costs. In effect, SKF provided a cost umbrella for the Japanese. As long as they operated beneath it, the Japanese could expand their product line and move into more varied applications.

Avoiding price competition by moving into higher margin products is called margin retreat—a common response to stepped-up competition that eventually leads to corporate suicide. As a company retreats, its costs rise as do its prices, thus "subsidizing" an aggressive competitor's expansion into the vacated position. The retreating company's revenue base stops growing and may eventually shrink to the point where it can no longer support the fixed cost of the operation. Retrenchment, restructuring, and further shrinkage follow in a cycle that leads to inevitable extinction.

SKF avoided this fate by adopting the Japanese strategy. After a review of its factories, the company focused each on those products it was best suited to manufacture. If a product did not fit a particular factory, it was either placed in another, more suitable plant or dropped altogether. This strategy not only halted SKF's retreat but also beat back the Japanese advance.

At the same time, however, leading Japanese manufacturers began to move toward a new source of competitive advantage—the flexible factory. Two developments drove this move. First, as they expanded and penetrated more markets, their narrow product lines began to pinch, limiting their ability to grow. Second, with growth limited, the economics of the focus strategy presented them with an unattractive choice: either reduce variety further or accept the higher costs of broader product lines.

In manufacturing, costs fall into two categories: those that respond to volume or scale and those that are driven by variety. Scale-related costs decline as volume increases, usually falling 15% to 25% per unit each time volume doubles. Variety-related costs, on the other hand, reflect the costs of complexity in manufacturing: setup, materials handling, inventory, and many of the overhead costs of a factory. In most cases, as variety increases, costs increase, usually at a rate of 20% to 35% per unit each time variety doubles.

The sum of the scale- and variety-related costs represents the total cost of manufacturing. With effort, managers can determine the optimum cost

Flexible manufacturing solved the dilemma; it produced both lower costs and greater variety.

point for their factories—the point where the combination of volume and variety yields the lowest total manufacturing cost for a particular plant. When markets are good, companies tend to edge toward increased variety in search of higher volumes, even though this will mean increased costs. When times are tough, companies pare their product lines, cutting variety to reduce costs.

In a flexible factory system, variety-driven costs start lower and increase more slowly as variety grows. Scale costs remain unchanged. Thus the optimum cost point for a flexible factory occurs at a higher volume and with greater variety than for a traditional factory. A gap emerges between the costs of the flexible and the traditional factory—a cost/variety gap that represents the competitive advantage of flexible production. Very simply, a flexible factory enjoys more variety with lower total costs than traditional factories, which are still forced to make the trade-off between scale and variety. (See "The Advantage of Flexible Manufacturing.")

Yanmar Diesel illustrates how this process works. In 1973, with the Japanese economy in recession, Yanmar Diesel was mired in red ink. Worse, there was no promise that once the recession had passed, the existing strategy and program would guarantee real improvement in the company's condition.

As a Toyota supplier, Yanmar was familiar with the automaker's flexible manufacturing system. Moreover, Yanmar was impressed with the automaker's ability to weather the recession without losing

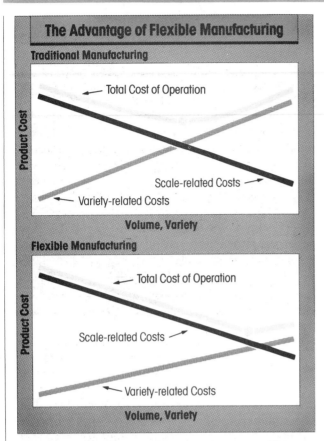

The Advantage of Flexible Manufacturing

Traditional Manufacturing

Product Cost

Total Cost of Operation

Scale-related Costs

Variety-related Costs

Volume, Variety

Flexible Manufacturing

Product Cost

Total Cost of Operation

Scale-related Costs

Variety-related Costs

Volume, Variety

For flexible factories, the optimum cost points occur at a higher volume and with higher variety than for traditional factories.

money. Yanmar decided to install the Toyota procedure in its own two factories. The changeover took less than five years and produced dramatic results: manufacturing costs declined 40% to 60%, depending on the product; factory break-even points dropped 80% to 50%; total manufacturing labor productivity improved by more than 100%.

But it was Yanmar's newfound capability in product variety that signaled the arrival of a unique strategic edge: during the restructuring Yanmar more than quadrupled its product line. With focused factories, Yanmar could have doubled productivity in such a short time only by reducing the breadth of the product line by 75%. The Toyota system made Yanmar's factories more flexible, reducing costs and producing a greater variety of products.

As its inventor, Taiichi Ohno, said, the Toyota production system was "born of the need to make many types of automobiles, in small quantities with the same manufacturing process." With its emphasis on just-in-time production, total quality control, employee decision making on the factory floor, and close supplier relations, the Toyota system gave the many Japanese manufacturers who adopted it in the mid-1970s a distinct competitive advantage.

A comparison of a U.S. company with a Japanese competitor in the manufacture of a particular automotive suspension component illustrates the nature and extent of the Japanese advantage. The U.S. company bases its strategy on scale and focus: it produces 10 million units per year—making it the world's largest producer—and offers only 11 types of finished parts. The Japanese company's strategy, on the other hand, is to exploit flexibility. It is both smaller and less focused: it manufactures only 3.5 million units per year but has 38 types of finished parts.

With one-third the scale and more than three times the product variety, the Japanese company also boasts total labor productivity that is half again that of its American competitor. Moreover, the unit cost of the Japanese manufacturer is less than half that of the U.S. company. But interestingly, the productivity

---

Yanmar's flexible factories cut costs and more than quadrupled its product line.

---

of the Japanese direct laborers is not as high as that of the U.S. workers, a reflection of the difference in scale. The Japanese advantage comes from the productivity of the overhead employees: with one-third the volume and three times the variety, the Japanese company has only one-eighteenth the overhead employees. (See "Flexible Manufacturing's Productivity Edge.")

In the late 1970s, Japanese companies exploited flexible manufacturing to the point that a new competitive thrust emerged—the variety war. A classic example of a variety war was the battle that erupted between Honda and Yamaha for supremacy in the motorcycle market, a struggle popularly known in Japanese business circles as the H-Y War. Yamaha ignited the H-Y War in 1981 when it announced the opening of a new factory which would make it the world's largest motorcycle manufacturer, a prestigious position held by Honda. But Honda had been concentrating its corporate resources on the automobile business and away from its motorcycle operation. Now, faced with Yamaha's overt and public challenge, Honda chose to counterattack.

Honda launched its response with the war cry, "Yamaha wo tsubusu!" ("We will crush, squash, slaughter Yamaha!") In the no-holds-barred battle that ensued, Honda cut prices, flooded distribution channels, and boosted advertising expenditures. Most important—and most impressive to consumers—Honda also rapidly increased the rate of change in its product line, using variety to bury Yamaha. At the start of the war, Honda had 60 models of motorcycles. Over the next 18 months, Honda introduced or replaced 113 models, effectively turning over its entire product line twice. Yamaha also began the war with 60 models; it was able to manage only 37 changes in its product line during those 18 months.

Honda's new product introductions devastated Yamaha. First, Honda succeeded in making motorcycle design a matter of fashion, where newness and freshness were important attributes for consumers. Second, Honda raised the technological sophistication of its products, introducing four-valve engines, composites, direct drive, and other new features. Next to a Honda, Yamaha products looked old, unattractive, and out of date. Demand for Yamaha products dried up; in a desperate effort to move them, dealers were forced to price them below cost. But even that didn't work. At the most intense point in the H-Y War, Yamaha had more than 12 months of inventory in its dealers' showrooms. Finally Yamaha surrendered. In a public statement, Yamaha President Eguchi announced, "We want to end the H-Y War. It is our fault. Of course there will be competition in the future but it will be based on a mutual recognition of our respective positions."

Honda didn't go unscathed either. The company's sales and service network was severely disrupted, requiring additional investment before it returned to a stable footing. However, so decisive was its victory that Honda effectively had as much time as it wanted to recover. It had emphatically defended its title as the world's largest motorcycle producer and done so in a way that warned Suzuki and Kawasaki not to challenge that leadership. Variety had won the war.

Time-Based Competitive Advantage

The strength of variety as a competitive weapon raises an interesting question. How could Japanese companies accommodate such rapid rates of change? In Honda's case, there could be only three possible answers. The company did one of the following:

1. Began the development of more than 100 new models 10 to 15 years before the attack.

2. Authorized a sudden, massive spending surge to develop and manufacture products on a crash basis.

3. Used structurally different methods to develop, manufacture, and introduce new products.

In fact, what Honda and other variety-driven competitors pioneered was time-based competitiveness. They managed structural changes that enabled their operations to execute their processes much faster. As a consequence, time became their new source of competitive advantage.

Flexible Manufacturing's Productivity Edge
(Automobile Suspension Component)

	U.S. Competitor	Japanese Competitor
Annual Volume	10M	3.5M
Employees		
Direct	107	50
Indirect	135	7
Total	242	57
Annual Units/Employee	43,100	61,400
Types of Finished Parts	11	38
Unit Cost for Comparable Part (index)	$100	$49

(1987 figures)

While time is a basic business performance variable, management seldom monitors its consumption explicitly—almost never with the same precision accorded sales and costs. Yet time is a more critical competitive yardstick than traditional financial measurements.

Today's new-generation companies compete with flexible manufacturing and rapid-response systems, expanding variety and increasing innovation. A company that builds its strategy on this cycle is a more powerful competitor than one with a traditional strategy based on low wages, scale, or focus. These older, cost-based strategies require managers to do whatever is necessary to drive down costs: move production to or source from a low-wage country; build new facilities or consolidate old plants to gain economies of scale; or focus operations down to the most economic subset of activities. These tactics reduce costs but at the expense of responsiveness.

In contrast, strategies based on the cycle of flexible manufacturing, rapid response, expanding variety, and increasing innovation are time based. Factories are close to the customers they serve. Organization structures enable fast responses rather than low costs and control. Companies concentrate on reducing if not eliminating delays and using their response advantages to attract the most profitable customers.

Many—but certainly not all—of today's time-based competitors are Japanese. Some of them are Sony, Matsushita, Sharp, Toyota, Hitachi, NEC, Toshiba, Honda, and Hino; time-based Western companies include Benetton, The Limited, Federal Express, Domino's Pizza, Wilson Art, and McDonald's. For these leading competitors, time has become the overarching measurement of performance. By reducing

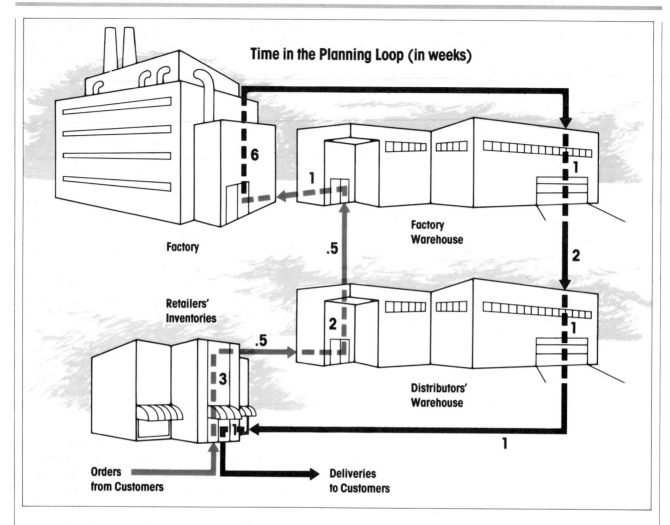

Time in the Planning Loop (in weeks)

Factory

Factory Warehouse

Retailers' Inventories

.5

.5

Distributors' Warehouse

Orders from Customers

Deliveries to Customers

the consumption of time in every aspect of the business, these companies also reduce costs, improve quality, and stay close to their customers.

Breaking the Planning Loop

Companies are systems; time connects all the parts. The most powerful competitors understand this axiom and are breaking the debilitating loop that strangles much of traditional manufacturing planning.

Traditional manufacturing requires long lead times to resolve conflicts between various jobs or activities that require the same resources. The long lead times, in turn, require sales forecasts to guide planning. But sales forecasts are inevitably wrong; by definition they are guesses, however informed. Naturally, as lead times lengthen, the accuracy of sales forecasts declines. With more forecasting errors, inventories balloon and the need for safety stocks at all levels increases. Errors in forecasting also mean more unscheduled jobs that have to be expedited, thereby

crowding out scheduled jobs. The need for longer lead times grows even greater and the planning loop expands even more, driving up costs, increasing delays, and creating system inefficiencies.

Managers who find themselves trapped in the planning loop often respond by asking for better forecasts and longer lead times. In other words, they treat the symptoms and worsen the problem. The only way to break the planning loop is to reduce the consumption of time throughout the system; that will, in turn, cut the need for lead time, for estimates, for safety stocks, and all the rest. After all, if a company could ever drive its lead time all the way to zero, it would have to forecast only the next day's sales. While that idea of course is unrealistic, successful time-based competitors in Japan and in the West have kept their lead times from growing and some have even reduced them, thereby diminishing the planning loop's damaging effects.

Thirty years ago, Jay W. Forrester of MIT published a pioneering article in HBR, "Industrial Dynamics: A Major Breakthrough for Decision Makers" (July-August 1958), which established a model of time's impact on an organization's performance. Using "industrial dynamics"—a concept originally developed for shipboard fire control systems—Forrester tracked the effects of time delays and decision rates within a simple business system consisting of a factory, a factory warehouse, a distributors' inventory, and retailers' inventories. The numbers in the illustration "Time in the Planning Loop" are the delays in the flow of information or product, measured in weeks. In this example, the orders accumulate at the retailer for three weeks, are in the mail for half a week, are delayed at the distributor for two weeks, go back into the mail for another half a week, and need eight weeks for processing at the factory and its warehouse. Then the finished product begins its journey back to the retailer. The cycle takes 19 weeks.

What distorts the system is time: lengthy delays inevitably create an inaccurate view of the market.

The system in this example is very stable—as long as retail demand is stable or as long as forecasts are accurate 19 weeks into the future. But if unexpected changes occur, the system must respond. The chart, also taken from the Forrester article, shows what happens to this system when a simple change takes place: demand goes up 10%, then flattens. Acting on new forecasts and seeking to cut delivery delays, the factory first responds by ramping up production 40%. When management realizes—too late—that it has overshot the mark, it cuts production 30%. Too late again it learns that it has overcorrected. This ramping up and cutting back continue until finally the system stabilizes, more than a year after the initial 10% increase.

What distorts the system so badly is time: the lengthy delay between the event that creates the new demand and the time when the factory finally receives the information. The longer that delay, the more distorted is the view of the market. Those distortions reverberate throughout the system, producing disruption, waste, and inefficiency.

These distortions plague business today. To escape them, companies have a choice: they can produce to forecast or they can reduce the time delays in the flow of information and product through the system. The traditional solution is to produce to forecast. The new approach is to reduce time consumption.

Because time flows throughout the system, focusing on time-based competitive performance results

in improvements across the board. Companies generally become time-based competitors by first correcting their manufacturing techniques, then fixing sales and distribution, and finally adjusting their approach to innovation. Ultimately, it becomes the basis for a company's overall strategy.

Time-Based Manufacturing

In general, time-based manufacturing policies and practices differ from those of traditional manufacturers along three key dimensions: length of production runs, organization of process components, and complexity of scheduling procedures.

When it comes to lot size, for instance, traditional factories attempt to maximize production runs while time-based manufacturers try to shorten their production runs as much as possible. In fact, many Japanese companies aim for run lengths of a single unit. The thinking behind this is as simple as it is fundamental to competitive success: reduced run lengths mean more frequent production of the complete mix of products and faster response to customers' demands.

Factory layout also contributes to time-based competitive advantage. Traditional factories are usually organized by process technology centers. For example, metal goods manufacturers organize their factories into shearing, punching, and braking departments; electronic assemblers have stuffing, wave soldering, assembly, testing, and packing departments. Parts move from one process technology center to the next. Each step consumes valuable time: parts sit, waiting to move; then move; then

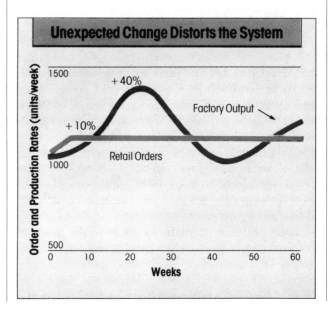

wait to be used in the next step. In a traditional manufacturing system, products usually receive value for only .05% to 2.5% of the time that they are in the factory. The rest of the time products sit waiting for something to happen.

Time-based factories, however, are organized by product. To minimize handling and moving of parts, the manufacturing functions for a component or a product are as close together as possible. Parts move from one activity to the next with little or no delay. Because the production process eliminates the need to pile and repile parts, they flow quickly and efficiently through the factory.

In traditional factories, scheduling is also a source of delay and waste. Most traditional factories use central scheduling that requires sophisticated materials resource planning and shop-floor control systems. Even though these systems are advanced, they still waste time: work orders usually flow to the factory floor on a monthly or weekly basis. In the meantime, parts can sit idle.

In time-based factories, local scheduling enables employees to make more production control decisions on the factory floor, without the time-consuming loop back to management for approval. Moreover, the combination of the product-oriented layout of the factory and local scheduling makes the total production process run more smoothly. Once a part starts through the production run, many of the requirements between manufacturing steps are purely automatic and require no intermediate scheduling.

Toyota went to work with its too-slow supplier, cutting response time from 15 days to 1.

These differences between traditional and time-based factories add up. Flexible factories enjoy big advantages in both productivity and time: labor productivity in time-based factories can be as much as 200% higher than in conventional plants; time-based factories can respond eight to ten times faster than traditional factories. Flexible production means significant improvements in labor and net-asset productivity. These, in turn, yield reductions of up to 20% in overall costs and increases in growth for much less investment.

Toyota offers a dramatic example of the kinds of improvements that leading time-based competitors are making. Dissatisfied with the response time of a supplier, Toyota went to work. It took the supplier 15 days to turn out a component after arrival of the raw

materials at its factory. The first step was to cut lot sizes, reducing response time to 6 days. Next Toyota streamlined the factory layout, reducing the number of inventory holding points. The response time fell to 3 days. Finally Toyota eliminated all work-in-progress inventories at the supplier's plant. New response time: 1 day.

Toyota, of course, is not alone in improving manufacturing response times. Matsushita cut the time needed to make washing machines from 360 hours to just 2; Honda slashed its motorcycle fabricating time by 80%; in North America, companies making motor controllers and electrical components for unit air conditioners have improved their manufacturing response times by 90%.

Time-Based Sales and Distribution

A manufacturer's next challenge is to avoid dissipation of factory performance improvements in other parts of the organization. In Jay Forrester's example of the planning loop, the factory and its warehouse accounted for roughly one-half of the system's time. In actuality today, the factory accounts for one-third to one-half of the total time—often the most "visible" portion of time. But other parts of the system are just as important, if less apparent. For example, in the Forrester system, sales and distribution consume as much or more time than manufacturing.

What Forrester modeled, the Japanese experienced. By the late 1970s, leading Japanese companies were finding that inefficient sales and distribution operations undercut the benefits of their flexible manufacturing systems. Toyota, which at that time was divided into two separate companies, Toyota Motor Manufacturing and Toyota Motor Sales, again makes this point. Toyota Motor Manufacturing could manufacture a car in less than 2 days. But Toyota Motor Sales needed from 15 to 26 days to close the sale, transmit the order to the factory, get the order scheduled, and deliver the car to the customer. By the late 1970s, the cost-conscious, competition-minded engineers at Toyota Manufacturing were angry at their counterparts at Toyota Motor Sales, who were frittering away the advantage gained in the production process. The sales and distribution function was generating 20% to 30% of a car's cost to the customer—more than it cost Toyota to manufacture the car!

Finally, in 1982 Toyota moved decisively to remedy the problem. The company merged Toyota Motor Manufacturing and Toyota Motor Sales. The company announced that it wanted to become "more marketing driven." While Toyota assured the public that the reorganization only returned it to its configuration in the 1950s, within 18 months all the Toyota Motor Sales directors retired. Their jobs were left vacant or filled by executives from Toyota Motor Manufacturing.

The company wasted no time in implementing a plan to cut delays in sales and distribution, reduce costs, and improve customer service. The old system, Toyota found, had handled customer orders in batches. Orders and other crucial information would accumulate at one step of the sales and distribution process before dispatch to the next level, which wasted time and generated extra costs.

To speed the flow of information, Toyota had to reduce the size of the information batches. The solution came from a company-developed computer system that tied its salespeople directly to the factory scheduling operation. This link bypassed several levels of the sales and distribution function and enabled the modified system to operate with very small batches of orders.

Toyota expected this new approach to cut the sales and distribution cycle time in half—from four to six weeks to just two to three weeks across Japan. (For the Tokyo and Osaka regions, which account for roughly two-thirds of Japan's population, the goal was to reduce cycle time to just two days.) But by 1987 Toyota had reduced system responsiveness to eight days, including the time required to make the car. In the Forrester example, this achievement is equivalent to cutting the 19-week cycle to 6 weeks. The results were predictable: shorter sales forecasts, lower costs, happier customers.

Time-Based Innovation

A company that can bring out new products three times faster than its competitors enjoys a huge advantage. Today, in one industry after another, Japanese manufacturers are doing just that to their Western competition:

■ In projection television, Japanese producers can develop a new television in one-third the time required by U.S. manufacturers.

■ In custom plastic injection molds, Japanese companies can develop the molds in one-third the time of U.S. competitors and at one-third the cost.

■ In autos, Japanese companies can develop new products in half the time—and with half as many people—as the U.S. and German competition.

To accomplish their fast-paced innovations, leading Japanese manufacturers have introduced a series of organizational techniques that precisely parallel their approach to flexible manufacturing:

■ In manufacturing, the Japanese stress short production runs and small lot sizes. In innovation, they favor smaller increments of improvement in new products, but introduce them more often—versus the Western approach of more significant improvements made less often.

■ In the organization of product development work, the Japanese use factory cells that are cross-functional teams. Most Western new product development activity is carried out by functional centers.

■ In the scheduling of work, Japanese factories stress local responsibility, just as product development scheduling is decentralized. The Western approach to both requires plodding centralized scheduling, plotting, and tracking.

The effects of this time-based advantage are devastating; quite simply, American companies are losing leadership of technology and innovation—supposedly this country's source of long-term advantage.

Unless U.S. companies cut new product cycles by 300%, Japanese manufacturers will easily out-innovate them.

Unless U.S. companies reduce their new product development and introduction cycles from 36-48 months to 12-18 months, Japanese manufacturers will easily out-innovate and outperform them. Taking the initiative in innovation will require even faster cycle times.

Residential air conditioners illustrate the Japanese ability to introduce more technological innovation in smaller increments—and how in just a few years these improvements add up to remarkably superior products. The Japanese introduce innovations in air conditioners four times faster than their American competitors; in technological sophistication the Japanese products are seven to ten years ahead of U.S. products.

Look at the changes in Mitsubishi Electric's three-horsepower heat pump between 1975 and 1985. From 1975 to 1979, the company did nothing to the product except change the sheet metal work, partly to improve efficiency but mostly to reduce materials costs. In 1979, the technological sophistication of the product was roughly equal to that of the U.S. competition. From this point on, the Japanese first established, and then widened the lead.

In 1980, Mitsubishi introduced its first major improvement: a new product that used integrated circuits to control the air-conditioning cycle. One year later, the company replaced the integrated circuits with microprocessors and added two important innovations to increase consumer demand. The first was "quick connect" freon lines. On the old product (and on the U.S. product), freon lines were made from copper tubing and cut to length, bent, soldered together, purged, and filled with freon—an operation requiring great skill to produce a reliable air conditioner. The Japanese substituted quick-connect freon lines—precharged hoses that simply clicked together. The second innovation was simplified wiring. On the old product (and still today on the U.S. product) the unit had six color-coded wires to connect. The advent of microprocessors made possible a two-wire connection with neutral polarity.

These two changes did not improve the energy-efficiency ratio of the product; nor were they intended to. Rather, the point was to fabricate a unit that would be simpler to install and more reliable, thereby broadening distribution and increasing demand. Because of these innovations, white-goods outlets could sell the new product, and local contractors could easily install it.

In 1982, Mitsubishi introduced a new version of the air conditioner featuring technological advances related to performance. A high-efficiency rotary compressor replaced the outdated reciprocating compressor. The condensing unit had louvered fins and inner fin tubes for better heat transfer. Because the balance of the system changed, all the electronics had to change. As a result, the energy-efficiency ratio improved markedly.

In 1983, Mitsubishi added sensors to the unit and more computing power, expanding the electronic

---

Mitsubishi's time-based approach left U.S. air-conditioner companies ten years behind.

---

control of the cycle and again improving the energy-efficiency ratio.

In 1984, Mitsubishi came out with another version of the product, this time with an inverter that made possible an even higher energy-efficiency ratio. The inverter, which requires additional electronics for the unit, allows unparalleled control over the speed of the electric motor, dramatically boosting the appliance's efficiency.

Using time-based innovation, Mitsubishi transformed its air conditioner. The changes came incrementally and steadily. Overall they gave Mitsu-

bishi—and other Japanese companies on the same track—the position of technological leadership in the global residential air-conditioning industry.

In 1985, a U.S. air-conditioner manufacturer was just debating whether to use integrated circuits in its residential heat pump. In view of its four- to five-year product development cycle, it could not have introduced the innovation until 1989 or 1990—putting the American company ten years behind the Japanese. Faced with this situation, the U.S. air-conditioner company followed the example of many U.S. manufacturers that have lost the lead in technology and innovation: it decided to source its air conditioners and components from its Japanese competition.

Time-Based Strategy

The possibility of establishing a response time advantage opens new avenues for constructing winning competitive strategies. At most companies, strategic choices are limited to three options:

1. Seeking coexistence with competitors. This choice is seldom stable, since competitors refuse to cooperate and stay put.

2. Retreating in the face of competitors. Many companies choose this course; the business press fills its pages with accounts of companies retreating by consolidating plants, focusing their operations, outsourcing, divesting businesses, pulling out of markets, or moving upscale.

3. Attacking, either directly or indirectly. The direct attack involves the classic confrontation—cut price and add capacity, creating head-on competition. Indirect attack requires surprise. Competitors either do not understand the strategies being used against them or they do understand but cannot respond—sometimes because of the speed of the attack, sometimes because of their inability to mount a response.

Of the three options, only an attack creates the opportunity for real growth. Direct attack demands superior resources; it is always expensive and potentially disastrous. Indirect attack promises the most gain for the least cost. Time-based strategy offers a powerful new approach for successful indirect attacks against larger, established competitors.

Consider the remarkable example of Atlas Door, a ten-year-old U.S. company. It has grown at an average annual rate of 15% in an industry with an overall annual growth rate of less than 5%. In recent years, its pretax earnings were 20% of sales, about five times the industry average. Atlas is debt free. In its tenth year the company achieved the number one competitive position in its industry.

The company's product: industrial doors. It is a product with almost infinite variety, involving limitless choices of width and height and material. Because of the importance of variety, inventory is almost useless in meeting customer orders; most doors can be manufactured only after the order has been placed.

Historically, the industry had needed almost four months to respond to an order for a door that was out of stock or customized. Atlas's strategic advantage was time: it could respond in weeks to any order. It had structured its order-entry, engineering, manufacturing, and logistics systems to move information and products quickly and reliably.

First, Atlas built just-in-time factories. These are fairly simple in concept. They require extra tooling and machinery to reduce changeover times and a fabrication process organized by product and scheduled to start and complete all of the parts at the same time. But even the performance of the factory—critical to the company's overall responsiveness—still only accounted for $2\frac{1}{2}$ weeks of the completed product delivery cycle.

Second, Atlas compressed time at the front end of the system, where the order first entered and was processed. Traditionally, when customers, distribu-

The industry needed almost four months to respond. Atlas could fill any order in just weeks.

tors, or salespeople called a door manufacturer with a request for price and delivery, they would have to wait more than one week for a response. If the desired door was not in stock, not in the schedule, or not engineered, the supplier's organization would waste even more time, pushing the search for an answer around the system.

Recognizing the opportunity to cut deeply into the time expenditure in this part of the system, Atlas first streamlined, then automated its entire order-entry, engineering, pricing, and scheduling processes. Today Atlas can price and schedule 95% of its incoming orders while the callers are still on the telephone. It can quickly engineer new special orders because it has preserved on computer the design and production data of all previous special orders—which

drastically reduces the amount of re-engineering necessary.

Third, Atlas tightly controlled logistics so that it always shipped only fully complete orders to construction sites. Orders require many components. Gathering all of them at the factory and making sure that they are with the correct order can be a time-consuming task. It is even more time-consuming, however, to get the correct parts to the job site *after* they have missed the initial shipment. Atlas developed a system to track the parts in production and the purchased parts for each order, ensuring arrival of all necessary parts at the shipping dock in time—a just-in-time logistics operation.

When Atlas started operations, distributors were uninterested in its product. The established distributors already carried the door line of a larger competitor; they saw no reason to switch suppliers except, perhaps, for a major price concession. But as a start-up, Atlas was too small to compete on price alone. Instead, it positioned itself as the door supplier of last resort, the company people came to if the established supplier could not deliver or missed a key date.

Of course, with industry lead times of almost four months, some calls inevitably came to Atlas. And when it did get a call, Atlas commanded a higher price because of its faster delivery. Atlas not only got a higher price but its time-based processes also yielded lower costs: it thus enjoyed the best of both worlds.

In ten short years, the company replaced the leading door suppliers in 80% of the distributors in the country. With its strategic advantage the company could be selective, becoming the house supplier for only the strongest distributors.

In the wake of this indirect attack, the established competitors have not responded effectively. The conventional view is that Atlas is a "garage shop operator" that cannot sustain its growth: competitors expect the company's performance to degrade to the industry average as it grows larger. But this response—or nonresponse—only reflects a fundamental lack of understanding of time as the source of competitive advantage. The extra delay in responding only adds to the insurmountable lead the indirect time-based attack has created. While the traditional companies track costs and size, the new competitor derives advantage from time, staying on the cutting edge, leaving its rivals behind.

Reprint 88410

The U.S. deregulated trains, planes, and more.
EC'92 can learn from the experience.

Strategic Choices for Newly Opened Markets

by Joel A. Bleeke

As 1992 approaches, markets are opening not just in Western Europe but throughout the world. In Eastern Europe, Asia, and North America, trade walls that have stood for decades are beginning to crumble in the face of political unrest and technological innovation. In anticipation of these changes, a do-or-die atmosphere is driving many European, Japanese, and U.S. companies to become broad-based competitors. And in the deal-oriented atmosphere that has ensued, aggressive competitors are often forced to make critical decisions fast on whether and how to expand into uncharted terrain.

Fortunately, a valuable map is available: U.S. companies' experience with deregulation over the past ten years. That experience shows clearly the pattern of competitive dynamics that unfolds when artificial constraints are suddenly lifted and new entrants are allowed to rush in. Consequently, it provides useful lessons not only for markets opening because of regulatory changes but also for markets such

Joel A. Bleeke is a director of McKinsey & Company and co-leader of McKinsey's International Management Center.

as telecommunications, semiconductors, and autos, which are becoming global in response to technological or other discontinuities.

Perhaps the most important of these lessons has to do with time. The U.S. companies' experience shows that managers who look only to the years immediately surrounding 1992 – or any other market opening – will make irreparable mistakes. Because the competitive environment changes twice – once when the market opens and again about five years later – a ten-year roadmap is essential.

This road map will direct many large competitors away from their traditional roles as broad-line players into new, more profitable roles as low-cost en-

> ## The opening of Europe may be even more traumatic than U.S. deregulation.

trants, focused-segment marketers, or providers of shared utilities. And for many, the map will include significant changes in course, since the actions required to survive in the early years of a market's opening are not the same as those that bring success in the second phase of open-market competition.

These lessons derive from a year-long study of the managerial implications of deregulation in U.S. airlines, financial services, long-distance telephone service, central-office switching, trucking, and railroads. The first part of this study involved a detailed assessment of the dynamics in each industry from its deregulation to the present (including an analysis of structural costs, industry cost curves, industry profitability, new entries, and exits). In the second part, my colleagues and I examined the management strategies of profitable and unprofitable companies to uncover common patterns. (The strategic choices we considered included pricing, breadth of product or service offerings, cost-reduction activities, and marketing strategies.)

In some ways, the opening of Europe and other global markets may be even more traumatic than U.S. deregulation. New entrants will not only be fledgling companies like People Express but also powerful organizations like American Airlines and Deutsche Bank. Given histories of local protection and the large number of strong across-the-board players that are planning to build beyond their national franchises, the competition (especially among global companies) may be far more painful than it was in the United States, where deregulation was largely a domestic event. The fact that major Japanese companies are planning investments that will meet local-content requirements – often at lower cost than existing European facilities – leads to that conclusion. So does the wave of cross-border merger and

> ## In deregulated markets, nearly all new entrants fail.
> ## So do many large competitors.

acquisition activity that has already begun, allowing less time for managers to think through their long-term game plans. Indeed, the strong alliances that are already forming across Europe suggest that the competitive situation may soon be dominated by powerful, broad-based competitors holding a series of local oligopolies and making new entry extremely difficult and costly.

Despite the differences, the U.S. experience with deregulation shows how the opening of once restricted markets leads to a new competitive world. Whether the market is in Canada, Eastern Europe, Asia, or the European Community matters less than the competitive dynamic its opening unleashes. And

in that competitive dynamic, undifferentiated size matters less than the strategic choices thoughtful managers make.

The Competitive Dynamics of Deregulation

Deregulation in the United States began in 1975, when the SEC abolished fixed rates for U.S. securities brokers. Before long, other industries were coping with deregulation as well: airlines in 1978, trucking and railroads in 1980, banking and telecommunications at intervals throughout the 1980s. In every instance, we can see the same set of competitive dynamics play itself out.

□ While the number of new entrants can be staggering, nearly all soon fail – along with many large existing competitors. No fewer than 215 new air carriers entered the market in the ten years following deregulation, compared with *no* new FAA-certified carriers in the preceding 40 years. But fewer than one-third of the new entrants and fewer than half (44%) of the existing competitors survived those ten years as independent entities. Arguably, only two of the new carriers (Midway Airlines and America West Airlines) have distinctive strong franchises today (and even Midway is suffering financially as a result of recent expansion beyond its Chicago hub). In trucking the story was much the same. From a steady level of 17,000 truckers in the 1960s and 1970s, the number of competitors rose to over 37,000 in 1987. At the same time, more than 72 companies, accounting for over $2 billion or 16% of industry revenues, shut down between 1980 and 1982 alone.

□ Industry profitability deteriorates rapidly as new entrants shatter pricing for all competitors for at least five years. The surprise is not entrants' starkly lower costs. (On average these were 40% to 50% below competitors' chiefly because the new companies carried less baggage such as seniority agreements, outmoded factories, and expensive distribution systems.) The surprise is new entrants' ability to destroy market pricing for everyone, even if they take only 10% to 15% of total market share. In the securities industry, for example, discount brokers captured less than 20% of consumer volume, but they forced a 30% reduction in market prices. Prices in the central-office and PBX-switching markets fell by 40% to 50%, yet low-cost entrants captured no more than 25% of the total market share.

□ The most attractive business segments often become the least attractive – and vice versa – as competitors all flock to the same markets and cross-subsidies unwind. In telecommunications, prices on the previously most profitable business, long-distance service, dropped 38% between 1984 and 1988, while prices on local service rose 43%. In air-

> **After deregulation, the most attractive businesses often become the least attractive – and vice versa.**

lines, prices on high-density, longer haul routes (like the Chicago to New York corridor) fell by 42%, while prices on previously less profitable, short-haul secondary routes climbed sharply. In the retail brokerage business, prices on institutional transactions dropped 30% on average in the year after deregulation, while prices on consumer transactions fell only 4%. In short, what appear to be less attractive strategies before deregulation often pay off after deregulation as savvy competitors avoid the rush of new entrants and anticipate the large price changes (both up and down) that soon occur.

☐ Variation in profitability between the best and worst performers widens dramatically and remains high. In time, the spread reflects the strongest companies' ability to gain on weaker competitors by rebuilding their franchises. From 1984 to 1988, for example, American Airlines earned $1.5 billion while Pan Am lost over $950 million. (As a benchmark, the nine largest carriers had aggregate profits of approximately $3.5 billion during this period.) But during the first five or so years, the variation occurs because the weak get weaker, not because the strong become more profitable. In the first three years after deregulation, for example, the least profitable railroads suffered massive losses (on the order of returns of negative 10% to 50%) after just about breaking even in the previous five years.

☐ Merger and acquisition activity often occurs in compressed waves that are driven by the demonstration effect of other acquisitions and by pressure to keep up with rivals that are doubling in size and/or scope. The first wave focuses on consolidating weak players, the second wave on combining the strong. In the brokerage industry, second-tier firms (numbers 11 to 25 in market share) grew rapidly in the three years surrounding deregulation by acquiring weaker competitors. But after raising its market share from 14% to 26%, this group began to lose ground before a second wave of acquisitions among the industry's largest firms.

☐ Only a small number of companies (no more than five to seven in the industries we examined) can re-main broad-based competitors. Most are forced to narrow their product range and spin off noncore activities to survive. The reasons are mostly financial: at the same time that profits are falling and cross-subsidies are unwinding, the cost of competing in each segment shoots up as new entrants increase competitive pressure and force established companies to invest heavily to improve productivity, research and development, marketing, and customer service. Given these pressures, many companies choose – or find it necessary – to focus on core activities in which they have strong skills and a competitive advantage.

The result is much greater segmentation within the industry, with each segment requiring its own set of skills and a distinctive business system. The trucking industry, for example, now consists of integrated less-than-truckload shippers, stand-alone, full-load carriers offering no consolidation services, and truck lessors. In brokerage, competitors have emerged to create related but distinct businesses in research, trading, and retail distribution.

Strategies for Survival, Strategies for Success

Looking back on ten years of deregulation, four distinct types of companies were able to survive and build profitable, sustainable market positions. They are: broad-based distribution companies that offer a wide range of products and services over an extensive geographic area; low-cost entrants that migrated over time to become specialty or customer segment-focused providers; focused-segment marketers that emphasize high levels of service at relatively high prices or target a very specific, defensible customer group; and shared utilities that focus on making economies of scale available to a large number of small competitors.

Except for some high-end marketers, successful companies in each of these categories pursued very different strategies in the first few years of deregulation than they did thereafter. Why the change in course? Changes in industry structure – and the innovations and initiative of sharp-witted managers.

In all the industries we studied, the early years of deregulation were characterized by shakeouts, restructuring, and the consolidation of position among survivors. During this period, flexibility (especially pricing flexibility) is the key to survival. Then the competitive situation changes. After five years of intense competition, the strain on industry performance has forced many of the weaker companies to exit. Larger companies have figured out how to offer low-cost products and services to compete with new rivals. The price gap between new entrants and existing companies has also diminished as the latter's cost-cutting efforts take effect. The result: new entries decline, the industry consolidates, and competition shifts away from purely price-based behavior. In this second phase, which is continuing in many industries today, leading companies move to build new oligopolies that can be every bit as powerful as those eliminated by deregulation. (The exhibit, "After Deregulation, Strategies Change," summarizes the key strategic choices these companies made.)

Broad-based distribution companies are deregulation's equivalent of large, multinational organizations. As a rule, more companies seek this role than are able to play it. Following deposit deregulation in 1981, for example, an informal survey of executives at the nation's largest banks showed that nearly all expected to be broad-based competitors ten years after deregulation. Yet, of necessity, most of the group moved away from broad-based competition throughout the 1980s, shedding overseas operations and, in several cases, selling consumer operations such as mortgage and credit card processing.

Broad-based competitors that did succeed understood their pricing in detail and were able to eliminate cross-subsidies and disaggregate pricing if competition demanded it. Equally important, they conserved resources and were willing to bide their time in moving to dominate their markets. Early critical actions for companies seeking this role include the following.

1. Improve pricing capability. Effective competitors assess the price sensitivity and underlying costs of serving specific customer segments and adjust pricing to protect these segments from new low-cost players. AT&T's price reductions for high-volume business customers reflected its recognition that these relationships were endangered by MCI's and Sprint's targeted marketing efforts. American Airlines became a leader in yield management by hiring a staff of over 100 people to manage the mix of seats and fares. While making it hard for business travelers to take advantage of cut-rate fares, American also moved to gain their loyalty by introducing the frequent flyer program.

2. Cut structural costs. In no instance could established broad-based companies reduce their costs to match those of low-cost entrants. But they could and did cut costs substantially. AT&T's employment has dropped roughly 20% since divestiture. American Airlines was among the first to introduce a two-tier wage structure, paying new pilots, flight attendants, and mechanics up to 50% less than industry averages.

3. Shift quickly toward new ways of differentiating service. U.S. Sprint aggressively installed digital fiber networks to provide high-quality service between major cities. Yellow Freight System improved its ability to consolidate less-than-truckload shipments by expanding from 248 trucking terminals in 1980 to 440 terminals in 1982. Federal Express introduced a computerized bar code system to track packages.

4. Conserve capital to maintain flexibility. The most costly mistake broad-based competitors made was overcommitting capital through acquisitions, major equipment purchases, or entry into new mar-

After Deregulation, Strategies Change

	Broad-Based Distribution Company	Low-Cost New Entrant	Focused-Segment Marketer	Shared Utility
Key Actions Early On	▪ Cut costs ▪ Differentiate service ▪ Improve pricing capabilities ▪ Increase marketing, product development ▪ Don't overcommit early	▪ Target the most profitable segments ▪ Eliminate structural costs ▪ Focus on price-sensitive customers and price-oriented advertising ▪ Outsource to limit the scope of operations ▪ Don't grow too fast	▪ Target nonprice-sensitive segments ▪ Bundle products ▪ Develop customer information systems ▪ Build personal relationships	▪ Identify separable, scale-intensive functions ▪ Sign up development partners to share costs, provide inputs ▪ Build a core set of clients
Five Years Later...	▪ Develop new oligopolies ▪ Use detailed pricing as a strategic weapon ▪ Preempt competitors via strategic alliances	▪ Move up the service-price ladder ▪ Identify new niches ▪ Maintain cost advantages ▪ Avoid competing in the core markets of broad-based competitors	▪ Continue to emphasize early actions ▪ Selectively expand into related segments ▪ Improve customer service ▪ Expand product features to support price	▪ Become the industry standard by building share ▪ Ensure participation and use by industry players, often by selling minority interests ▪ Move to a high-service, high-price position while increasing customer dependence on the shared utility
Examples	American Airlines Merrill Lynch	Midway Airlines Charles Schwab	Hambrecht & Quist Northern Trust Goldman, Sachs	SABRE SWIFT Telerate Reuters

kets, leaving themselves too thin a cushion to weather the profit storm. IU International, for example, expanded rapidly in the less-than-truckload business by acquiring Ryder and Pacific Intermountain Express. After losing over $125 million in two years trying to build a national carrier, the business was divested.

United hurt its competitive position in airlines by its costly acquisitions of Hertz and Westin. These nonairline holdings were sold in 1987, but by then American had been able to outpace United's growth in revenue passenger miles due in part to this diversion. In contrast to United's capital-consuming acquisitions, American grew mostly from within, conserving its cash to build existing businesses and using affiliations rather than acquisitions to extend its reach.

The key point is that during the profit squeeze that follows deregulation, capital markets often close for new funding because of low industry profitability. As a result, capital becomes scarce in deregulating industries, and conserving capital during the early years is essential for survival. This is less true later on, however, when a different set of strategic choices becomes critical for success. Of these, the most important is identifying new ways to increase market clout and to develop new local oligopolies.

At first, as we have seen, low-cost entrants and focused-segment marketers threaten existing broadline players, and many giants topple as they fail to react quickly enough. But it is crucial not to underestimate the power of large competitors over time to

 Never underestimate the power of large competitors to make big better again.

make big better again. In the deregulated airline industry, the use of hub control, computerized yield-management systems, and frequent flyer programs have been powerful tools for competitors to regain clout and pricing power. The top eight airlines now control 92% of revenue passenger miles compared with 80% before deregulation. (By 1988, American alone accounted for about 20% of the airline industry's market value compared with approximately 7% in 1978.) Local oligopolies are also apparent at many major hubs: in St. Louis, TWA controlled 82% of the traffic in 1988 compared with 43% in 1979. The same

year, USAir controlled 36 of Pittsburgh's 51 gates and held an 85% market share compared with 48% in 1979. By 1990, United and American represented 80% of the flights from Chicago's O'Hare.

The reemergence of oligopolies is also evident in the securities industry, where the top 25 firms increased their share of capital to 63% in 1985 compared with 51% in 1980 and 43% on "May Day" in 1975. At the same time, these firms made deep pockets more important by escalating the role of risk capital in securities trading and mergers and acquisitions. In trucking, the top ten less-than-truckload carriers held a 50% market share in 1987 compared with 35% in 1980, enabling them to gain economies of scale by leveraging their spending on freight terminals and information systems.

In rebuilding market power, finely detailed pricing capabilities continue to play a critical role. Pricing can be used defensively, to protect profits by discouraging competitors who enter home turf, and offensively, to maximize profitability from uncontested markets. In airlines, this kind of capability makes the chances of a new entrant modeled on People Express virtually nil. By 1981, the 600,000 fares incorporated in American's computer system in 1977 had risen to 1.6 million, allowing it to meet low prices for selected routes and passenger segments without endangering its broad revenue base. Similarly, truckers filed over 1.2 million tariffs in 1987 compared with an average of 185,000 independent tariffs per year in the early 1980s.

Low-cost new entrants were the catalyst for the competitive battles that followed deregulation. But successful entrants almost always migrated relatively quickly to specialty or segment-focused competition rather than pursue a pure low-cost strategy. Among the reasons for changing strategy were the reactions of existing competitors, the appearance of "faster guns" with even lower cost structures, and the slow-but-steady rise of the companies' own structural costs.

As we have seen, low-cost entrants compete with cost structures that are fundamentally different from those of existing competitors. They have lower wage schedules, more flexible employment arrangements, and often no unions. Simpler manufacturing and distribution systems eliminate many costs of complexity. Low-cost entrants streamline their businesses and leave decisions to line managers supported by little or no staff. They also tend to outsource products and supplies. Discount brokers let clearing agents handle many of their transactions, for example, rather than build their own internal systems. Similarly, low-cost airlines avoided building computer systems, leased gates, and paid other carriers to handle their maintenance. Over time, of course, new entrants begin to develop their own structural costs as employees become more senior and facilities age. But successful players in deregulated industries continue to control expenses tightly, even when they are no longer competing on price alone.

Other critical choices that low-cost entrants make early on are to target the most profitable segments of a business—those that are cross-subsidizing other segments—and to focus on price and price advertising. In their early years, low-cost entrants are no-frills suppliers. They do not offer service, just rock-bottom price. In addition, they manage their growth. People Express failed in part because it expanded too quickly, consuming capital that was needed later to support price competition. By the end of 1985, less than five years after its founding, People Express had grown to 3,400 employees and 78 planes with enough seats to rank as the ninth largest airline in the United States. Capacity doubled in 1984 alone, and the acquisitions continued in 1985 and 1986. Yet by the end of 1984, earlier profits had already given way to red ink as the airline was unable to fill its seats even at loss-leader fares.

The most dangerous mistake low-cost entrants can make is to take on broad-based competitors in their sensitive core markets where their larger rivals will use all their resources to defend their turfs. Most new entrants are bruised severely when the giants react, and all but a few fail. Midway Airlines's recent attempt to enter the Milwaukee-Chicago market illustrates the power of pricing against new entrants. On Monday, May 1, 1989, Midway began offering jet service from Milwaukee to its own hub at Midway Airport in Chicago. On Thursday, June 8, Midway cut its Milwaukee fares to increase its passenger loads. But Milwaukee is a hub for Northwest Airlines. By Tuesday, June 13, Northwest had not only matched Midway's fares but also cut *all* its fares on flights to and from Midway. By Friday, June 16, Midway was forced to cut back its promotion in Milwaukee to restore its pricing in Chicago.

Longer term, the key to survival for low-cost players lies in finding a viable migration route to a position as a broad-based competitor (as MCI has done) or a focused-segment provider. Identifying new niches can play a part in this migration. Midway Airlines is now the third largest carrier in Chicago. While initially it concentrated on price, today it emphasizes service, especially the convenience of near-to-downtown Midway Airport. The company's strategy has migrated away from pure low cost to a price-value trade-off that features convenience. Yet its market clout reaches just so far: recent efforts to expand to a second hub in Philadelphia have met with tough responses from the majors.

Implicit in this migration, of course, is movement up the service-price ladder. While maintaining acceptable prices, Charles Schwab now offers a range of money market and mutual funds, retirement accounts, and CDs as well as customer help lines and quotation services that increase cost but still offer a

Successful low-cost entrants don't compete on price for very long.

reasonable price-value trade-off. U.S. Sprint features the superior quality of fiber-optic lines. MCI has systematically built skills in new product areas like "800" lines and international service, while marketing heavily to profitable corporate customers and keeping a tight hold on headquarters expense.

Migration is difficult, however, and many companies fail as their consumer image becomes blurred. Continental Airlines seems to be caught in this dilemma as it tries to change its image from a cut-rate provider to a full-service airline oriented toward business travelers. Since many passengers still see the airline as a low-cost option, Continental is finding that it must offer special (and costly) incentives to lure business trade.

Focused-segment marketers target a specific set of customers or products, emphasizing service levels that are unavailable elsewhere at relatively high prices. Because success in pursuing this strategy largely depends on identifying the right niche and building strong personal relationships, many companies do not need to shift direction five years out. They can continue to develop initiatives that are effective early on.

In general, the closer the personal relationship in the sales channel between the customer and the provider, the less price sensitive the customer (and segment) is likely to be. Once these customers have been identified, segment marketers often develop a broad range of products for the customer group and encourage cross-selling. Bundling products and increasing product complexity help segment marketers by reducing price sensitivity and by creating opportunities to deepen personal relationships. Sales of corporate banking services to middle-market customers by regional banks are a good example of such product bundling.

Successful focused-segment marketers also develop customer information systems with an emphasis on databases and customer profitability lev-

els. The relationship databases used by regional banks for upscale accounts, the customer files that make frequent flyer programs possible, and Merrill Lynch's Cash Management Account for its securities customers are all good examples of such systems.

Other essential pieces of this strategy include: (1) selectively expanding beyond existing segments into closely related segments or markets, as many regional banks have done in rolling up local community banks; (2) identifying new approaches and ways to measure service performance such as turnaround time, reprocess time, and error logs; and (3) developing new product features such as the extended product guarantees, car rental insurance, and high credit limits that now come with costly credit cards to support a premium price. In every instance, the intent is the same: to lock in attractive customers through product attributes and customized service.

Shared utilities are the last—and newest—of the strategic groups that emerged from deregulation. Shared utilities offer new entrants and other competitors the advantages of scale by sharing costs across many companies. They are usually created as competitive pressures generate demand for new information, services, or inputs that cannot be met by small, individual companies. Relatively few places for shared utilities exist in each industry. But for those companies that can identify and capitalize on an opportunity, the strategy is most attractive.

Ironically, in the years immediately following deregulation, many observers predicted that only a few large companies would survive in each industry. But these observers never imagined the growth of shared

> Deregulation pundits never anticipated companies like Telerate that make advantages of scale available to everyone.

utilities that would make many of the advantages of size available to everyone. Telerate, for example, provides government bond and foreign exchange quotations and financial market news instantly around the world from its home in New York, thereby making it possible for small- and medium-size traders to have many of the information advantages that come from scale. Telerate's average return on equity between 1985 and 1988 was more than 20%.

Similarly, Centex Telemanagement, a telecommunications remarketer in California, is now one of Pacific Bell's top customers. The company purchases telephone time in large blocks and resells it to smaller companies at attractive rates.

The first step for a would-be shared utility is to identify discrete functions with heavy fixed costs that cannot easily be developed in-house by new or small competitors. Computer expenses are often the basis for a shared utility like Dallas-based Hogan Systems, which provides systems support for small- and medium-size commercial banks.

Next comes signing up development partners to help build the utility by sharing costs or contributing proprietary information. Most deregulation-inspired shared utilities had such partners in their early years. Telerate shared development with a U.S. primary securities dealer, in part to get access to real-time trading information. Globex, the new utility for off-hours futures and options trading, has links with Reuters, the Chicago Mercantile Exchange, and the Chicago Board of Trade. Equally critical is building a set of core clients among the utility's largest users and working to ensure their loyalty through superior service. Telerate's early penetration of major trading rooms was a key to its later success.

As the service gains momentum, making sure that it becomes the industry standard is crucial. For many utilities, that means growing fast enough to meet the demands of customers and build a large installed base. Even though many customers initially had complaints about Telerate's service, it became the industry standard because it could handle extremely rapid growth in the number of terminals, information sources, and customers it had outstanding.

Unhappily for most competitors, shared utilities are natural monopolies. So while they offer attractive opportunities during the first phase of open-market activity, eventually less effective producers are driven out of business by the scale required for satisfactory performance. Those that are largest, with the greatest ability to spread costs across a broad base, survive. The rest do not. This shakeout is now occurring in airline computer reservation systems. It is also taking place in global rating of debt securities, where the strength of Moody's and Standard & Poor's has made it hard for European-based and Asian-based entrants to prosper.

Because they dominate their markets, shared utilities have great pricing flexibility and often generate extraordinary returns. As a result, they can easily become the target of envy, prompting powerful customers to consider creating a rival. In fact, a consortium of securities firms and investment banks has recently been discussing the possibility of creating a new shared utility to compete with Telerate and Reuters in the market for U.S. government securities pricing information.

To avoid encouraging rivals and to support their revenue base, utilities often move to supply high levels of customer service and personal contact in exchange for their high price. They also seek to lock in their product or service: for example, by expanding the number of individual users who receive their services at a given company. Selling part of the shared utility to customers and suppliers may also help to ensure continued use and profitability while reducing the resentment associated with high returns.

When Global Markets Open

The patterns of competition that characterized deregulation in the United States are already emerging in Western Europe. In the airline industry, early liberalization of flights between London and Amsterdam led to a 37% increase in capacity and an effective drop in prices of 16% on what had been a highly profitable route. Ryanair, a new low-cost player, has entered the Dublin-London market with round-trip fares that are approximately half those of Aer Lingus. Trans European Airways, Europe's second largest charter airline, has applied to fly scheduled routes at discount prices out of Belgium.

The wave of merger, acquisition, and alliance activity that followed U.S. deregulation is also well underway. Air France has acquired control of UTA and Air Inter to become the largest airline in continental Europe. British Airways and KLM are each seeking a 20% stake in Sabena World Airlines. Similar alliances are emerging in telecommunications and financial services, suggesting that the powerful series of local oligopolies that characterize the second phase of open-market competition are already developing, even before 1992.

Europe's competitive evolution is also being speeded up by the fact that many of the new entrants are mighty international competitors like Honda or American Airlines. These competitors will be able to capitalize quickly on current differences in global efficiency across markets. Pilots of some continental European airlines, for example, are paid, on average, more than twice what their counterparts at major U.S. airlines receive. Yet the productivity of U.S. airlines, measured by revenue passenger miles per employee, is more than double that of the European airlines. As markets open, these differences will be largely equalized.

The exact dynamics of market openings will vary, of course, from country to country. But the new competitive structure that market opening creates remains the same, not only for deregulating markets but also for markets experiencing other discontinuities. The oil crisis of the 1970s, for example, made possible a rush of new Japanese auto entrants into the United States. And while these companies initially entered as low-cost players, they soon recognized the need to migrate to positions as focused-segment marketers and broad-based competitors in order to survive as others entered with even lower costs.

Whether in Canada, Eastern Europe, the EC, Asia, or the United States, opening markets will cause rapid changes in the character of profitable companies as cost cutting, pricing, and market segmentation become far more important than undifferentiated size. Managers who use the lessons of U.S. deregulation wisely should be able to avoid many of the hard landings that so often surround market openings.

Author's note: I thank my colleague David Ernst for his contribution to this article.

Reprint 90502

THE POLITICS OF BUSINESS

How An Industry Builds Political Advantage

by DAVID B. YOFFIE

Silicon Valley goes to Capitol Hill.

No U.S. company or industry is immune from the impact of decisions made in Washington. But many corporate executives still act as if politics is an exercise in crisis management – something to worry about after trouble comes.

Ignoring Washington until you need it may have worked 25 years ago. Today it is a prescription for failure. Divisions within the executive branch, the erosion of party discipline on Capitol Hill, and the sprawling power of congressional staffs have rendered obsolete once reliable channels of access and influence. Increased political competition among businesses further complicates the situation. In the early 1960s, fewer than 150 companies maintained Washington offices. Today the number is close to 700. Some 2,500 companies have other forms of Washington representation, and more than 15,000 lobbyists work the halls of Congress and the regulatory agencies.

Executives must bring to politics the same long-term perspectives they apply to marketing and investment decisions. This is especially true for companies or industries whose size and reach don't provide a natural base of influence. Manufacturers of steel, automobiles, or textiles expect a sympathetic hearing in Washington – too many jobs in too many congressional districts are at stake. But politics is very different for smaller industries that don't affect millions of people, don't have employees spread across the country, or can't draw on the clout of national labor unions.

Like a superior business strategy to niche players in a crowded market, intelligent and carefully executed political strategies are crucial for smaller industries to succeed in Washington. The challenge is to create and sustain political advantage – to develop a stable and constructive relationship that makes Washington an ally in the battle for global competitiveness. The process of building political advantage requires high-level executive attention and action. If government is important to an industry's competitive future, political activism must be a business priority.

The political effectiveness of the semiconductor industry shows what it takes to succeed. The design and manufacture of semiconductors is a small industry by any standard. Merchant suppliers (companies that sell chips to other companies) employ fewer than 115,000 U.S. workers and generate revenues of $12 billion – just over 10% of the revenues of General Motors. Employment is focused geographically; more than half the industry's work force lives in Arizona, California, and Texas. And most of the top semiconductor companies were founded by self-assured entrepreneurs dedicated to the virtues of

David B. Yoffie is an associate professor at the Harvard Business School, where he specializes in business-government relations and international trade. He is also the author of Power & Protectionism: Strategies of the Newly Industrializing Countries *(Columbia University Press, 1983). For HBR, he has previously written on industrial policy and on countertrade.*

small enterprise and corporate self-reliance. For much of their early history, these driven industrialists resisted outside alliances of any sort, especially with Washington. These are hardly the ingredients from which political juggernauts are fashioned.

Yet semiconductor companies have compiled one of the most impressive political performance records of the 1980s. In 1983, the industry established an ambitious agenda for government action: more favorable tax treatment, relaxed antitrust regulation of joint research and development, greater protection of chip designs, and several tough policies to promote fair trade. The industry had realized these objectives and more by the end of 1987. (See the insert, "Big Results for a Small Industry.")

The track record has been most striking on the trade front. The semiconductor industry has nursed serious grievances about Japanese trade practices since the mid-1970s. Once they decided to act, U.S. companies needed less than two years to convince Washington to take aggressive action on their behalf.

The formal campaign began in June 1985, when the Semiconductor Industry Association (SIA) filed for relief under Section 301 of the Trade Act of 1974. Section 301 authorizes the president to penalize countries that deny U.S. products fair access to their markets. Fourteen months later, the United States

Why did semiconductor companies succeed in Washington when other industries came away disappointed?

and Japan signed an accord that gave the industry the assistance it sought. The Japanese agreed to open their markets to foreign semiconductors and to stop selling chips below cost. In April 1987, concluding that Japan was violating the accord, the Reagan administration approved $300 million in punitive sanctions—the first such penalties against Japan since World War II. This series of measures is unprecedented for its swiftness, severity, and agreement with industry recommendations.

Why have semiconductor companies succeeded in Washington when other industries of comparable and greater size (telecommunications equipment, footwear, automobile parts) have not? There are no magic formulas for influencing government. Political environments change, public officials come and go, opponents and allies shift overnight. But the semiconductor industry's experiences illuminate

four general principles for making things happen in Washington:

1. *Companies need a united front.* Small industries must develop and maintain alliances among competitors, suppliers, and customers. Such ties expand the range of affected constituencies, increase the resources available for political action, and defuse potential sources of opposition.

2. *Government allies are essential.* Friends inside the government are as important as corporate allies. An industry should identify and cultivate executive branch agencies and members of Congress with stakes in its agenda. This means crafting positions that will appeal to targeted officials and factoring their interests and agendas into the industry's own political calculations. An industry should also identify potential adversaries in government and take steps to minimize their impact.

3. *CEOs have a special role to play.* A visible, persuasive, accessible CEO is often more effective than dozens of hired political guns. Top executives can overcome "barriers to entry" in Washington. In the early stages of political activism, gaining access to public officials and raising industry visibility can be especially difficult. Lobbyists often struggle to get time with a senator or a cabinet member. Business leaders can get to them more easily. When CEOs make promises, they can deliver; lobbyists are only messengers. Politicians know this.

4. *Political action by company executives is more effective than trade association efforts.* Trade associations can play important roles in setting agendas, monitoring political developments, and establishing contacts in Washington. But company managers—senior executives, middle managers, plant supervisors—should be on the front lines. Managers understand the details and subtleties of their industry; it's their livelihood. And precisely because it's their livelihood, they may be more driven to get results.

The modern semiconductor industry was born in 1959 with the invention of the integrated circuit. The industry has experienced three phases of political engagement. The first 15 years were marked by an arm's-length relationship with government. U.S. companies were global technology leaders in all segments of the chip market, industry revenues exploded, and many millionaires were born. During this expansion period, NASA and the Pentagon were important customers, but chip makers wanted the government's business—not its meddling.

This attitude began to change in the mid-1970s with the first stirrings of foreign competition. During the 1975 recession, U.S. semiconductor companies scaled back plans to add production capacity much as they had in previous recessions. Then, when the economy rallied, they were caught short of capacity. This time the Japanese rushed in to meet excess demand. When Japanese success in commodity chips threatened to put certain U.S. producers out of business, a few of them turned to Washington for help. But their proposals for government intervention fell on deaf ears.

Gradually, as Japanese competition seemed to verge on domination, more chip makers began to look to Washington. U.S. companies accounted for 55% of world semiconductor production in 1978; by

> **Semiconductor executives saw that their market position would deteriorate further without Washington's help.**

1987, their share had dropped to 44%. During this same period, Japanese market share rose from 28% to 50%. Alarmed by these trends, semiconductor companies made political activism a priority.

Trade policy has been an issue of particular urgency. Its importance was rooted in one of the industry's most striking characteristics—that production costs for most products declined by 30% for every doubling of cumulative volume. This is because semiconductor manufacturing lines frequently turned out more defective than sound chips. With new products, yields were often as low as 25%, even for the best companies. As products matured, however, yields would run as high as 90%.

The need to raise yields led companies to manufacture high-volume products that could act as "technology drivers." It was generally believed that skills learned in manufacturing large quantities of a simple product could be transferred to more complicated, higher value-added devices and help "drive" the company down a steep learning curve. Dynamic random access memory (DRAM) chips, a 1971 American invention, were the most widely used technology driver for many years. Other technology drivers included static random access memory (SRAM) chips and erasable programmable read only memory (EPROM) chips.

During the past ten years, however, U.S. companies have lost market share in each of these critical products. In 1975, for example, U.S. companies accounted for 90% of world DRAM shipments. By 1987, their share was just over 20%, an erosion suffered almost exclusively at the hands of the Japanese.

U.S. merchant producers have articulated two basic objections to Japanese practices. First, for decades U.S. companies have been unable to increase their 10% share of the Japanese market, despite wide swings in the dollar's value and their consistent success in Europe against the Japanese. De facto exclusion from Japan, which by 1986 had become the world's largest market for semiconductors, put American manufacturers at a serious competitive disadvantage in technology drivers. Second, U.S. companies claimed that the Japanese were selling commodity chips in the United States below production costs. This alleged dumping not only cost U.S. companies market share, it also put tremendous pressure on industry profits. U.S. merchant producers lost a staggering $2 billion in 1985 and 1986. This dismal outcome was largely the result of a global industry downturn (Japanese producers also lost $2 billion), but dumping in the U.S. market made a bad situation worse.

It's easy to see why most semiconductor executives eventually agreed that the trade situation and their collective market position would deteriorate further without aggressive intervention from Washington. The challenge became translating the goal of fair trade into the reality of government policy.

Stand United

A crucial choice for executives trying to build political advantage is whether to advance the interests of their own companies or to support industrywide initiatives. Political activism is expensive, so only big corporations can consider a company-based agenda. The startup investment for a bare-bones Washington operation—an office, a secretary, and a full-time lobbyist—typically runs about $1 million.

Even for large companies, industrywide campaigns are often preferable for issues where rivals share common political interests. For small companies, forging common political ground is a necessity. A politician evaluating a proposal from business usually searches for answers to several basic questions: What will the proposal cost? What sectors of the economy benefit? What sectors lose? No politician wants to help one industry if it means antagonizing three others. That's why coalitions are so important from a strategic perspective. Just as powerful suppliers and customers squeeze profit margins in the marketplace, unrestrained political competition among rivals, suppliers, and customers usually reduces everyone's influence.

The defeat of several early proposals for government assistance taught semiconductor industry leaders the importance of building coalitions. During

Big Results for a Small Industry

The performance of the semiconductor industry in Washington during the past five years compares favorably with the recent political success of any domestic industry, regardless of size. Here is a selective catalog of legislation and executive actions adopted since 1983 that bolstered the competitive position of U.S. semiconductor manufacturers.

October 1984. President Reagan signs the National Cooperative Research Act after the House and Senate approve it unanimously. The law, clearing a legal path for the industry's Sematech research consortium, eases antitrust restrictions against joint research and development.

October 1984. The Trade and Tariff Act of 1984 becomes law. An important provision of this omnibus trade statute clarifies that denial of "fair and equitable market access" is a basis to petition for relief under Section 301 of the Trade Act of 1974. The law also instructs the president to negotiate reductions in barriers to trade in services and high-technology products, and it specifically authorizes lower tariffs on semiconductors.

November 1984. President Reagan signs the Semiconductor Chip Protection Act. For the first time, semiconductor companies get statutory protection against duplication of their chip designs. Enforcement of the act is potentially worth millions of dollars in additional profits to U.S. companies, which have been fighting low-priced competition from foreign-made chips.

March 1985. The United States and Japan eliminate tariffs on imported semiconductors. This agreement took two years to negotiate, even though tariffs were so modest that their elimination was not expected to affect chip prices. The biggest impact was improved profits for U.S. producers, which were paying a duty on chips sent abroad for final assembly and then shipped back for sale in the U.S. market, and lower overhead associated with these shipments.

August 1986. The United States and Japan sign a landmark agreement on trade in semiconductors that reflects virtually all the Semiconductor Industry Association's demands. The Japanese pledge to lift their purchases of foreign-made chips to slightly more than 20% of their market over a five-year period, effectively doubling U.S. sales to Japan. In addition, the U.S. Commerce Department establishes a system to monitor production costs and prices for Japanese chips and to set fair market values. The Japanese agree not to sell chips outside their home market below these levels.

April 1987. President Reagan imposes $300 million in sanctions on Japanese products in response to alleged violations of the semiconductor accord. He raises duties on a number of products—including portable computers, selected power hand tools, and some color television sets—to 100% of their value. In June and November, after determining that the Japanese were no longer dumping chips, the president lifts some of the sanctions. Other sanctions remain in place to signal continued U.S. displeasure with the slow improvement in U.S. access to the Japanese semiconductor market.

November 1987. Congress includes $100 million in the fiscal 1988 defense appropriations bill to help underwrite the Sematech research consortium. Sematech's Austin, Texas facilities focus on reestablishing U.S. leadership in semiconductor chip manufacture. The goal is to develop leading-edge chip-making techniques, based exclusively on U.S. materials and technology, by 1993.

---

the first 20 years of the industry's existence, it had no organization to represent its interests in Washington. Some companies belonged to large electronics trade associations, but these groups' agendas did not reflect semiconductor industry priorities. So in 1977, five leading merchant producers of high-volume chips—Advanced Micro Devices (AMD), Fairchild, Intel, Motorola, and National Semiconductor—founded the Semiconductor Industry Association.

The SIA and individual companies floated several initiatives against Japan during the late 1970s, and political leaders did what political leaders invariably do. They sought the reactions of other players in the industry as well as outside constituencies. In this case, the key outside constituency was the biggest buyers of chips—giant computer builders like Hewlett-Packard and Digital Equipment. The users' primary concern was maintaining reasonable prices and flexible supplies. Invariably, they opposed SIA initiatives, which effectively doomed the proposals. A string of defeats convinced semiconductor leaders that they had to expand their base of business support.

The process of building coalitions took two forms. Merchant producers cultivated active support from companies and industry associations that had opposed previous SIA initiatives. They also worked to discourage active opposition. If a company or association could not endorse a semiconductor proposal, it might be persuaded at least not to undermine it.

One important step in the coalition-building process was expanding the industry's trade association membership. SIA leaders had been working to increase membership since 1977, but in the early 1980s they made a particular effort to enroll the large captive producers of chips. (Captive producers build chips primarily for use in their own products.) IBM joined the SIA in December 1980, and during the next few years, so did other big captive producers. By 1985, the SIA had 48 members with combined revenues of more than $100 billion. The organization included some large merchant producers like Texas Instruments that had initially resisted joining the group, smaller companies building custom chips, major chip buyers like Control Data and NCR (most of which also produced their own chips), and giant captive producers like IBM and Digital Equipment.

The most important new member, of course, was IBM, the world's largest manufacturer and consumer of semiconductors. IBM never played a leadership role on trade issues, but the company's envoy conveyed to the SIA what positions IBM could and could not live with. Moreover, IBM's membership gave the SIA a level of credibility and visibility in Washington that it had never before enjoyed.

Find the right political channels. Cultivate government allies. Don't provoke likely adversaries.

Collecting in one organization large and small merchant producers, captive producers, and important users also created a means by which each industry segment could develop a better understanding of other segments' interests and priorities. Debates within the SIA were, in effect, a negotiating process that produced consensus on particular initiatives. Even if a member company was unenthusiastic about a final SIA proposal, it was unlikely to sabotage the initiative in Washington. It had participated in the internal debates and understood how and why the SIA had reached the position.

The evolution of the Section 301 petition is a case in point. Agreement on the terms of the complaint took three years of bargaining among SIA members. A critical issue was whether trade sanctions should be proposed and, if so, how severe they should be. Some large merchant companies favored an outright embargo on certain commodity chips, or at least the imposition of high tariffs and stiff fines, unless Japan met a timetable for increased U.S. access to its markets. Large users like IBM and Hewlett-Packard re-

jected this proposal outright. Merchant suppliers realized that user opposition would pose huge political obstacles, as it had with previous initiatives, so IBM's and other companies' objections carried great weight in the SIA.

The petition filed in June 1985 did not advocate punitive embargoes, tariffs, or other restrictions on chip supplies. It proposed two tough but constructive policies. First, it demanded a commitment that by the early 1990s the U.S. share of the Japanese semiconductor market increase commensurately with the U.S. position in the rest of the world. Penalties for noncompliance were left vague, although the SIA made it clear that it expected penalties if negotiations failed. Second, the petition suggested a monitoring system to ensure that Japanese companies were not selling chips below cost in the United States or elsewhere. All SIA members could live with these positions.

The process of building coalitions – or at least of neutralizing potential opposition – extended beyond industry borders. George Scalise, chief administrative officer of AMD and chairman of the SIA's public policy committee, worked hard to secure an endorsement of the 301 suit from the American Electronics Association. The AEA, which has been a Washington presence for decades, represents some 2,800 companies with $305 billion in global sales. Scalise understood that strong opposition from the electronics group might doom the 301 action.

The AEA never fully embraced the SIA position, but it did issue a letter supporting the objectives of the trade case. Coordination with the AEA was also important after adoption of the August 1986 trade agreement. Prices for certain DRAMs quickly skyrocketed, which shook up small chip buyers. The SIA established a subcommittee within the AEA to address user concerns and dampen possible calls for repeal of the agreement.

Target Government Allies

A sound marketing strategy balances product positioning, distribution channels, and reasonable prices. A sound political strategy has similar balances. An industry must position a proposed course of action so as to appeal to the customer (White House officials, regulators, or members of Congress), target the most effective channels of influence (congressional committees, executive agencies, or the courts), and impose reasonable costs on taxpayers and other constituencies. Pushing the right buttons, identifying government allies, and working hard not to antagonize potential adversaries are all essential. Failure in any area usually dooms the entire initiative.

The semiconductor industry paid close attention to all three areas. The 301 complaint's primary objective was opening foreign markets rather than closing U.S. doors. This positioning meant the trade action appealed simultaneously to "Japan bashers" and free traders. It certainly satisfied the White House, which liked the idea of appeasing protectionist sentiment on Capitol Hill by supporting a trade initiative that rejected quotas and tariffs. Representatives and senators with protectionist leanings were also satisfied. Even legislators whose districts included no semiconductor employment were attracted to the cause. They could go home and tell voters they were being tough on Japan, and not antagonize other corporate interests. In short, virtually every set of actors in Washington had something to gain by supporting the skillfully crafted industry position, and few had anything to lose.

As for distribution, the industry used a number of complementary political channels. A common strategy of smaller industries is to avoid "politicized" channels (Congress and the White House), where votes matter, and pursue "administrative" channels (the courts and regulatory agencies), where cases are won or lost on their merits. When the data are clear and convincing and the issue is a one-time problem, administrative remedies are usually adequate. If the objective is to make government an ongoing ally, however, companies and industries must tap political channels and find ways to build alliances with public officials.

A Section 301 petition is one of the more politicized avenues for relief under the trade laws. The U.S. trade representative rules on the merits of the case, and the president determines appropriate sanctions. But the law leaves much room for maneuver. The trade representative can postpone the decision for up to one year, and the president can choose not to act even in the face of a favorable ruling. So the semiconductor industry took steps to heighten the visibility of its trade complaint and the costs of complacency.

One tactic was for companies to file their own trade actions, even without SIA endorsement. Days after the SIA filed the 301, Micron Technology charged that Japanese companies were dumping 64K DRAMs. A few months later, three industry leaders (Intel, AMD, and National Semiconductor) accused the Japanese of dumping EPROMs. Even the Commerce Department, anxious to get tough with the Japanese, initiated its own dumping complaint on 256K and higher DRAMs in December. By the end of 1985, the U.S. government faced four separate complaints on unfair semiconductor trade practices, which put even more pressure on the administration and the Japanese to reach an accommodation.

Capitol Hill was another focus. Congress has no direct role in complaints filed under the trade laws, but the SIA approached representatives and senators to support the 301 petition by lobbying the administration and drawing media attention to the issue of unfair trade practices. The association set a very specific

 Even the most loyal customers need attention from top brass. So do politicians.

objective: develop legislative support that was bipartisan, bicameral, and as geographically broad as possible. The result was the Congressional Support Group, a caucus composed of ten representatives and ten senators, ten Democrats and ten Republicans, from states including California, Missouri, Florida, and Pennsylvania. The legislators applied pressure on the White House by making telephone calls, lobbying members of the cabinet, and pushing the trade representative to become more involved in the trade dispute.

The SIA also persuaded 180 representatives and senators—including the entire delegations from several states with heavy semiconductor employment—to send letters (drafted by the SIA's general counsel) to the administration. Meanwhile, the California delegation met with the Japanese ambassador to the United States to emphasize the gravity of the issue. By the time the White House decided to negotiate a semiconductor agreement, the SIA had made as many allies inside the government as it had developed among suppliers and customers.

Many political observers believe that the Pentagon figured prominently in the semiconductor dispute. They argue that microelectronics is so important to high-technology weapons and communications systems that the Defense Department must have been the natural ally of U.S. chip producers. How could the Pentagon tolerate Japanese domination of a commodity dubbed the "oil of the 1980s"?

The truth is, the Defense Department never weighed in strongly on semiconductor trade policy. One of the department's long-standing priorities was to persuade Japan to increase its military spending; trade disputes wouldn't advance this goal. The SIA understood this and kept its distance from the defense establishment until after trade issues were settled. Later, when it was looking for funding for its Sematech research consortium, the industry enlisted the Pentagon's support. The fiscal 1988 defense appropriations bill included $100 million for Sematech.

Get CEOs Involved

Broad membership in an association or informal coalition helps build legitimacy in Washington. Effective political targeting further improves the odds of success. But who does the work?

Here again, semiconductor companies made the right moves at the right times. Even before they had forged an industry consensus on trade policy, they had worked hard to establish a beachhead in Washington. Like companies in so many other industries, chip makers turned to political activism only after troubling market trends had surfaced. Like the marketplace, however, politics usually rewards early movers. The first companies that enter political life make the campaign contributions, build the key congressional ties, and establish the reputations that translate into access and influence. Latecomers can find themselves at the end of a very long line.

The semiconductor industry recognized it needed a distinct approach. So it called on the charisma and persuasiveness of its senior executives, who proved to be a very valuable resource. Their technical achievements and business celebrity gave them great visibility on Capitol Hill. Chairmen, presidents, and other high-ranking executives traveled to Washington to meet with cabinet secretaries, senators, and members of Congress and to testify before congressional committees. Especially prominent from 1979 through 1981 were Robert Noyce, vice chairman of Intel, Charles Sporck, CEO of National Semiconductor, W. Jerry Sanders III, chairman of Advanced Micro Devices, and Motorola Chairman Robert Galvin.

These men opened many doors that might have been closed to lobbyists or lower ranking businesspeople. Noyce, for example, is something of a legend in the electronics world. A multimillionaire, co-inventor of the integrated circuit, he was general manager of Fairchild Semiconductor during its rise in the 1960s and one of the founders of Intel. The Washington establishment wanted to get to know him as much as he wanted to develop political contacts. Noyce spent 20% of his time during the early 1980s on political action. He and his colleagues in effect softened up Washington for the formal campaign that began in 1985.

Politically engaged CEOs are an effective weapon against the ever-increasing Washington barriers to entry. They are also important for maintaining political ties. Even the most loyal customers need periodic attention from top brass; so do politicians. Noyce and his industry peers still visit Washington a few times a year, every year, to stay close to the players.

Put Managers on Front Lines

Of course, top executives can't do the whole job. Over the long term, companies face another critical choice: whether to rely on their trade association's staff and paid lobbyists or to involve other corporate managers. The nature of the agenda determines the right answer.

When an industry is involved in maintaining the political status quo—staying in touch with Capitol Hill, conducting routine public relations, monitoring the regulatory agencies—the best strategy is to use trade association professionals. Large groups like the National Association of Manufacturers and the Food Marketing Institute exist mainly to keep tabs on Washington and influence technical regulations and

Japan sells more chips...
(percent share of world DRAM shipments)

	United States	Japan	Europe
1980	57%	41%	2%
1982	53	43	4
1984	38	56	6
1986	18	75	3
1987	22	65	3

Source: Dataquest Inc., February 1988. Figures refer to units shipped, not revenues. Some years do not add up to 100% because of shipments from other regions.

...and buys more too
(semiconductor consumption in millions of dollars)

	N. America	Japan	Europe
1980	$ 6,053	$ 3,383	$ 3,686
1982	6,970	4,082	3,167
1984	13,139	8,845	4,805
1986	10,201	12,356	5,532
1987*	11,743	14,239	6,780

*Estimated

Source: Dataquest Inc., August 1987.

bills. It makes sense for large association staffs to run these activities. As the issues become more urgent, however, and the political agenda moves from reacting to initiating new policies, managers should become involved directly. The more consequential the issue, the higher the level of manager needed.

The semiconductor industry never had the luxury of maintaining the political status quo. By the time it turned its attention to Washington, the trade situation was urgent. So the companies agreed to dedicate money and some of their own people to government relations. Time and again, managers from the large manufacturers came to Washington to support the trade initiative. Chip producers and users, including AMD, Digital Equipment, General Instruments, Harris Corporation, Intel, International Rectifier, Motorola, National Semiconductor, Rockwell International, and Texas Instruments committed executives to help build congressional support, visit trade officials, generate press releases, and for other work to build political bridges. AMD's George Scalise devoted 25% of his time to managing the trade case.

Washington lawyer Alan Wolff, a former deputy special trade representative, supplemented these industry lobbying efforts. The combination of experienced outside counsel and hands-on executive involvement proved powerful. Wolff provided the SIA with government contacts and a good feel for what agencies would be open to what positions. But many of the foot soldiers in the campaign were company managers whose expertise and commitment made them very persuasive with public officials.

This pattern of direct executive action explains why the SIA has remained such a lean organization. Despite its ambitious political agenda, the SIA employs only six professionals and two government affairs executives. Its annual budget runs less than $1 million, and the association doesn't have a Washington office. The Japanese, on the other hand, reportedly spent between $30 and $50 million lobbying against the trade initiatives.

In less than a decade, the semiconductor industry has built a constructive and nonadversarial relationship with Congress and the executive branch. These ties have produced a series of policy initiatives which, while not ideal, have had overwhelmingly positive consequences for the industry. U.S. semiconductor companies still have serious competitive problems, including quality and manufacturing costs. But government intervention has improved short-term profitability and cash flows and long-term prospects for research and development.

The work of the semiconductor industry in Washington is not over. For government to be a reliable ally and partner, the relationship must be stable and ongoing. A shotgun approach to politics – get what you want and don't return until you need something else – simply won't suffice. So the industry remains mobilized. The SIA and member companies continue to monitor Japanese chip prices and foreign access to the Japanese market and to supply the data to Washington. This vigilance helps explain why the Reagan administration imposed the sanctions in

> **If U.S. companies really want to be competitive, the semiconductor experience must become the rule – not the exception.**

April 1987. Literally hundreds of violations of similar agreements have occurred over the past 30 years, but no administration has taken action as severe as the semiconductor sanctions.

Most American companies continue to have an adversarial relationship with Washington. Business leaders complain about government bureaucracy and inefficiencies. Public officials complain about special interest groups maneuvering for their own side deals, making it impossible to fashion coherent national policy. Even in the semiconductor case, business-government relations have not always been smooth. Some companies have worked to undermine SIA proposals; certain government officials have tried to obstruct semiconductor policies.

We must build more constructive business-government relationships in the United States, which means not always assuming that government is the enemy. Many public officials are eager to help business in the battle for global competitiveness, especially when business frames its proposals in a way that appeals to the officials' own agendas and priorities. The process of building political advantage may be especially challenging for smaller companies and industries, but it is far from impossible, especially if they focus their efforts. Semiconductor companies did not try to shape the entire range of policies affecting them. They targeted certain issues that were central to their future and where their case was strongest.

Not every industry can expect to duplicate the semiconductor producers' success in Washington. But if U.S. companies are serious about regaining world competitiveness, the semiconductor experience must become the rule, not the exception. ▽

Reprint 88314

From competitive advantage to corporate strategy

Michael E. Porter

Corporate strategy, the overall plan for a diversified company, is both the darling and the stepchild of contemporary management practice – the darling because CEOs have been obsessed with diversification since the early 1960s, the stepchild because almost no consensus exists about what corporate strategy is, much less about how a company should formulate it.

The track record of corporate strategies has been dismal.

A diversified company has two levels of strategy: business unit (or competitive) strategy and corporate (or companywide) strategy. Competitive strategy concerns how to create competitive advantage in each of the businesses in which a company competes. Corporate strategy concerns two different questions: what businesses the corporation should be in and how the corporate office should manage the array of business units.

Corporate strategy is what makes the corporate whole add up to more than the sum of its business unit parts.

The track record of corporate strategies has been dismal. I studied the diversification records of 33 large, prestigious U.S. companies over the 1950-1986 period and found that most of them had divested many more acquisitions than they had kept.

The corporate strategies of most companies have dissipated instead of created shareholder value.

The need to rethink corporate strategy could hardly be more urgent. By taking over companies and breaking them up, corporate raiders thrive on failed corporate strategy. Fueled by junk bond financing and growing acceptability, raiders can expose any company to takeover, no matter how large or blue chip.

Recognizing past diversification mistakes, some companies have initiated large-scale restructuring programs. Others have done nothing at all. Whatever the response, the strategic questions persist. Those who have restructured must decide what to do next to avoid repeating the past; those who have done nothing must awake to their vulnerability. To survive, companies must understand what good corporate strategy is.

A sober picture

While there is disquiet about the success of corporate strategies, none of the available evidence satisfactorily indicates the success or failure of corporate strategy. Most studies have approached the question by measuring the stock market valuation of

Michael E. Porter is professor of business administration at the Harvard Business School and author of Competitive Advantage *(Free Press, 1985) and* Competitive Strategy *(Free Press, 1980).*

Exhibit I   **Diversification profiles of
33 leading U.S. companies**

Company	Number total entries	All entries into new industries	Percent acqui-sitions	Percent joint ventures	Percent start-ups
ALCO Standard	221	165	99 %	0 %	1 %
Allied Corp.	77	49	67	10	22
Beatrice	382	204	97	1	2
Borden	170	96	77	4	19
CBS	148	81	67	16	17
Continental Group	75	47	77	6	17
Cummins Engine	30	24	54	17	29
Du Pont	80	39	33	16	51
Exxon	79	56	34	5	61
General Electric	160	108	47	20	33
General Foods	92	53	91	4	6
General Mills	110	102	84	7	9
W.R.Grace	275	202	83	7	10
Gulf & Western	178	140	91	4	6
IBM	46	38	18	18	63
IC Industries	67	41	85	3	12
ITT	246	178	89	2	9
Johnson & Johnson	88	77	77	0	23
Mobil	41	32	53	16	31
Procter & Gamble	28	23	61	0	39
Raytheon	70	58	86	9	5
RCA	53	46	35	15	50
Rockwell	101	75	73	24	3
Sara Lee	197	141	96	1	4
Scovill	52	36	97	0	3
Signal	53	45	67	4	29
Tenneco	85	62	81	6	13
3M	144	125	54	2	45
TRW	119	82	77	10	13
United Technologies	62	49	57	18	24
Westinghouse	129	73	63	11	26
Wickes	71	47	83	0	17
Xerox	59	50	66	6	28
Total	**3,788**	**2,644**			
Average	**114.8**	**80.1**	**70.3 %**	**7.9 %**	**21.8 %**

Note:
Beatrice, Continental Group, General Foods, RCA, Scovill, and Signal were taken over as the study was being completed. Their data cover the period up through takeover but not subsequent divestments.

Entries into new industries that represented entirely new fields	Percent acquisitions	Percent joint ventures	Percent start-ups
56	100 %	0 %	0 %
17	65	6	29
61	97	0	3
32	75	3	22
28	65	21	14
19	79	11	11
13	46	23	31
19	37	0	63
17	29	6	65
29	48	14	38
22	86	5	9
27	74	7	19
66	74	5	21
48	88	2	10
16	19	0	81
17	88	6	6
50	92	0	8
18	56	0	44
15	60	7	33
14	79	0	21
16	81	19	6
19	37	21	42
27	74	22	4
41	95	2	2
12	92	0	8
20	75	0	25
26	73	8	19
34	71	3	56
28	64	11	25
17	23	17	39
36	61	3	36
22	68	0	32
18	50	11	39
906			
27.4	67.9 %	7.0 %	25.9 %

Note:
The percentage averages may not add up
to 100% because of rounding off.

mergers, captured in the movement of the stock prices of acquiring companies immediately before and after mergers are announced.

These studies show that the market values mergers as neutral or slightly negative, hardly cause for serious concern.[1] Yet the short-term market reaction is a highly imperfect measure of the long-term success of diversification, and no self-respecting executive would judge a corporate strategy this way.

Studying the diversification programs of a company over a long period of time is a much more telling way to determine whether a corporate strategy has succeeded or failed. My study of 33 companies, many of which have reputations for good management, is a unique look at the track record of major corporations. (For an explanation of the research, see the insert "Where the Data Come From.") Each company entered an average of 80 new industries and 27 new fields. Just over 70% of the new entries were acquisitions, 22% were start-ups, and 8% were joint ventures. IBM, Exxon, Du Pont, and 3M, for example, focused on start-ups, while ALCO Standard, Beatrice, and Sara Lee diversified almost solely through acquisitions (Exhibit I has a complete rundown).

My data paint a sobering picture of the success ratio of these moves (see Exhibit II). I found that on average corporations divested more than half their acquisitions in new industries and more than 60% of their acquisitions in entirely new fields. Fourteen companies left more than 70% of all the acquisitions they had made in new fields. The track record in unrelated acquisitions is even worse—the average divestment rate is a startling 74% (see Exhibit III). Even a highly respected company like General Electric divested a very high percentage of its acquisitions, particularly those in new fields. Companies near the top of the list in Exhibit II achieved a remarkably low rate of divestment. Some bear witness to the success of well-thought-out corporate strategies. Others, however, enjoy a lower rate simply because they have not faced up to their problem units and divested them.

I calculated total shareholder returns (stock price appreciation plus dividends) over the period of the study for each company so that I could compare them with its divestment rate. While companies near the top of the list have above-average shareholder returns, returns are not a reliable measure of diversification success. Shareholder return often depends heavily on the inherent attractiveness of companies' base industries. Companies like CBS and General Mills had extremely profitable base businesses that subsidized poor diversification track records.

I would like to make one comment on the use of shareholder value to judge performance. Linking shareholder value quantitatively to diversification performance only works if you compare the shareholder value that is with the shareholder value that might have been without diversification. Because such a comparison is virtually impossible to make, my own measure of diversification success – the number of units retained by the company – seems to be as good an indicator as any of the contribution of diversification to corporate performance.

My data give a stark indication of the failure of corporate strategies.[2] Of the 33 companies, 6 had been taken over as my study was being completed (see the note on *Exhibit II*). Only the lawyers, investment bankers, and original sellers have prospered in most of these acquisitions, not the shareholders.

Premises of corporate strategy

Any successful corporate strategy builds on a number of premises. These are facts of life about diversification. They cannot be altered, and when ignored, they explain in part why so many corporate strategies fail.

Competition occurs at the business unit level. Diversified companies do not compete; only their business units do. Unless a corporate strategy places primary attention on nurturing the success of each unit, the strategy will fail, no matter how elegantly constructed. Successful corporate strategy must grow out of and reinforce competitive strategy.

Diversification inevitably adds costs and constraints to business units. Obvious costs such as the corporate overhead allocated to a unit may not be as important or subtle as the hidden costs and constraints. A business unit must explain its decisions to top management, spend time complying with planning and other corporate systems, live with parent company guidelines and personnel policies, and forgo the opportunity to motivate employees with direct equity ownership. These costs and constraints can be reduced but not entirely eliminated.

Shareholders can readily diversify themselves. Shareholders can diversify their own portfolios of stocks by selecting those that best match their preferences and risk profiles.[3] Shareholders can often diversify more cheaply than a corporation because they can buy shares at the market price and avoid hefty acquisition premiums.

These premises mean that corporate strategy cannot succeed unless it truly adds value – to business units by providing tangible benefits that offset the inherent costs of lost independence and to

shareholders by diversifying in a way they could not replicate.

Passing the essential tests

To understand how to formulate corporate strategy, it is necessary to specify the conditions under which diversification will truly create shareholder value. These conditions can be summarized in three essential tests:

1 **The attractiveness test.** The industries chosen for diversification must be structurally attractive or capable of being made attractive.

2 **The cost-of-entry test.** The cost of entry must not capitalize all the future profits.

3 **The better-off test.** Either the new unit must gain competitive advantage from its link with the corporation or vice versa.

Of course, most companies will make certain that their proposed strategies pass some of these tests. But my study clearly shows that when companies ignored one or two of them, the strategic results were disastrous.

How attractive is the industry?

In the long run, the rate of return available from competing in an industry is a function of its underlying structure, which I have described in another HBR article.[4] An attractive industry with a high average return on investment will be difficult to enter because entry barriers are high, suppliers and buyers have only modest bargaining power, substitute products or services are few, and the rivalry among competitors is stable. An unattractive industry like steel will have structural flaws, including a plethora of substitute materials, powerful and price-sensitive buyers, and excessive rivalry caused by high fixed costs and a large group of competitors, many of whom are state supported.

Diversification cannot create shareholder value unless new industries have favorable structures that support returns exceeding the cost of capital. If the industry doesn't have such returns, the company must be able to restructure the industry or gain a sustainable competitive advantage that leads to returns well above the industry average. An industry need not be attractive before diversification. In fact, a

Where the data come from

We studied the 1950-1986 diversification histories of 33 large diversified U.S. companies. They were chosen at random from many broad sectors of the economy.

To eliminate distortions caused by World War II, we chose 1950 as the base year and then identified each business the company was in. We tracked every acquisition, joint venture, and start-up made over this period – 3,788 in all. We classified each as an entry into an entirely new sector or field (financial services, for example), a new industry within a field the company was already in (insurance, for example), or a geographic extension of an existing product or service. We also classified each new field as related or unrelated to existing units. Then we tracked whether and when each entry was divested or shut down and the number of years each remained part of the corporation.

Our sources included annual reports, 10K forms, the F&S Index, and Moody's, supplemented by our judgment and general knowledge of the industries involved. In a few cases, we asked the companies specific questions.

It is difficult to determine the success of an entry without knowing the full purchase or start-up price, the profit history, the amount and timing of ongoing investments made in the unit, whether any write-offs or write-downs were taken, and the selling price and terms of sale. Instead, we employed a relatively simple way to gauge success: *whether the entry was divested or shut down.* The underlying assumption is that a company will gen-

erally not divest or close down a successful business except in a comparatively few special cases. Companies divested many of the entries in our sample within five years, a reflection of disappointment with performance. Of the comparatively few divestments where the company disclosed a loss or a gain, the divestment resulted in a reported loss in more than half the cases.

The data in *Exhibit I* cover the entire 1950-1986 period. However, the divestment ratios in *Exhibit II* and *Exhibit III* do not compare entries and divestments over the entire period because doing so would overstate the success of diversification. Companies usually do not shut down or divest new entries immediately but hold them for some time to give them an opportunity to succeed. Our data show that the average holding period is five to slightly more than ten years, though many divestments occur within five years. To accurately gauge the success of diversification, we calculated the percentage of entries made by 1975 and by 1980 that were divested or closed down as of January 1987. If we had included more recent entries, we would have biased upward our assessment of how successful these entries had been.

As compiled, these data probably understate the rate of failure. Companies tend to announce acquisitions and other forms of new entry with a flourish but divestments and shutdowns with a whimper, if at all. We have done our best to root out every such transaction, but we have undoubtedly missed some. There may also be new entries that we did not uncover, but our best impression is that the number is not large.

---

company might benefit from entering before the industry shows its full potential. The diversification can then transform the industry's structure.

In my research, I often found companies had suspended the attractiveness test because they had a vague belief that the industry "fit" very closely with their own businesses. In the hope that the corporate "comfort" they felt would lead to a happy outcome, the companies ignored fundamentally poor industry structures. Unless the close fit allows substantial competitive advantage, however, such comfort will turn into pain when diversification results in poor returns. Royal Dutch Shell and other leading oil companies have had this unhappy experience in a number of chemicals businesses, where poor industry structures overcame the benefits of vertical integration and skills in process technology.

Another common reason for ignoring the attractiveness test is a low entry cost. Sometimes the buyer has an inside track or the owner is anxious to sell. Even if the price is actually low, however, a one-

shot gain will not offset a perpetually poor business. Almost always, the company finds it must reinvest in the newly acquired unit, if only to replace fixed assets and fund working capital.

Diversifying companies are also prone to use rapid growth or other simple indicators as a proxy for a target industry's attractiveness. Many that rushed into fast-growing industries (personal computers, video games, and robotics, for example) were burned because they mistook early growth for long-term profit potential. Industries are profitable not because they are sexy or high tech; they are profitable only if their structures are attractive.

What is the cost of entry?

Diversification cannot build shareholder value if the cost of entry into a new business eats up its expected returns. Strong market forces,

Exhibit II	**Acquisition track records of leading U.S. diversifiers ranked by percent divested**

Company	All acquisitions in new industries	Percent made by 1980 and then divested	Percent made by 1975 and then divested	Acquisitions in new industries that represented entirely new fields	Percent made by 1980 and then divested	Percent made by 1975 and then divested
Johnson & Johnson	59	17 %	12 %	10	33 %	14 %
Procter & Gamble	14	17	17	11	17	17
Raytheon	50	17	26	13	25	33
United Technologies	28	25	13	10	17	0
3M	67	26	27	24	42	45
TRW	63	27	31	18	40	38
IBM	7	33	0*	3	33	0*
Du Pont	13	38	43	7	60	75
Mobil	17	38	57	9	50	50
Borden	74	39	40	24	45	50
IC Industries	35	42	50	15	46	44
Tenneco	50	43	47	19	27	33
Beatrice	198	46	45	59	52	51
ITT	159	52	52	46	61	61
Rockwell	55	56	57	20	71	71
Allied Corp.	33	57	45	11	80	67
Exxon	19	62	20*	5	80	50*
Sara Lee	135	62	65	39	80	76
General Foods	48	63	62	19	93	93
Scovill	35	64	77	11	64	70
Signal	30	65	63	15	70	67
ALCO Standard	164	65	70	56	72	76
W.R. Grace	167	65	70	49	71	70
General Electric	51	65	78	14	100	100
Wickes	38	67	72	15	73	70
Westinghouse	46	68	69	22	61	59
Xerox	33	71	79	9	100	100
Continental Group	36	71	72	15	60	60
General Mills	86	75	73	20	65	60
Gulf & Western	127	79	78	42	75	72
Cummins Engine	13	80	80	6	83	83
RCA	16	80	92	7	86	100
CBS	54	87	89	18	88	88
Total	**2,021**			**661**		
Average per company†	**61.2**	**53.4 %**	**56.5 %**	**20.0**	**61.2 %**	**61.1 %**

*Companies with three or fewer acquisitions by the cutoff year.

†Companies with three or fewer acquisitions by the cutoff year are excluded from the average to minimize statistical distortions.

Note:
Beatrice, Continental Group, General Foods, RCA, Scovill, and Signal were taken over as the study was being completed. Their data cover the period up through takeover but not subsequent divestments.

however, are working to do just that. A company can enter new industries by acquisition or start-up. Acquisitions expose it to an increasingly efficient merger market. An acquirer beats the market if it pays a price not fully reflecting the prospects of the new unit. Yet multiple bidders are commonplace, information flows rapidly, and investment bankers and other intermediaries work aggressively to make the market as efficient as possible. In recent years, new financial instruments such as junk bonds have brought new buyers into the market and made even large companies vulnerable to takeover. Acquisition premiums are high and reflect the acquired company's future prospects—sometimes too well. Philip Morris paid more than four times book value for Seven-Up Company, for example. Simple arithmetic meant that profits had to more than quadruple to sustain the preacquisition ROI. Since there proved to be little Philip Morris could add in marketing prowess to the sophisticated marketing wars in the soft-drink industry, the result was the unsatisfactory financial performance of Seven-Up and ultimately the decision to divest.

In a start-up, the company must overcome entry barriers. It's a real catch-22 situation, however, since attractive industries are attractive because their entry barriers are high. Bearing the full cost of the entry barriers might well dissipate any potential profits. Otherwise, other entrants to the industry would have already eroded its profitability.

In the excitement of finding an appealing new business, companies sometimes forget to apply the cost-of-entry test. The more attractive a new industry, the more expensive it is to get into.

Will the business be better off?

A corporation must bring some significant competitive advantage to the new unit, or the new unit must offer potential for significant advantage to the corporation. Sometimes, the benefits to the new unit accrue only once, near the time of entry, when the parent instigates a major overhaul of its strategy or installs a first-rate management team. Other diversification yields ongoing competitive advantage if the new unit can market its product through the well-developed distribution system of its sister units, for instance. This is one of the important underpinnings of the merger of Baxter Travenol and American Hospital Supply.

When the benefit to the new unit comes only once, the parent company has no rationale for holding the new unit in its portfolio over the long term. Once the results of the one-time improvement are clear, the diversified company no longer adds value to offset the inevitable costs imposed on the unit. It is best to sell the unit and free up corporate resources.

The better-off test does not imply that diversifying corporate risk creates shareholder value in and of itself. Doing something for shareholders that they can do themselves is not a basis for corporate strategy. (Only in the case of a privately held company, in which the company's and the shareholder's risk are the same, is diversification to reduce risk valuable for its own sake.) Diversification of risk should only be a by-product of corporate strategy, not a prime motivator.

Executives ignore the better-off test most of all or deal with it through arm waving or trumped-up logic rather than hard strategic analysis. One reason is that they confuse company size with shareholder value. In the drive to run a bigger company, they lose sight of their real job. They may justify the suspension of the better-off test by pointing to the way they manage diversity. By cutting corporate staff to the bone and giving business units nearly complete autonomy, they believe they avoid the pitfalls. Such thinking misses the whole point of diversification, which is to create shareholder value rather than to avoid destroying it.

Concepts of corporate strategy

The three tests for successful diversification set the standards that any corporate strategy must meet; meeting them is so difficult that most diversification fails. Many companies lack a clear concept of corporate strategy to guide their diversification or pursue a concept that does not address the tests. Others fail because they implement a strategy poorly.

My study has helped me identify four concepts of corporate strategy that have been put into practice—portfolio management, restructuring, transferring skills, and sharing activities. While the concepts are not always mutually exclusive, each rests on a different mechanism by which the corporation creates shareholder value and each requires the diversified company to manage and organize itself in a different way. The first two require no connections among business units; the second two depend on them. (See *Exhibit IV*.) While all four concepts of strategy have succeeded under the right circumstances, today some make more sense than others. Ignoring any of the concepts is perhaps the quickest road to failure.

Portfolio management

The concept of corporate strategy most in use is portfolio management, which is based primar-

Exhibit III	**Diversification performance in joint ventures, start-ups, and unrelated acquisitions**
	Companies in same order as in Exhibit II

Company	Joint ventures as a percent of new entries	Percent made by 1980 and then divested	Percent made by 1975 and then divested	Start-ups as a percent of new entries	Percent made by 1980 and then divested
Johnson & Johnson	0 %	†	†	23 %	14 %
Procter & Gamble	0	†	†	39	0
Raytheon	9	60 %	60 %	5	50
United Technologies	18	50	50	24	11
3M	2	100*	100*	45	2
TRW	10	20	25	13	63
IBM	18	100*	†	63	20
Du Pont	16	100*	†	51	61
Mobil	16	33	33	31	50
Borden	4	33	33	19	17
IC Industries	3	100*	100*	13	80
Tenneco	6	67	67	13	67
Beatrice	1	†	†	2	0
ITT	2	0*	†	8	38
Rockwell	24	38	42	3	0
Allied Corp.	10	100	75	22	38
Exxon	5	0	0	61	27
Sara Lee	1	†	†	4	75
General Foods	4	†	†	6	67
Scovill	0	†	†	3	100
Signal	4	†	†	29	20
ALCO Standard	0	†	†	1	†
W.R. Grace	7	33	38	10	71
General Electric	20	20	33	33	33
Wickes	0	†	†	17	63
Westinghouse	11	0*	0*	26	44
Xerox	6	100*	100*	28	50
Continental Group	6	67	67	17	14
General Mills	7	71	71	9	89
Gulf & Western	4	75	50	6	100
Cummins Engine	17	50	50	29	0
RCA	15	67	67	50	99
CBS	16	71	71	17	86
Average per company‡	**7.9 %**	**50.3 %**	**48.9 %**	**21.8 %**	**44.0 %**

*Companies with two or fewer entries.

†No entries in this category.

‡Average excludes companies with two or fewer entries to minimize statistical distortions.

Note:
Beatrice, Continental Group, General Foods, RCA, Scovill, and Signal were taken over as the study was being completed. Their data cover the period up through takeover but not subsequent divestments.

Percent made by 1975 and then divested	Acquisitions in unrelated new fields as a percent of total acquisitions in new fields	Percent made by 1980 and then divested	Percent made by 1975 and then divested
20 %	0 %	†	†
0	9	†	†
50	46	40 %	40 %
20	40	0*	0*
3	33	75	86
71	39	71	71
22	33	100*	100*
61	43	0*	0*
56	67	60	100
13	21	80	80
30	33	50	50
80	42	33	40
0	63	59	53
57	61	67	64
0	35	100	100
29	45	50	0
19	100	80	50*
100*	41	73	73
50	42	86	83
100*	45	80	100
11	67	50	50
†	63	79	81
71	39	65	65
44	36	100	100
57	60	80	75
44	36	57	67
56	22	100	100
0	40	83	100
80	65	77	67
100	74	77	74
0	67	100	100
55	36	100	100 .
80	39	100	100
40.9 %	46.1 %	74.0 %	74.4 %

ily on diversification through acquisition. The corporation acquires sound, attractive companies with competent managers who agree to stay on. While acquired units do not have to be in the same industries as existing units, the best portfolio managers generally limit their range of businesses in some way, in part to limit the specific expertise needed by top management.

The acquired units are autonomous, and the teams that run them are compensated according to unit results. The corporation supplies capital and works with each to infuse it with professional management techniques. At the same time, top management provides objective and dispassionate review of business unit results. Portfolio managers categorize units by potential and regularly transfer resources from units that generate cash to those with high potential and cash needs.

In a portfolio strategy, the corporation seeks to create shareholder value in a number of ways. It uses its expertise and analytical resources to spot attractive acquisition candidates that the individual shareholder could not. The company provides capital on favorable terms that reflect corporatewide fund-raising ability. It introduces professional management skills and discipline. Finally, it provides high-quality review and coaching, unencumbered by conventional wisdom or emotional attachments to the business.

The logic of the portfolio management concept rests on a number of vital assumptions. If a company's diversification plan is to meet the attractiveness and cost-of-entry tests, it must find good but undervalued companies. Acquired companies must be truly undervalued because the parent does little for the new unit once it is acquired. To meet the better-off test, the benefits the corporation provides must yield a significant competitive advantage to acquired units. The style of operating through highly autonomous business units must both develop sound business strategies and motivate managers.

In most countries, the days when portfolio management was a valid concept of corporate strategy are past. In the face of increasingly well-developed capital markets, attractive companies with good managements show up on everyone's computer screen and attract top dollar in terms of acquisition premium. Simply contributing capital isn't contributing much. A sound strategy can easily be funded; small to medium-size companies don't need a munificent parent.

Other benefits have also eroded. Large companies no longer corner the market for professional management skills; in fact, more and more observers believe managers cannot necessarily run anything in the absence of industry-specific knowledge and experience. Another supposed advantage of the portfolio management concept—dispassionate review—rests on similarly shaky ground since the added value of review alone is questionable in a portfolio of sound companies.

The benefit of giving business units complete autonomy is also questionable. Increasingly, a company's business units are interrelated, drawn together by new technology, broadening distribution channels, and changing regulations. Setting strategies of units independently may well undermine unit performance. The companies in my sample that have succeeded in diversification have recognized the value of interrelationships and understood that a strong sense of corporate identity is as important as slavish adherence to parochial business unit financial results.

But it is the sheer complexity of the management task that has ultimately defeated even the best portfolio managers. As the size of the company grows, portfolio managers need to find more and more deals just to maintain growth. Supervising dozens or even hundreds of disparate units and under chain-letter pressures to add more, management begins to make mistakes. At the same time, the inevitable costs of being part of a diversified company take their toll and unit performance slides while the whole company's ROI turns downward. Eventually, a new management team is installed that initiates wholesale divestments and pares down the company to its core businesses. The experiences of Gulf & Western, Consolidated Foods (now Sara Lee), and ITT are just a few comparatively recent examples. Reflecting these realities, the U.S. capital markets today reward companies that follow the portfolio management model with a "conglomerate discount"; they value the whole less than the sum of the parts.

In developing countries, where large companies are few, capital markets are undeveloped, and professional management is scarce, portfolio management still works. But it is no longer a valid model for corporate strategy in advanced economies. Nevertheless, the technique is in the limelight today in the United Kingdom, where it is supported so far by a newly energized stock market eager for excitement. But this enthusiasm will wane—as well it should. Portfolio management is no way to conduct corporate strategy.

Restructuring

Unlike its passive role as a portfolio manager, when it serves as banker and reviewer, a company that bases its strategy on restructuring becomes an active restructurer of business units. The new businesses are not necessarily related to existing units. All that is necessary is unrealized potential.

The restructuring strategy seeks out undeveloped, sick, or threatened organizations or industries on the threshold of significant change. The parent intervenes, frequently changing the unit management team, shifting strategy, or infusing the company with

new technology. Then it may make follow-up acquisitions to build a critical mass and sell off unneeded or unconnected parts and thereby reduce the effective acquisition cost. The result is a strengthened company or a transformed industry. As a coda, the parent sells off the stronger unit once results are clear because the parent is no longer adding value and top management decides that its attention should be directed elsewhere. (See the insert "An Uncanny British Restructurer" for an example of restructuring.)

A strong sense of corporate identity is as important as slavish adherence to business unit financial results.

When well implemented, the restructuring concept is sound, for it passes the three tests of successful diversification. The restructurer meets the cost-of-entry test through the types of company it acquires. It limits acquisition premiums by buying companies with problems and lackluster images or by buying into industries with as yet unforeseen potential. Intervention by the corporation clearly meets the better-off test. Provided that the target industries are structurally attractive, the restructuring model can create enormous shareholder value. Some restructuring companies are Loew's, BTR, and General Cinema. Ironically, many of today's restructurers are profiting from yesterday's portfolio management strategies.

To work, the restructuring strategy requires a corporate management team with the insight to spot undervalued companies or positions in industries ripe for transformation. The same insight is necessary to actually turn the units around even though they are in new and unfamiliar businesses.

These requirements expose the restructurer to considerable risk and usually limit the time in which the company can succeed at the strategy. The most skillful proponents understand this problem, recognize their mistakes, and move decisively to dispose of them. The best companies realize they are not just acquiring companies but restructuring an industry. Unless they can integrate the acquisitions to create a whole new strategic position, they are just portfolio managers in disguise. Another important difficulty surfaces if so many other companies join the action that they deplete the pool of suitable candidates and bid their prices up.

Perhaps the greatest pitfall, however, is that companies find it very hard to dispose of business units once they are restructured and performing well.

Exhibit IV   Concepts of corporate strategy

	Portfolio management	Restructuring	Transferring skills	Sharing activities
Strategic prerequisites	Superior insight into identifying and acquiring undervalued companies Willingness to sell off losers quickly or to opportunistically divest good performers when buyers are willing to pay large premiums Broad guidelines for and constraints on the types of units in the portfolio so that senior management can play the review role effectively A private company or undeveloped capital markets Ability to shift away from portfolio management as the capital markets get more efficient or the company gets unwieldy	Superior insight into identifying restructuring opportunities Willingness and capability to intervene to transform acquired units Broad similarities among the units in the portfolio Willingness to cut losses by selling off units where restructuring proves unfeasible Willingness to sell units when restructuring is complete, the results are clear, and market conditions are favorable	Proprietary skills in activities important to competitive advantage in target industries Ability to accomplish the transfer of skills among units on an ongoing basis Acquisitions of beachhead positions in new industries as a base	Activities in existing units that can be shared with new business units to gain competitive advantage Benefits of sharing that outweigh the costs Both start-ups and acquisitions as entry vehicles Ability to overcome organizational resistance to business unit collaboration
Organizational prerequisites	Autonomous business units A very small, low-cost, corporate staff Incentives based largely on business unit results	Autonomous business units A corporate organization with the talent and resources to oversee the turnarounds and strategic repositionings of acquired units Incentives based largely on acquired units' results	Largely autonomous but collaborative business units High-level corporate staff members who see their role primarily as integrators Cross-business-unit committees, task forces, and other forums to serve as focal points for capturing and transferring skills Objectives of line managers that include skills transfer Incentives based in part on corporate results	Strategic business units that are encouraged to share activities An active strategic planning role at group, sector, and corporate levels High-level corporate staff members who see their roles primarily as integrators Incentives based heavily on group and corporate results
Common pitfalls	Pursuing portfolio management in countries with efficient capital marketing and a developed pool of professional management talent Ignoring the fact that industry structure is not attractive	Mistaking rapid growth or a "hot" industry as sufficient evidence of a restructuring opportunity Lacking the resolve or resources to take on troubled situations and to intervene in management Ignoring the fact that industry structure is not attractive Paying lip service to restructuring but actually practicing passive portfolio management	Mistaking similarity or comfort with new businesses as sufficient basis for diversification Providing no practical ways for skills transfer to occur Ignoring the fact that industry structure is not attractive	Sharing for its own sake rather than because it leads to competitive advantage Assuming sharing will occur naturally without senior management playing an active role Ignoring the fact that industry structure is not attractive

Human nature fights economic rationale. Size supplants shareholder value as the corporate goal. The company does not sell a unit even though the company no longer adds value to the unit. While the transformed units would be better off in another company that had related businesses, the restructuring company instead retains them. Gradually, it becomes a portfolio manager. The parent company's ROI declines as the need for reinvestment in the units and normal business risks eventually offset restructuring's one-shot gain. The perceived need to keep growing intensifies the pace of acquisition; errors result and standards fall. The restructuring company turns into a conglomerate with returns that only equal the average of all industries at best.

Transferring skills

The purpose of the first two concepts of corporate strategy is to create value through a company's relationship with each autonomous unit. The corporation's role is to be a selector, a banker, and an intervenor.

The last two concepts exploit the interrelationships between businesses. In articulating them, however, one comes face-to-face with the often ill-defined concept of synergy. If you believe the text of the countless corporate annual reports, just about anything is related to just about anything else! But imagined synergy is much more common than real synergy. GM's purchase of Hughes Aircraft simply because cars were going electronic and Hughes was an electronics concern demonstrates the folly of paper synergy. Such corporate relatedness is an ex post facto rationalization of a diversification undertaken for other reasons.

Portfolio management is no way to conduct corporate strategy.

Even synergy that is clearly defined often fails to materialize. Instead of cooperating, business units often compete. A company that can define the synergies it is pursuing still faces significant organizational impediments in achieving them.

But the need to capture the benefits of relationships between businesses has never been more important. Technological and competitive developments already link many businesses and are creating new possibilities for competitive advantage. In such sectors as financial services, computing, office equipment, entertainment, and health care, interrelationships among previously distinct businesses are perhaps the central concern of strategy.

To understand the role of relatedness in corporate strategy, we must give new meaning to this often ill-defined idea. I have identified a good way to start—the value chain.[5] Every business unit is a collection of discrete activities ranging from sales to accounting that allow it to compete. I call them value activities. It is at this level, not in the company as a whole, that the unit achieves competitive advantage.

I group these activities in nine categories. *Primary* activities create the product or service, deliver and market it, and provide after-sale support. The categories of primary activities are inbound logistics, operations, outbound logistics, marketing and sales, and service. *Support* activities provide the input and infrastructure that allow the primary activities to take place. The categories are company infrastructure, human resource management, technology development, and procurement.

The value chain defines the two types of interrelationships that may create synergy. The first is a company's ability to transfer skills or expertise among similar value chains. The second is the ability to share activities. Two business units, for example, can share the same sales force or logistics network.

The value chain helps expose the last two (and most important) concepts of corporate strategy. The transfer of skills among business units in the diversified company is the basis for one concept. While each business unit has a separate value chain, knowledge about how to perform activities is transferred among the units. For example, a toiletries business unit, expert in the marketing of convenience products, transmits ideas on new positioning concepts, promotional techniques, and packaging possibilities to a newly acquired unit that sells cough syrup. Newly entered industries can benefit from the expertise of existing units and vice versa.

These opportunities arise when business units have similar buyers or channels, similar value activities like government relations or procurement, similarities in the broad configuration of the value chain (for example, managing a multisite service organization), or the same strategic concept (for example, low cost). Even though the units operate separately, such similarities allow the sharing of knowledge.

Of course, some similarities are common; one can imagine them at some level between almost any pair of businesses. Countless companies have fallen into the trap of diversifying too readily because of similarities; mere similarity is not enough.

Transferring skills leads to competitive advantage only if the similarities among businesses meet three conditions:

1   The activities involved in the businesses are similar enough that sharing expertise is meaningful. Broad similarities (marketing intensiveness, for example, or a common core process technology such as bending metal) are not a sufficient basis for diversification. The resulting ability to transfer skills is likely to have little impact on competitive advantage.

2   The transfer of skills involves activities important to competitive advantage. Transferring skills in peripheral activities such as government relations or real estate in consumer goods units may be beneficial but is not a basis for diversification.

3   The skills transferred represent a significant source of competitive advantage for the receiving unit. The expertise or skills to be transferred are both advanced and proprietary enough to be beyond the capabilities of competitors.

The transfer of skills is an active process that significantly changes the strategy or operations of the receiving unit. The prospect for change must be specific and identifiable. Almost guaranteeing that no shareholder value will be created, too many companies

An uncanny
British restructurer

Hanson Trust, on its way to becoming Britain's largest company, is one of several skillful followers of the restructuring concept. A conglomerate with units in many industries, Hanson might seem on the surface a portfolio manager. In fact, Hanson and one or two other conglomerates have a much more effective corporate strategy. Hanson has acquired companies such as London Brick, Ever Ready Batteries, and SCM, which the city of London rather disdainfully calls "low tech."

Although a mature company suffering from low growth, the typical Hanson target is not just in any industry; it has an attractive structure. Its customer and supplier power is low and rivalry with competitors moderate. The target is a market leader, rich in assets but formerly poor in management. Hanson pays little of the present value of future cash flow out in an acquisition premium and reduces purchase price even further by aggressively selling off businesses that it cannot improve. In this way, it recoups just over a third of the cost of a typical acquisition during the first six months of ownership. Imperial Group's plush properties in London lasted barely two months under Hanson ownership, while Hanson's recent sale of Courage Breweries to Elders recouped £1.4 billion of the original £2.1 billion acquisition price of Imperial Group.

Like the best restructurers, Hanson approaches each unit with a modus operandi that it has perfected through repetition.

Hanson emphasizes low costs and tight financial controls. It has cut an average of 25% of labor costs out of acquired companies, slashed fixed overheads, and tightened capital expenditures. To reinforce its strategy of keeping costs low, Hanson carves out detailed one-year financial budgets with divisional managers and (through generous use of performance-related bonuses and share option schemes) gives them incentive to deliver the goods.

It's too early to tell whether Hanson will adhere to the last tenet of restructuring – selling turned-around units once the results are clear. If it succumbs to the allure of bigness, Hanson may take the course of the failed U.S. conglomerates.

etary expertise across units. This makes certain the company can offset the acquisition premium or lower the cost of overcoming entry barriers.

The industries the company chooses for diversification must pass the attractiveness test. Even a close fit that reflects opportunities to transfer skills may not overcome poor industry structure. Opportunities to transfer skills, however, may help the company transform the structures of newly entered industries and send them in favorable directions.

The transfer of skills can be one-time or ongoing. If the company exhausts opportunities to infuse new expertise into a unit after the initial post-acquisition period, the unit should ultimately be sold. The corporation is no longer creating shareholder value. Few companies have grasped this point, however, and many gradually suffer mediocre returns. Yet a company diversified into well-chosen businesses can transfer skills eventually in many directions. If corporate management conceives of its role in this way and creates appropriate organizational mechanisms to facilitate cross-unit interchange, the opportunities to share expertise will be meaningful.

By using both acquisitions and internal development, companies can build a transfer-of-skills strategy. The presence of a strong base of skills sometimes creates the possibility for internal entry instead of the acquisition of a going concern. Successful diversifiers that employ the concept of skills transfer may, however, often acquire a company in the target industry as a beachhead and then build on it with their internal expertise. By doing so, they can reduce some of the risks of internal entry and speed up the process. Two companies that have diversified using the transfer-of-skills concept are 3M and Pepsico.

Sharing activities

The fourth concept of corporate strategy is based on sharing activities in the value chains among business units. Procter & Gamble, for example, employs a common physical distribution system and sales force in both paper towels and disposable diapers. McKesson, a leading distribution company, will handle such diverse lines as pharmaceuticals and liquor through superwarehouses.

The ability to share activities is a potent basis for corporate strategy because sharing often enhances competitive advantage by lowering cost or raising differentiation. But not all sharing leads to competitive advantage, and companies can encounter deep organizational resistance to even beneficial sharing possibilities. These hard truths have led many companies to reject synergy prematurely and retreat to the false simplicity of portfolio management.

are satisfied with vague prospects or faint hopes that skills will transfer. The transfer of skills does not happen by accident or by osmosis. The company will have to reassign critical personnel, even on a permanent basis, and the participation and support of high-level management in skills transfer is essential. Many companies have been defeated at skills transfer because they have not provided their business units with any incentives to participate.

Transferring skills meets the tests of diversification if the company truly mobilizes propri-

A cost-benefit analysis of prospective sharing opportunities can determine whether synergy is possible. Sharing can lower costs if it achieves economies of scale, boosts the efficiency of utilization, or helps a company move more rapidly down the learning curve. The costs of General Electric's advertising, sales, and after-sales service activities in major appliances are low because they are spread over a wide range of appliance products. Sharing can also enhance the potential for differentiation. A shared order-processing system, for instance, may allow new features and services that a buyer will value. Sharing can also reduce the cost of differentiation. A shared service network, for example, may make more advanced, remote servicing technology economically feasible. Often, sharing will allow an activity to be wholly reconfigured in ways that can dramatically raise competitive advantage.

Sharing must involve activities that are significant to competitive advantage, not just any activity. P&G's distribution system is such an instance in the diaper and paper towel business, where products are bulky and costly to ship. Conversely, diversification based on the opportunities to share only corporate overhead is rarely, if ever, appropriate.

Sharing activities inevitably involves costs that the benefits must outweigh. One cost is the greater coordination required to manage a shared activity. More important is the need to compromise the design or performance of an activity so that it can be shared. A salesperson handling the products of two business units, for example, must operate in a way that is usually not what either unit would choose were it independent. And if compromise greatly erodes the unit's effectiveness, then sharing may reduce rather than enhance competitive advantage.

Many companies have only superficially identified their potential for sharing. Companies also merge activities without consideration of whether they are sensitive to economies of scale. When they are not, the coordination costs kill the benefits. Companies compound such errors by not identifying costs of sharing in advance, when steps can be taken to minimize them. Costs of compromise can frequently be mitigated by redesigning the activity for sharing. The shared salesperson, for example, can be provided with a remote computer terminal to boost productivity and provide more customer information. Jamming business units together without such thinking exacerbates the costs of sharing.

Despite such pitfalls, opportunities to gain advantage from sharing activities have proliferated because of momentous developments in technology, deregulation, and competition. The infusion of electronics and information systems into many industries creates new opportunities to link businesses. The corporate strategy of sharing can involve both acquisition and internal development. Internal development is of-

Adding value with hospitality

Marriott began in the restaurant business in Washington, D.C. Because its customers often ordered takeouts on the way to the national airport, Marriott eventually entered airline catering. From there, it jumped into food service management for institutions. Marriott then began broadening its base of family restaurants and entered the hotel industry. More recently, it has moved into restaurants, snack bars, and merchandise shops in airport terminals and into gourmet restaurants. In addition, Marriott has branched out from its hotel business into cruise ships, theme parks, wholesale travel agencies, budget motels, and retirement centers.

Marriott's diversification has exploited well-developed skills in food service and hospitality. Marriott's kitchens prepare food according to more than 6,000 standardized recipe cards; hotel procedures are also standardized and painstakingly documented in elaborate manuals. Marriott shares a number of important activities across units. A shared procurement and distribution system for food serves all Marriott units through nine regional procurement centers. As a result, Marriott earns 50% higher margins on food service than any other hotel company. Marriott also has a fully integrated real estate unit that brings corporatewide power to bear on site acquisitions as well as on the designing and building of all Marriott locations.

Marriott's diversification strategy balances acquisitions and start-ups. Start-ups or small acquisitions are used for initial entry, depending on how close the opportunities for sharing are. To expand its geographic base, Marriott acquires companies and then disposes of the parts that do not fit.

Apart from this success, it is important to note that Marriott has divested 36% of both its acquisitions and its start-ups. While this is an above-average record, Marriott's mistakes are quite illuminating. Marriott has largely failed in diversifying into gourmet restaurants, theme parks, cruise ships, and wholesale travel agencies. In the first three businesses, Marriott discovered it could not transfer skills despite apparent similarities. Standardized menus did not work well in gourmet restaurants. Running cruise ships and theme parks was based more on entertainment and pizzazz than the carefully disciplined management of hotels and midprice restaurants. The wholesale travel agencies were ill fated from the start because Marriott had to compete with an important customer for its hotels and had no proprietary skills or opportunities to share with which to add value.

ten possible because the corporation can bring to bear clear resources in launching a new unit. Start-ups are less difficult to integrate than acquisitions. Companies using the shared-activities concept can also make acquisitions as beachhead landings into a new industry and then integrate the units through sharing with other units. Prime examples of companies that have diversified via using shared activities include P&G, Du Pont, and IBM. The fields into which each has diversified are a cluster of tightly related units. Marriott illustrates both successes and failures in sharing activities over time. (See the insert "Adding Value with Hospitality.")

Following the shared-activities model requires an organizational context in which business unit collaboration is encouraged and reinforced. Highly autonomous business units are inimical to such collaboration. The company must put into place a variety of what I call horizontal mechanisms—a strong sense of corporate identity, a clear corporate mission statement that emphasizes the importance of integrating business unit strategies, an incentive system that rewards more than just business unit results, cross-business-unit task forces, and other methods of integrating.

A corporate strategy based on shared activities clearly meets the better-off test because business units gain ongoing tangible advantages from others within the corporation. It also meets the cost-of-entry test by reducing the expense of surmounting the barriers to internal entry. Other bids for acquisitions that do not share opportunities will have lower reservation prices. Even widespread opportunities for sharing activities do not allow a company to suspend the attractiveness test, however. Many diversifiers have made the critical mistake of equating the close fit of a target industry with attractive diversification. Target industries must pass the strict requirement test of having an attractive structure as well as a close fit in opportunities if diversification is to ultimately succeed.

Choosing a corporate strategy

Each concept of corporate strategy allows the diversified company to create shareholder value in a different way. Companies can succeed with any of the concepts if they clearly define the corporation's role and objectives, have the skills necessary for meeting the concept's prerequisites, organize themselves to manage diversity in a way that fits the strategy, and find themselves in an appropriate capital market environment. The caveat is that portfolio management is only sensible in limited circumstances.

A company's choice of corporate strategy is partly a legacy of its past. If its business units are in unattractive industries, the company must start from scratch. If the company has few truly proprietary skills or activities it can share in related diversification, then its initial diversification must rely on other concepts. Yet corporate strategy should not be a once-and-for-all choice but a vision that can evolve. A company should choose its long-term preferred concept and then proceed pragmatically toward it from its initial starting point.

Both the strategic logic and the experience of the companies I studied over the last decade suggest that a company will create shareholder value through diversification to a greater and greater extent as its strategy moves from portfolio management toward sharing activities. Because they do not rely on superior insight or other questionable assumptions about the company's capabilities, sharing activities and transferring skills offer the best avenues for value creation.

Sharing allows activities to change completely in ways that increase competitive advantage.

Each concept of corporate strategy is not mutually exclusive of those that come before, a potent advantage of the third and fourth concepts. A company can employ a restructuring strategy at the same time it transfers skills or shares activities. A strategy based on shared activities becomes more powerful if business units can also exchange skills. As the Marriott case illustrates, a company can often pursue the two strategies together and even incorporate some of the principles of restructuring with them. When it chooses industries in which to transfer skills or share activities, the company can also investigate the possibility of transforming the industry structure. When a company bases its strategy on interrelationships, it has a broader basis on which to create shareholder value than if it rests its entire strategy on transforming companies in unfamiliar industries.

My study supports the soundness of basing a corporate strategy on the transfer of skills or shared activities. The data on the sample companies' diversification programs illustrate some important characteristics of successful diversifiers. They have made a disproportionately low percentage of unrelated acquisitions, *unrelated* being defined as having no clear opportunity to transfer skills or share important activities (see *Exhibit III*). Even successful diversifiers such as 3M, IBM, and TRW have terrible records when they have strayed into unrelated acquisitions. Successful acquirers diversify into fields, each of which is related to many others. Procter & Gamble and IBM, for example, operate in 18 and 19 interrelated fields respectively and so enjoy numerous opportunities to transfer skills and share activities.

Companies with the best acquisition records tend to make heavier-than-average use of start-ups and joint ventures. Most companies shy away from modes of entry besides acquisition. My results cast doubt on the conventional wisdom regarding start-ups. *Exhibit III* demonstrates that while joint ventures are about as risky as acquisitions, start-ups are not. Moreover, successful companies often have very good records with start-up units, as 3M, P&G, Johnson & Johnson, IBM, and United Technologies illustrate. When a company has the internal strength to start up a unit, it can be safer and less costly to launch a company than to rely solely on an acquisition and then have to deal with the problem of integration. Japanese diversification histories support the soundness of start-up as an entry alternative.

My data also illustrate that none of the concepts of corporate strategy works when industry structure is poor or implementation is bad, no matter how related the industries are. Xerox acquired companies in related industries, but the businesses had poor structures and its skills were insufficient to provide enough competitive advantage to offset implementation problems.

An action program

To translate the principles of corporate strategy into successful diversification, a company must first take an objective look at its existing businesses and the value added by the corporation. Only through such an assessment can an understanding of good corporate strategy grow. That understanding should guide future diversification as well as the development of skills and activities with which to select further new businesses. The following action program provides a concrete approach to conducting such a review. A company can choose a corporate strategy by:

1 Identifying the interrelationships among already existing business units.

A company should begin to develop a corporate strategy by identifying all the opportunities it has to share activities or transfer skills in its existing portfolio of business units. The company will not only find ways to enhance the competitive advantage of existing units but also come upon several possible diversification avenues. The lack of meaningful interrelationships in the portfolio is an equally important finding, suggesting the need to justify the value added by the corporation or, alternately, a fundamental restructuring.

2 Selecting the core businesses that will be the foundation of the corporate strategy.

Successful diversification starts with an understanding of the core businesses that will serve as the basis for corporate strategy. Core businesses are those that are in an attractive industry, have the potential to achieve sustainable competitive advantage, have important interrelationships with other business units, and provide skills or activities that represent a base from which to diversify.

The company must first make certain its core businesses are on sound footing by upgrading management, internationalizing strategy, or improving technology. My study shows that geographic extensions of existing units, whether by acquisition, joint venture, or start-up, had a substantially lower divestment rate than diversification.

The company must then patiently dispose of the units that are not core businesses. Selling them will free resources that could be better deployed elsewhere. In some cases disposal implies immediate liquidation, while in others the company should dress up the units and wait for a propitious market or a particularly eager buyer.

3 Creating horizontal organizational mechanisms to facilitate interrelationships among the core businesses and lay the groundwork for future related diversification.

Top management can facilitate interrelationships by emphasizing cross-unit collaboration, grouping units organizationally and modifying incentives, and taking steps to build a strong sense of corporate identity.

4 Pursuing diversification opportunities that allow shared activities.

This concept of corporate strategy is the most compelling, provided a company's strategy passes all three tests. A company should inventory activities in existing business units that represent the strongest foundation for sharing, such as strong distribution channels or world-class technical facilities. These will in turn lead to potential new business areas. A company can use acquisitions as a beachhead or employ start-ups to exploit internal capabilities and minimize integrating problems.

5 Pursuing diversification through the transfer of skills if opportunities for sharing activities are limited or exhausted.

Companies can pursue this strategy through acquisition, although they may be able to use start-ups if their existing units have important skills they can readily transfer.

Such diversification is often riskier because of the tough conditions necessary for it to work. Given the uncertainties, a company should avoid diversifying on the basis of skills transfer alone. Rather it should also be viewed as a stepping-stone to subsequent diversification using shared activities. New industries should be chosen that will lead naturally to other businesses. The goal is to build a cluster of related and mutually reinforcing business units. The strategy's logic implies that the company should not set the rate of return standards for the initial foray into a new sector too high.

6   Pursuing a strategy of restructuring if this fits the skills of management or no good opportunities exist for forging corporate interrelationships.

When a company uncovers undermanaged companies and can deploy adequate management talent and resources to the acquired units, then it can use a restructuring strategy. The more developed the capital markets and the more active the market for companies, the more restructuring will require a patient search for that special opportunity rather than a headlong race to acquire as many bad apples as possible. Restructuring can be a permanent strategy, as it is with Loew's, or a way to build a group of businesses that supports a shift to another corporate strategy.

7   Paying dividends so that the shareholders can be the portfolio managers.

Paying dividends is better than destroying shareholder value through diversification based on shaky underpinnings. Tax considerations, which some companies cite to avoid dividends, are hardly legitimate reason to diversify if a company cannot demonstrate the capacity to do it profitably.

Creating a corporate theme

Defining a corporate theme is a good way to ensure that the corporation will create shareholder value. Having the right theme helps unite the efforts of business units and reinforces the ways they interrelate as well as guides the choice of new businesses to enter. NEC Corporation, with its "C&C" theme, provides a good example. NEC integrates its computer, semiconductor, telecommunications, and consumer electronics businesses by merging computers and communication.

It is all too easy to create a shallow corporate theme. CBS wanted to be an "entertainment company," for example, and built a group of businesses related to leisure time. It entered such industries as toys, crafts, musical instruments, sports teams, and hi-fi retailing. While this corporate theme sounded good, close listening revealed its hollow ring. None of these businesses had any significant opportunity to share activities or transfer skills among themselves or with CBS's traditional broadcasting and record businesses. They were all sold, often at significant losses, except for a few of CBS's publishing-related units. Saddled with the worst acquisition record in my study, CBS has eroded the shareholder value created through its strong performance in broadcasting and records.

Moving from competitive strategy to corporate strategy is the business equivalent of passing through the Bermuda Triangle. The failure of corporate strategy reflects the fact that most diversified companies have failed to think in terms of how they really add value. A corporate strategy that truly enhances the competitive advantage of each business unit is the best defense against the corporate raider. With a sharper focus on the tests of diversification and the explicit choice of a clear concept of corporate strategy, companies' diversification track records from now on can look a lot different.

References

1 The studies also show that sellers of companies capture a large fraction of the gains from merger. See Michael C. Jensen and Richard S. Ruback, "The Market for Corporate Control: The Scientific Evidence," *Journal of Financial Economics*, April 1983, p. 5, and Michael C. Jensen, "Takeovers: Folklore and Science," HBR November-December 1984, p. 109.

2 Some recent evidence also supports the conclusion that acquired companies often suffer eroding performance after acquisition. See Frederick M. Scherer, "Mergers, Sell-Offs and Managerial Behavior," in *The Economics of Strategic Planning*, ed. Lacy Glenn Thomas (Lexington, Mass.: Lexington Books, 1986), p. 143, and David A. Ravenscraft and Frederick M. Scherer, "Mergers and Managerial Performance," paper presented at the Conference on Takeovers and Contests for Corporate Control, Columbia Law School, 1985.

3 This observation has been made by a number of authors. See, for example, Malcolm S. Salter and Wolf A. Weinhold, *Diversification Through Acquisition* (New York: Free Press, 1979).

4 See Michael E. Porter, "How Competitive Forces Shape Strategy," HBR March-April 1979, p. 86.

5 Michael E. Porter, *Competitive Advantage* (New York: Free Press, 1985).

Reprint 87307

Author's note: The research for this article was done with the able assistance of my research associate Cheng G. Ong. Malcolm S. Salter, Andrall E. Pearson, A. Michael Keehner, and the Monitor Company also provided helpful comments.

*Strategy isn't beating
the competition; it's serving
customers' real needs.*

Getting Back to Strategy

by Kenichi Ohmae

"Competitiveness" is the word most commonly uttered these days in economic policy circles in Washington and most European capitals. The restoration of competitive vitality is a widely shared political slogan. Across the Atlantic, the sudden nearness of 1992 and the coming unification of the Common Market focus attention on European industries' ability to compete against global rivals. On both continents, senior managers, who started to wrestle with these issues long before politicians got hold of them, search actively for successful models to follow, for examples of how best to play the new competitive game. With few exceptions, the models they have found and the examples they are studying are Japanese.

To many Western managers, the Japanese competitive achievement provides hard evidence that a successful strategy's hallmark is the creation of sustainable competitive advantage by beating the competition. If it takes world-class manufacturing to win, runs the lesson, you have to beat competitors with your factories. If it takes rapid product development, you have to beat them with your labs. If it takes mastery of distribution channels, you have to beat them with your logistics systems. No matter what it takes, the goal of strategy is to beat the competition.

After a painful decade of losing ground to the Japanese, managers in the United States and Europe have learned this lesson very well indeed. As a guide to action, it is clear and compelling. As a metric of performance, it is unambiguous. It is also wrong.

Of course, winning the manufacturing or product development or logistics battle is no bad thing. But it is not really what strategy is—or should be—about. Because when the focus of attention is on ways to beat the competition, it is inevitable that strategy gets defined primarily in terms of the competition. For instance, if the competition has recently brought out an electronic kitchen gadget that slices, dices, and brews coffee, you had better get one just like it into your product line—and get it there soon. If the competition has cut production costs, you had better get out your scalpel. If they have just started to run national ads, you had better call your agency at once. When you go toe-to-toe with competitors, you cannot let them build up any kind of advantage. You must match their every move. Or so the argument goes.

Of course it is important to take the competition into account, but in making strategy that should not come first. It cannot come first. First comes painstaking attention to the needs of customers. First comes close analysis of a company's real degrees of freedom in responding to those needs. First comes the willingness to rethink, fundamentally, what products are and what they do, as well as how best to organize the business system that designs, builds, and markets them. Competitive realities are what you test possible strategies against; you define them in terms of customers. Tit-for-tat responses to what competi-

> ## Remember Sun Tzu's advice: the smartest strategy in war avoids a battle.

tors do may be appropriate, but they are largely reactive. They come second, after your real strategy. Before you test yourself against competition, strategy takes shape in the determination to create value for customers.

It also takes shape in the determination to *avoid* competition whenever and wherever possible. As the great Sun Tzu observed 500 years before Christ, the

Kenichi Ohmae heads McKinsey's office in Tokyo. He is the author of The Mind of the Strategist: The Art of Japanese Business *(McGraw-Hill, 1982),* Triad Power: The Coming Shape of Global Competition *(Free Press, 1985), and* Beyond National Borders *(Dow Jones-Irwin, 1987). This is the first in a series of articles on strategy by Mr. Ohmae that will appear in HBR.*

smartest strategy in war is the one that allows you to achieve your objectives without having to fight. In just three years, for example, Nintendo's "family computer" sold 12 million units in Japan alone, during which time it had virtually no competition at all. In fact, it created a vast network of companies working to help it succeed. Ricoh supplied the critical Zylog chips; software houses produced special games to play on it like Dragon Quest I, II, and III. Everyone was making too much money to think of creating competition.

The visible clashing between companies in the marketplace—what managers frequently think of as strategy—is but a small fragment of the strategic whole. Like an iceberg, most of strategy is submerged, hidden out of sight. The visible part can foam and froth with head-to-head competition. But most of it is intentionally invisible—beneath the surface where value gets created, where competition gets avoided. Sometimes, of course, the foam and froth of direct competition cannot be avoided. The product is right, the company's direction is right, the perception of value is right, and managers have to buckle down and fight it out with competitors. But in my experience, managers too often and too willingly launch themselves into old-fashioned competitive battles. It's familiar ground. They know what to do, how to fight. They have a much harder time seeing when an effective customer-oriented strategy could avoid the battle altogether.

The Big Squeeze

During the late 1960s and early 1970s, most Japanese companies focused their attention on reducing costs through programs like quality circles, value engineering, and zero defects. As these companies went global, however, they began to concentrate instead on differentiating themselves from their competitors. This heavy investment in competitive differentiation has now gone too far; it has already passed the point of diminishing returns—too many models, too many gadgets, too many bells and whistles.

Today, as a result, devising effective customer-oriented strategies has a special urgency for these companies. A number of the largest and most successful face a common problem—the danger of being trapped between low-cost producers in the NIEs (newly industrialized economies) and high-end producers in Europe. While this threat concerns managers in all the major industrial economies, in Japan, where the danger is most immediate and pressing, it has quickly led companies to rethink their familiar

strategic goals. As a consequence, they are rediscovering the primary importance of focusing on customers—in other words, the importance of getting back to what strategy is really about.

In Japan today, the handwriting is on the wall for many industries: the strategic positioning that has served them so well in the past is no longer tenable. On one side, there are German companies making

The Japanese are caught between high-value products and low-cost entries.

top-of-the-line products like Mercedes or BMW in automobiles, commanding such high prices that even elevated cost levels do not greatly hurt profitability. On the other are low-price, high-volume producers like Korea's Hyundai, Samsung, and Lucky Goldstar. These companies can make products for less than half what it costs the Japanese. The Japanese are being caught in the middle: they are able neither to command the immense margins of the Germans nor to undercut the rock-bottom wages of the Koreans. The result is a painful squeeze.

If you are the leader of a Japanese company, what can you do? I see three possibilities. First, because Korean productivity is still quite low, you can challenge them directly on costs. Yes, their wages are often as little as one-seventh to one-tenth of yours. But if you aggressively take labor content out of your products, you can close or even reverse the cost gap. In practice, this means pushing hard—and at considerable expense—toward full automation, unmanned operations, and totally flexible manufacturing systems.

Examples prove that it can be done. NSK (Nikon Seiko), which makes bearings, has virtually removed its work force through an extensive use of computer-integrated manufacturing linked directly with the marketplace. Mazak Machinery has taken almost all the labor content out of key components in its products. Fujitsu Fanuc has so streamlined itself that it has publicly announced that it can break even with as little as 20% capacity utilization and can compete successfully with a currency as strong as 70 yen to the dollar.

This productivity-through-automation route is one way to go. In fact, for commodity products such as bearings it may be the only way. Once you start down this path, however, you have to follow it right to the end. No turning back. No stopping. Because Korean wages are so low that nothing less than a total commitment to eliminating labor content will suffice. And China, with wage rates just one-fifth of those in the newly industrialized economies, is not far behind Korea and Taiwan in such light industries as textiles, footwear, and watchbands. Although the currencies of the newly industrialized economies are now moving up relative to the dollar, the difference in wage rates is still great enough to require the fiercest kind of across-the-board determination to get rid of labor content.

A second way out of the squeeze is for you to move upmarket where the Germans are. In theory this might be appealing; in practice it has proven very hard for the Japanese to do. Their corporate cultures simply do not permit it. Just look, for example, at what happened with precision electronic products like compact disk players. As soon as the CD reached the market, customers went crazy with demand. Everybody wanted one. It was a perfect opportunity to move upscale with a ''Mercedes'' compact disk player. What did the Japanese do? Corporate culture and instinct took over, and they cut prices down to about one-fifth of what U.S. and European companies were going to ask for their CDs. Philips, of course, was trying to keep prices and margins up, but the Japanese were trying to drive them down. The Western companies wanted to make money; the Japanese instinct was to build share at any cost.

This is foolishness—or worse. Of course, it is perfectly clear why the Japanese respond this way. They are continuing to practice the approach that served them well in the past when they were playing the low-cost market entry game that the Koreans are playing now. It's the game they know how to play. But now there's a new game, and the Japanese companies have new positions. The actions that made sense for a low-cost player are way off course for a company trying to play at the high end of the market.

There is another reason for this kind of self-defeating behavior. Sony is really more worried about Matsushita than about Philips, and Matsushita is

> **You've got 40% of the global piano market—but demand is dropping 10% each year. What's your strategy?**

more worried about Sanyo. This furious internal competition fuels the Japanese impulse to slash prices whenever possible. That's also why it's so difficult for Japanese companies to follow the German route. To do it, they have to buck their own history. It means going their own way, and guarding against the instinct to backpedal, to do what their domestic competitors are doing.

Hard as it is, a number of companies *are* going their own way quite successfully. Some, like Seiko in its dogfight with Casio and Hong Kong-based watchmakers, had been badly burned in the low-price game and are now moving to restore profits at the high end of the market. Others, like Honda, Toyota, and Nissan in the automobile industry, are launching more expensive car lines and creating second dealer channels in the United States through which to compete directly for the upscale ''German'' segment. Still others, like Nakamichi in tape recorders, have always tried to operate at the high end and have never given in on price. Such companies are, however, very rare. Instinct runs deep. Japanese producers tend to compete on price even when they do not have to.

For most companies, following the Korean or German approach is neither an appealing nor a sustainable option. This is not only true in Japan but also in all the advanced industrial economies, if for different reasons. What sets Japanese companies apart is the consideration that they may have less room to maneuver than others, given their historical experience and present situation. For all these companies, there is a pressing need for a middle strategic course, a way to flourish without being forced to go head-to-head with competitors in either a low-cost or an upmarket game. Such a course exists—indeed, it leads managers back to the heart of what strategy is about: creating value for customers.

Five-Finger Exercise

Imagine for a moment that you are head of Yamaha, a company that makes pianos. What are your strategic choices? After strenuous and persistent efforts to become the leading producer of high-quality pianos, you have succeeded in capturing 40% of the global piano market. Unfortunately, just when you finally became the market leader, overall demand for pianos started to decline by 10% every year. As head of Yamaha, what do you do?

A piano is a piano. In most respects, the instrument has not changed much since Mozart. Around the world, in living rooms and dens and concert halls and rehearsal halls, there are some 40 million pianos. For the most part they simply sit. Market growth is stagnant, in polite terms. In business terms, the industry is already in decline; and Korean producers are now coming on-line with their usual low-cost offerings. Competing just to hold share is not an attractive prospect. Making better pianos will not help much; the market has only a limited ability to absorb additional volume. What do you do? What can you do?

According to some analysts, the right move would be to divest the business, labeling it a dog that no longer belongs in the corporate portfolio. But Yamaha reacted differently. Rather than selling the business, Yamaha thought long and hard about how to create value for customers. It took that kind of effort – the answers were far from obvious.

What Yamaha's managers did was look – they took a hard look at the customer and the product. What they saw was that most of these 40 million pianos sit around idle and neglected – and out of tune – most of the time. Not many people play them anymore. No one seems to have a lot of time anymore – and one thing learning to play the piano takes is lots of time. What sits in the homes of these busy people is a large piece of furniture that collects dust. Instead of music, it may even produce guilt. Certainly it is not a functioning musical instrument. No matter how good you are at strategy, you won't be able to sell that many new pianos – no matter how good they are – in such an environment. If you want to create value for customers, you're going to have to find ways to add value to the millions of pianos already out there.

So what do you do? What Yamaha did was to remember the old player piano – a pleasant idea with a not very pleasant sound. Yamaha worked hard to develop a sophisticated, advanced combination of digital and optical technology that can distinguish among 92 different degrees of strength and speed of key touch from pianissimo to fortissimo. Because the technology is digital, it can record and reproduce each keystroke with great accuracy, using the same kind of 3½" disks that work on a personal computer. That means you can now record live performances by the pianists of your choice – or buy such recordings on a computerlike diskette – and then, in effect, invite the artists into your home to play the same compositions on your piano. Yamaha's strategy used technology to create new value for piano customers.

Think about it. For about $2,500 you can retrofit your idle, untuned, dust-collecting piece of oversized furniture so that great artists can play it for you in the privacy of your own home. You can invite your friends over and entertain them as well – and showcase the latest in home entertainment technology. If you are a flutist, you can invite someone over to accompany you on the piano and record her performance. Then, even when she is not there, you can practice the piece with full piano accompaniment.

Furthermore, if you have a personal computer at home in Cambridge and you know a good pianist living in California, you can have her record your favorite sonata and send it over the phone; you simply download it onto your computer, plug the diskette into your retrofitted piano, and enjoy her performance. Or you can join a club that will send you the concert that a Horowitz played last night at Carnegie Hall to listen to at home on your own piano. There are all kinds of possibilities.

In terms of the piano market, this new technology creates the prospect of a $2,500 sale to retrofit each of 40 million pianos – not bad for a declining industry. In fact, the potential is even greater because there are also the software recordings to market.

Yamaha started marketing this technology last April, and sales in Japan have been explosive. This was a stagnant industry, remember, an industry which had suffered an annual 10% sales decline in each of the past five years. Now it's alive again – but in a different way. Yamaha did not pursue all the usual routes: it didn't buckle down to prune costs, proliferate models, slice overhead, and all the other usual approaches. It looked with fresh eyes for chances to create value for customers. And it found them.

It also found something else: it learned that the process of discovering value-creating opportunities is itself contagious. It spreads. For instance, now that customers have pianos that play the way Horowitz played last night at Carnegie Hall, they want their instrument tuned to professional standards. That means a tuner visits every six months and generates substantial additional revenue. (And it is substantial. Globally, the market for tuning is roughly $1.6 billion annually, a huge economic opportunity long ignored by piano manufacturers and distributors.) Yamaha can also give factory workers who might otherwise lose their jobs a chance to be tuners.

As the piano regains popularity, a growing number of people will again want to learn how to play the instrument themselves. And that means tutorials, piano schools, videocassettes, and a variety of other revenue-producing opportunities. Overall, the potential growth in the piano industry, hardware and software, is much bigger than anyone previously recognized. Creating value for the customer was the key that unlocked it.

But what about people's reluctance today to spend the time to learn piano the old-fashioned way? We are a society that prizes convenience, and as the many years of declining piano sales illustrate, learning to play a musical instrument is anything but convenient. Listening to music, as opposed to making music, is more popular than ever. Look at all the people going to school or to the office with earphones on; music is everywhere. It's not interest in music that's going down; it's the interest in spending years of disciplined effort to master an instrument. If you asked people if they would like to be able to play an instrument like the piano, they'd say yes. But most feel as if

> **Kao used R&D to change the map of the Japanese bath product industry.**

they've already missed the opportunity to learn. They're too old now; they don't have the time to take years of lessons.

With the new digital and sound-chip technologies, they don't have to. Nor do they have to be child prodigies. For $1,500 they can buy a Klavinova, a digital electronic piano, that allows them to do all kinds of wonderful things. They can program it to play and then croon along. They can program it to play the left hand part and join in with a single finger. They can listen to a tutorial cassette that directs which keys to push. They can store instructions in the computer's memory so that they don't have to play all the notes and chords simultaneously. Because the digital technology makes participation easy and accessible, "playing" the instrument becomes fun. Technology removes the learning barrier. No wonder this digital

segment is now much bigger than the traditional analog segment of the market.

Most piano manufacturers, however, are sticking with traditional acoustic technologies and leaving their futures to fate. Faced with declining demand, they fight even harder against an ever more aggressive set of competitors for their share of a shrinking pie. Or they rely on government to block imports. Yamaha has not abandoned acoustic instruments; it is now the world leader in nearly all categories of acoustic and "techno" musical instruments. What it did, however, was to study its music-loving customers and to build a strategy based on delivering value linked to those customers' inherent interest in music. It left nothing to fate. It got back to strategy.

Cleaning Up

This is how you chart out a middle course between the Koreans and the Germans. This is how you revitalize an industry. More to the point, this is how you create a value-adding strategy: not by setting out to beat the competition but by setting out to understand how best to provide value for customers.

Kao is a Japanese toiletry company that spends 4% of its revenues on fundamental R&D, studying skin, hair, blood, circulation—things like that. (This 4% may, at first, sound low, but it excludes personnel cost. This matters because as many as 2,800 of the company's 6,700 or so employees are engaged in R&D.) Recently it developed a new product that duplicates the effect of a Japanese hot spring. A hot spring has a high mineral content under extreme pressure. Even the right chemicals thrown into a hot bath will not automatically give you the same effect. Babu, Kao's new bath additive, actually produces the same kind of improvement in circulation that a hot spring provides. It looks like a jumbo-sized Alka-Seltzer tablet. When you throw one Babu into a bath, it starts to fizz with carbon dioxide bubbles as minerals dissolve in the hot water.

Kao's strategy was to offer consumers something completely different from traditional bath gel. Because of its effects on overall health and good circulation, Babu competes on a different ground. In fact, it wiped out the old Japanese bath gel and additives industry in a single year. It's the only product of its kind that now sells in Japan. There is no competition because potential competitors cannot make anything like it. Kao is playing a different game.

For the new breed of Japanese companies, like Yamaha and Kao, strategy does not mean beating the competition. It means working hard to understand a customer's inherent needs and then rethinking what a category of product is all about. The goal is to develop the right product to serve those needs—not just a better version of competitors' products. In fact, Kao pays far less attention to other toiletry companies than it does to improving skin condition, circulation, or caring for hair. It now understands hair so well that its newest hair tonic product, called Success, falls somewhere between cosmetics and medicine. In that arena, there is no competition.

Brewing Wisdom

Getting back to strategy means getting back to a deep understanding of what a product is about. Some time back, for example, a Japanese home appliance company was trying to develop a coffee percolator. Should it be a General Electric-type percolator, executives wondered? Should it be the same drip-type that Philips makes? Larger? Smaller? I urged them to ask a different kind of question: Why do people drink coffee? What are they looking for when they do? If your objective is to serve the customer better, then shouldn't you understand why that customer drinks coffee in the first place? Then you know what kind of percolator to make.

The answer came back: good taste. I then asked the company's engineers what they were doing to help the consumer enjoy good taste in a cup of coffee. They said they were trying to design a good percolator. I asked them what influences the taste of a cup of coffee. No one knew. That became the next question we had to answer. It turns out that lots of things can affect taste—the beans, the temperature, the water. We did our homework and discovered all the things that affect taste. For the engineers, each factor represented a strategic degree of freedom in designing a percolator—that is, a factor about which something can be done. With beans, for instance, you can have different degrees of quality or freshness. You can grind them in various ways. You can produce different grain sizes. You can distribute the grains differently when pouring hot water over them.

Of all the factors, water quality, we learned, made the greatest difference. The percolator in design at the time, however, didn't take water quality into account at all. Everyone had simply assumed that customers would use tap water. We discovered next that the grain distribution and the time between grinding the beans and pouring in the water were crucial. As a result, we began to think about the product and its necessary features in a new way. It *had* to have a built-in dechlorinating function. It *had* to have a built-in grinder. All the customer should have to do is pour in water and beans; the machine should handle the rest. That's the way to assure great taste in a cup of coffee.

To start you have to ask the right questions and set the right kinds of strategic goals. If your only concern is that General Electric has just brought out a percolator that brews coffee in ten minutes, you will get your engineers to design one that brews it in seven minutes. And if you stick with that logic, market research will tell you that instant coffee is the way to go. If the General Electric machine consumes only a little electricity, you will focus on using even less.

Conventional marketing approaches won't solve the problem. You can get any results you want from the consumer averages. If you ask people whether they want their coffee in ten minutes or seven, they will say seven, of course. But it's still the wrong question. And you end up back where you started, trying to beat the competition at its own game. If your primary focus is on the competition, you will never step back and ask what the customer's inherent needs are or what the product really is about. Personally, I would much rather talk with three housewives for two hours each on their feelings about, say, washing machines than conduct a 1,000-person survey on the same topic. I get much better insight and perspective on what they are really looking for.

Taking Pictures

Back in the mid-1970s, single-lens reflex (SLR) cameras started to become popular, and lens-shutter cameras declined rapidly in popularity. To most people, the lens-shutter model looked cheap and nonprofessional and it took inferior quality pictures. These opinions were so strong that one camera company with which I was working had almost decided to pull out of the lens-shutter business entirely. Everyone knew that the trend was toward SLR and that only a better version of SLR could beat the competition.

I didn't know. So I asked a few simple questions: Why do people take pictures in the first place? What are they really looking for when they take pictures? The answer was simple. They were not looking for a good camera. They were looking for good pictures. Cameras—SLR or lens-shutter—and film were not the end products that consumers wanted. What they wanted were good pictures.

Why was it so hard to take good pictures with a lens-shutter camera? This time, no one knew. So we went to a film lab and collected a sample of some 18,000 pictures. Next we identified the 7% or so that

"It's from a car rental outfit that wants to arrange an annual Blessing of the Fleet."

were not very good; then we tried to analyze why each of these picture-taking failures had occurred. We found some obvious causes – even some categories of causes. Some failures were the result of poor distance adjustment. The company's design engineers addressed that problem in two different ways: they added a plastic lens designed to keep everything in focus beyond three feet (a kind of permanent focus), and they automated the focus process.

Another common problem with the bad pictures was not enough light. The company built a flash right into the camera. That way, the poor fellow who left his flash attachment on a closet shelf could still be equipped to take a good picture. Still another problem was the marriage of film and camera. Here the engineers added some grooves on the side of the film cartridges so that the camera could tell how sensitive the film is to light and could adjust. Double exposure was another common problem. The camera got a self-winder.

In all, we came up with some 200 ideas for improving the lens-shutter camera. The result – virtually a whole new approach to the product – helped revitalize the business. Today, in fact, the lens-shutter market is bigger than that for SLRs. And we got there

because we did a very simple thing: we asked what the customer's inherent needs were and then re-thought what a camera had to be in order to meet them. There was no point slugging it out with competitors. There was no reason to leave the business. We just got back to strategy – based on customers.

Making Dinner

There is no mystery to this process, no black box to which only a few gurus have access. The questions that have to be asked are straightforward, and the place to start is clear. Awhile ago, some people came to me with a set of excellent ideas for designing kitchen appliances for Japanese homes. They knew cooking, and their appliances were quite good. After some study, however, I told them not to go ahead.

What I did was to go and visit several hundred houses and apartments and take pictures of the kitchens. The answer became clear: there was no room. There were even things already stacked on top of the refrigerators. The counters were already full. There was no room for new appliances, no matter how appealing their attributes.

Thinking about these products, and understanding the customer's needs, however, did produce a different idea: build this new equipment into something that is already in the kitchen. That way there is no new demand for space. What that led to, for example, was the notion of building a microwave oven into a regular oven. Everyone looked at the pictures of 200 kitchens and said, no space. The alternative was, re-think the product.

Aching Heads, Bad Logic

Looking closely at a customer's needs, thinking deeply about a product – these are no exotic pieces of strategic apparatus. They are, as they have always been, the basics of sound management. They have just been neglected or ignored. But why? Why have so many managers allowed themselves to drift so far away from what strategy is really about?

Think for a moment about aching heads. Is my headache the same as yours? My cold? My shoulder pain? My stomach discomfort? Of course not. Yet when a pharmaceutical company asked for help to improve its process for coming up with new products, what it wanted was help in getting into its development pipeline new remedies for standard problems like headache or stomach pain. It had assembled a list of therapeutic categories and was eager to match them up with appropriate R&D efforts.

No one had taken the time, however, to think about how people with various discomforts actually feel. So we asked 50 employees in the company to fill out a questionnaire – throughout a full year – about how they felt physically at all times of the day every day of the year. Then we pulled together a list of the symptoms described, sat down with the company's scientists, and asked them, item by item: Do you know why people feel this way? Do you have a drug

Simply providing aspirin for every headache isn't strategy.

for this kind of symptom? It turned out that there were no drugs for about 80% of the symptoms, these physical awarenesses of discomfort. For many of them, some combination of existing drugs worked just fine. For others, no one had ever thought to seek a particular remedy. The scientists were ignoring tons of profit.

Without understanding customers' needs – the specific types of discomfort they were feeling – the company found it all too easy to say, "Headache? Fine, here's a medicine, an aspirin, for headache. Case closed. Nothing more to do there. Now we just have to beat the competition in aspirin." It was easy not to take the next step and ask, "What does the headache feel like? Where does it come from? What is the underlying cause? How can we treat the cause, not just

the symptom?" Many of these symptoms, for example, are psychological and culture-specific. Just look at television commercials. In the United States, the most common complaint is headache; in the United Kingdom, backache; in Japan, stomachache. In the United States, people say that they have a splitting headache; in Japan it is an ulcer. How can we truly understand what these people are feeling and why?

The reflex, of course, is to provide a headache pill for a headache – that is, to assume that the solution is simply the reverse of the diagnosis. That is bad medicine and worse logic. It is the kind of logic that reinforces the impulse to direct strategy toward beating the competition, toward cutting costs when making traditional musical instruments or adding a different ingredient to the line of traditional soaps. It is the kind of logic that denies the need for a detailed understanding of intrinsic customer needs. It leads to forklift trucks that pile up boxes just fine but do not allow the operators to see directly in front of them. It leads to dishwashers that remove everything but the scorched eggs and rice that customers most want to get rid of. It leads to pianos standing idle and gathering dust.

Getting back to strategy means fighting that reflex, not giving in to it. It means resisting the easy answers in the search for better ways to deliver value to customers. It means asking the simple-sounding questions about what products are about. It means, in short, taking seriously the strategic part of management. ▽

Reprint 88609

Marketing and finance are complementary – when the analysis is right.

Must Finance and Strategy Clash?

by Patrick Barwise, Paul R. Marsh, and Robin Wensley

Marketers and finance people seldom see eye to eye. The marketers say, "This product will open up a whole new market segment." Finance people respond, "It's a bad investment. The IRR is only 8%." Why are they so often in opposition?

The financial criteria used to decide if a project will be profitable are entirely consistent with the tenets of competitive marketing analysis. Correctly applied, good financial analysis complements rather than contradicts good marketing analysis. In practice, though, the analysis usually falls short. That explains why a strategic investment's projected returns are so often out of line with the marketing and strategic logic.

From a financial perspective, a good investment is one with a positive net present value – that is, one whose value exceeds its costs. While marketers often think a project's NPV is merely the result of financial arithmetic, in reality, it is derived from strategic marketing issues. To have a positive NPV, a project must pass two tests[1]: Does the product or service have enough value to enough customers to support prices and volumes that exceed the costs of supplying it – including the opportunity cost of capital? This question is central to postwar marketing and the "marketing concept." Second, does the company have enough sources of sustainable competitive advantage to exploit, develop, and defend the opportunity? This reflects marketing's more recent emphasis

on competitive strategy. The trick, then, is to encourage an investment decision-making process in which the financial analysis highlights rather than masks these two fundamental marketing questions.

Consider Fashion Bathrooms, a disguised but real division of a diversified engineering company that makes traditional cast-iron bathtubs. The CEO and her senior managers were considering new investments. One option was to adopt a novel proprietary casting process to make lighter bathtubs that could compete better against plastic ones. The $20 million investment seemed wise from a marketing perspective, but the investment's NPV came to a negative $2 million.

> **Good analysis ties the details of strategy to the financial implications.**

A debate ensued. Some top managers put their faith in the numbers. They believed that although the project would produce a superior product in many respects, its capital requirements were excessive. To the CEO and some others, however, Project

1. Patrick Barwise, Paul Marsh, and Robin Wensley, "Strategic Investment Decisions," *Research in Marketing*, vol. 9, 1987, pp. 1-57.

Patrick Barwise is senior lecturer in marketing, and Paul R. Marsh is deputy principal, faculty dean, and professor of management and finance – both at London Business School. Robin Wensley is chairman of Warwick Business School, where he teaches strategic marketing.

Lightweight still made intuitive sense. They wanted to go ahead with it despite the negative returns. As the marketing director put it, "There are some investments you have to make simply to stay in business – regardless of their rate of return."

In the end, what was good for Fashion Bathrooms in a marketing sense was also good for it financially. The initial analysis simply failed to reflect that reality. To sharpen the financial analysis, the managers returned to the marketing strategy and delved deeper into it. Now the financial analysis helped clarify the marketing issues to be reconsidered.

Good project evaluation considers *all* the relevant factors, including hard-to-quantify costs and benefits. It also takes into account the more neglected consequences of *not* investing. It recognizes the value of opening up options and, by not arbitrarily restricting the time horizon or setting discount rates too high, avoids undervaluing long-term projects. Understanding project evaluation is easy. Doing it is the real challenge.

Use the Right Base Case

Finance theory assumes that a project will be evaluated against its base case, that is, what will happen if the project is not carried out. Managers tend to explore fully the implications of adopting the project but usually spend less time considering the likely outcome of not making the investment. Yet unless the base case is realistic, the incremental cash flows – the difference between the "with" and the "without" scenarios – will mislead.

Often companies implicitly assume that the base case is simply a continuation of the status quo, but this assumption ignores market trends and competitor behavior. It also neglects the impact of changes the company might make anyway, like improving operations management.

Using the wrong base case is typical of product launches in which the new product will likely erode the market for the company's existing product line. Take Apple Computer's introduction of the Macintosh SE. The new PC had obvious implications for sales of earlier generation Macintoshes. To analyze the incremental cash flows arising from the new product, Apple would have needed to count the lost contribution from sales of its existing products as a cost of the launch.

Wrongly applied, however, this approach would equate the without case to the status quo: it would assume that without the SE, sales of existing Macintoshes would continue at their current level. In the

competitive PC market, however, nothing stands still. Competitors like IBM would likely innovate and take share away from the earlier generation Macintoshes – which a more realistic base case would have reflected. Sales of existing products would decline even in the base case.

Consider investments in the marketing of existing brands through promotions, media budgets, and the like. They are often sold as if they were likely to lead to ever-increasing market share. But competitors will also be promoting their brands, and market shares across the board still have to add up to 100%. Still, such an investment is not necessarily wasted. It may just need a more realistic justification: although the investment is unlikely to increase sales above existing levels, it may prevent sales from falling. Marketers who like positive thinking may not like this defensive argument, but it is the only argument that makes economic sense in a mature market.

In situations like this, when the investment is needed just to maintain market share, the returns may be high in comparison with the base case, but the company's reported profits may still go down. Senior managers are naturally puzzled at apparently netting only 5% on a project that had promised a 35% return.[2] Without the investment, however, the profit picture would have looked even worse, especially in the longer term.

Some projects disappoint for other reasons. Sometimes the original proposals are overoptimistic, partly because the base case is implicit or defined incorrectly. That is, if managers are convinced that the investment is sound and are frustrated because the figures fail to confirm their intuition, they may overinflate projections of sales or earnings. But misstating the base case and then having to make unrealistic projections are unlikely to cancel each other out; they merely cloud the analysis.

The base case against which Fashion Bathrooms first compared Project Lightweight implicitly assumed that sales would stay the same without the investment. In fact, sales were declining. When managers reevaluated the project using the correct base case, the negative NPV disappeared. The finance director also began to question the discount rate. He had at first used a high rate because the volumes and therefore the cost savings seemed very uncertain. At the time, Fashion Bathrooms had two plants, both running below capacity. Project Lightweight would upgrade one, so only products made at that plant would benefit from the new efficiencies. The finance director realized, however, that Fashion Bathrooms could shift all production to the upgraded plant until

2. Joseph L. Bower, *Managing the Resource Allocation Process* (Boston: Harvard Business School Press, 1986), p.13.

it hit full capacity. That way, the company would be sure to get the full savings. The second plant would handle only the overflow.

Other managers at Fashion Bathrooms thought that exiting the business was a more relevant base case. This alternative proved to be unattractive. The company would face heavy closure costs, and its plants had few alternative uses and therefore very low resale value.

Define the Project Boundaries

Advising managers to get the base case right is like telling them to get the project right. Obviously, the advice is grossly simplistic. One difficult task, for instance, is defining the project's boundaries: What is the correct without case – exiting the business, carrying on as things are now, improving distribution and marketing? And what is the right version of the project? Usually, there are several quite different ways of implementing it.

The project's boundaries tend to shift during the course of the analysis. Different players view the investment differently. For the CEO of Fashion Bathrooms, the without case was the dismal prospect of soldiering on in a declining market, while the investment was a way to improve morale and signal a commitment to stay in business. The manager of the plant that would not be upgraded saw things differently. While the without case would allow his factory to maintain its production level, the with case was a sure route to reduced output and diminished personal status – or even the loss of his job.

In principle, managers should take a corporate perspective when considering incremental costs and benefits. In practice, this is unrealistic. Unit managers' own responsibilities and self-interest will influence their perception of the project and color the way they define and analyze the proposal.

A project may look good at the business unit level because it shifts costs or steals share from another unit. From the corporate perspective, such a project would be less appealing. Fashion Bathrooms' parent company had a minimal share of the plastic bathtub market, so management ignored any erosion that Project Lightweight might cause. Had the plastics division been larger or more important, corporate management would have wanted the analysis to include the loss for the plastics division as well as the gain for the cast-iron bathtub division.

One might expect the boundaries of a project to be defined more broadly at the corporate level than at the business unit level. This is not always the case.

"Hey, what a great desk! I almost wish I were a scribe, instead of a Pharisee."

The CEO of Fashion Bathrooms, for instance, proposed the ambitious idea of combining marketing for the plastic and cast-iron divisions. The parent company board discouraged her from pursuing this course. It wanted her to narrow her focus and first sort out the operating and marketing problems at Fashion Bathrooms.

Choose an Appropriate Time Horizon

Project boundaries are also defined in terms of time. A project's financial analysis often extends over whichever is shorter: the assets' physical economic life or some arbitrary time horizon, like ten years. In the final year, the analysis may include minimal salvage values for the largest tangible assets. But financial appraisals seldom explain why a particular time horizon was chosen, even when the numbers are sensitive to the project's assumed life.

Strategic projects seldom have short or even easily defined lives. A plant built to manufacture a new branded product will eventually have to be replaced, but the product's value to the company, if successful, may easily outlast the plant. Or the plant's replacement date may extend beyond the time horizon used to appraise the project. None of this matters as long as the financial appraisal includes full economic terminal value rather than salvage amounts. The terminal value should reflect the cash flows over the remaining life of the existing plant or the value of the brand when the plant is replaced.

Some managers argue that it is pointless to look beyond ten years since cash flows will have only a small present value when discounted and since no one can accurately forecast that far ahead. But if terminal values are large, as they are for many strategic investments, they will be significant even when discounted. And that such values are notoriously hard to forecast is little reason to ignore them. Many strategic investments are designed to build a market position, a research capability, a reputation, or a brand name. Assuming that these assets are worthless beyond some arbitrary horizon fails to reflect the strategic reality.

The bathtub managers were fully aware that they had chosen an arbitrary time horizon for evaluating Project Lightweight. Their choice of ten years was purely pragmatic: there were ten columns on the company's capital-budgeting appraisal form. Since ten years was also the standard life over which plant and machinery were depreciated, they inserted no terminal value for the upgraded plant. In reality, however, the upgraded plant would last longer than ten years, and the market for cast-iron bathtubs was projected to continue well into the future.

Evaluate Options

Strategic investments usually go beyond exploitation of a particular opportunity. They open up options that extend even further into the future than the original project. When, for instance, Nestlé was considering its takeover of Rowntree, it paid close attention to the intangible assets. Nestlé was particularly interested in Rowntree's brands because of the marketing and distribution options they provided, especially in Europe in the run up to 1992.

Obviously, options stemming from investments in R&D, know-how, brand names, test markets, and channel developments have value beyond the initial investment. Less obvious is the value of the options to create subsequent products that complement or are based on existing ones.

Financial theorists and professionals have long been interested in valuing financial options like puts

3. See Stewart C. Myers, "Finance Theory and Financial Strategy," *Interfaces*, January-February 1984, pp. 126-137.

4. *Principles of Corporate Finance*, 3rd edition (New York: McGraw-Hill, 1988), p. 258.

5. Paul R. Marsh, Patrick Barwise, Kathryn Thomas, and Robin Wensley, "Managing Strategic Investment Decisions," in *Competitiveness and the Management Process*, ed. Andrew Pettigrew (Oxford: Basil Blackwell, 1988).

and calls, warrants, and convertible bonds; valuation models for these options are well-known. More recently, however, theorists and practitioners have acknowledged the importance of options on real assets.[3] But quantitative models for valuing these kinds of options are almost impossible to apply in

A product brand may outlast the factory. Do you give it a terminal value?

practice, since truly strategic options are so vague and often depend on a manager's vision of what might happen.

Financial appraisals of strategic investments therefore usually focus on the opportunity at hand and seldom try to value market opportunities that the investment may create. Businesspeople try to compensate for this when it comes to making the real decision. As Richard A. Brealey and Stewart C. Myers wrote, "Businesspeople often act smarter than they talk....They may make correct decisions, but they may not be able to explain them in the language of finance."[4]

Fashion Bathrooms was well aware of the options that Project Lightweight could open for its cast-iron bathtub business. First was the possibility of modernizing the company's second plant by introducing the casting process there as well. The attractiveness of this action would depend on the success of the company in reversing the market decline. Second, Fashion Bathrooms could use the same brand name to produce complementary products like washbasins and shower trays. The company made no attempt to value these opportunities, partly because they were just ideas with a small chance of being implemented and partly because Project Lightweight already appeared financially worthwhile.

Unbundle the Costs and Benefits

Almost any strategic investment can be regarded as a bundle of component subprojects, each with different costs and benefits. It is useful to recognize this and unbundle the subprojects. Doing so simplifies the analysis and helps managers make forecasts and assumptions explicit. It may also help the proposers come up with a better alternative.

Take an investment in a highly competitive market, like a Main Street retailing operation. The investment is a combination of two things: an investment in real estate and an investment in retailing skills. Yet financial evaluations normally lump these together, showing the total project as an initial investment in real estate plus shop-fitting costs, a stream of retailing profits, and a terminal value for the real estate and retailing business. A common problem with this formulation is that an overoptimistic terminal value for the real estate can make a bad retailing investment look good; a pessimistic value can make an efficient retailing operation look like a loser.

An alternative analysis would view the investment as two related projects. The first is a straight real estate investment, which includes the initial cost, a stream of rental receipts, and a terminal value. The second is a retailing investment, which involves the initial shop-fitting costs, the stream of retailing profits net of the rental, and the terminal value of the retailing operation.

Unless the company has a genuine competitive advantage in real estate, the NPV of the investment in real estate in the highly competitive Main Street market will probably be zero. Using the assumption of a zero NPV and given the purchase price and market rentals, managers can find the terminal value of the property. This shifts the focus to the second project, where the company may indeed have a competitive advantage. By stripping out the initial cost and the terminal values of the real estate and replacing these with the market rental, that is, with the opportunity cost of renting the space to another tenant, the company can evaluate the pure retailing project without the bias of an optimistic or pessimistic assumption about future real estate prices.

Performing the analysis this way clarifies the investment decision and avoids misleading forecasts. It also raises questions that might otherwise go unasked. In the Main Street deal, for example, it raises questions like: Would it be better to rent rather than buy the real estate? Or is it better to forgo the retailing project and invest in the real estate only?

Many strategic investments come packaged with investments in highly competitive and risky markets: overseas investments in manufacturing facilities may come with investments in foreign currency, investments in natural resource extraction may come with an investment in the resource itself, and so on. The best approach is to separate the investments in which the company has some competitive advantage from those in a highly competitive market and for which the NPV is likely to be zero.

Projects are also often bundled for political reasons. Proposers may include under the project umbrella a smaller project that would be hard to justify by itself. In one packaged-goods company, the executives buried in a large cost-saving investment a staff and office space upgrade and an investment in a new computer system. Although related to the cost-saving project, these additions were not essential to it. In such cases, project evaluators should proceed with caution. Unbundling is a useful analytic discipline, but it may be counterproductive to do it too explicitly. In our experience, managers often indulge in this kind of bundling to gain approval for genuinely worthwhile projects that are hard to justify in their own right. If they are forced to quantify the benefits of each subproject separately, some good projects may never see the light of day.

What gets included in or excluded from a project also depends on the proposers' need to end up with financial forecasts that are good enough to gain acceptance but not so good as to become an embarrassment later. It is often assumed that managers use optimistic revenue and cost projections if the project

Some investments are really two. Do you analyze them separately?

doesn't look profitable enough and do the opposite if it looks too profitable. According to our research, managers are in fact more likely to influence the numbers by redefining the project's boundaries.[5] They realize this is less likely to give hostages to fortune.

A highly profitable project will tend to be justified on the basis of its direct benefits but may also carry many indirect costs for such things as new computers or site refurbishment. Conversely, the proposer of a marginal project will tie in as many direct, quantifiable benefits as he or she can and exclude all indirect costs. This way, managers get corporate support for most of their projects without seriously compromising the decision-making process.

The management team at Fashion Bathrooms recognized the importance of project unbundling. Project Lightweight offered cost savings through a reduction in raw materials costs. On the other hand, it also promised quality improvements that would lead to increased sales. The CEO asked the finance director to rework the figures to determine if the project could be justified on the basis of cost savings alone – a benefit much easier to measure than incremental sales growth.

Unfortunately, cost savings alone were not enough. The project made sense only if the quality improvements could boost sales. This realization provoked further soul-searching. The managers reevaluated the quality improvements and asked themselves what evidence they had that sales would in fact benefit.

The quality improvements were twofold. First, the new bathtubs would be thinner and 35% lighter, making them easier to transport and install. Since plumbers and builders often make the buying decision, this feature was important. Second, the new casting process would create a smoother, shinier finish. But would these improvements really lead to more sales?

Fashion Bathrooms responded to this classic marketing problem by conducting market research. The results were revealing. Some people found many advantages in cast-iron bathtubs: they didn't flex and pull away from the wall, they looked better than shiny plastic, and they were more durable. But some complained of having to choose between a white cast-iron bathtub and a 20-week wait for a colored one. Others didn't even know that cast-iron bathtubs were available and that they had some advantages over plastic.

Would customers value the planned quality improvements? A lighter tub might seem less solid; a shiny finish might make it look just like a plastic tub. The evidence was shaky.

Ultimately Better Investments

In the end, Fashion Bathrooms shelved Project Lightweight. When managers scrutinized the analysis itself – not just the numbers it produced – they considered a new set of questions: Does Fashion Bathrooms have a sustainable competitive advantage? Why do people buy a particular type of bathtub? Was the company delivering what the market wanted, when it wanted it? And was Fashion Bathrooms helping to create a strong brand image for quality cast-iron bathtubs? These are the issues that are most important to strategic marketing.

When Fashion Bathrooms answered the questions and redid the financial analysis, things fell into place. The numbers demonstrated the benefits of investing

When finance and marketing conflict, retrace the analysis.

in intangible assets like brand image, market position, customer franchise, and distribution channels, and of investing to improve factory organization, styling, production control, color mix, and, above all, delivery.

The Fashion Bathrooms story illustrates that in marketing and operations, detail matters. Good investments come from a detailed understanding of both the market and the company's operating and competitive capabilities. Used sensibly, finance helps bring these into the open. Financial analysis also helps clarify the project's boundaries by addressing issues like the base case, the time horizon, and future strategic options – all of which are as much strategic and market based as they are financial. Finance gives them a common language and framework.

Unfortunately, the financial analysis is all too often "pinned on" afterward, rather like the tail on the donkey in the children's game. An interactive process that relates the product-market specifics to the wider financial implications is not only a requirement for sound strategic investment decisions but also a powerful source of organizational learning. ⊟

Planning
Corporate Strategy

Value analysis is a useful planning tool —
when rigorous strategy analysis goes with it.

Putting Strategy into Shareholder Value Analysis

by George S. Day and Liam Fahey

Does shareholder value analysis deserve its enormous popularity of recent years? Is it a reliable measure of a strategy's true potential to create wealth for shareholders? The answer depends on how companies use it. SVA *can* effectively translate a strategy into cash flow — but only when the analysis is linked to a full understanding of the company's strategy alternatives.

Proponents of SVA claim it is superior to any other method of analyzing the financial consequences of strategies and hold it up as the decade's most important contribution to corporate planning. Companies like Westinghouse, Dexter, Signode, and Trinova have had great success with it, financial theorists endorse it, a consulting industry has been built on it.

George S. Day is the executive director of the Marketing Science Institute in Cambridge, Massachusetts and is a professor at the University of Toronto. His forthcoming book, Market-Driven Strategy: Processes for Creating Value *(Free Press, 1990), uses the ideas in this article. Liam Fahey is associate professor of management policy at Boston University's School of Management. His most recent book is* The Strategic Planning Management Reader *(Prentice-Hall, 1989).*

But SVA has a long list of detractors. At the top of that list are operating managers, who tend to be far less enthusiastic about SVA than their more senior counterparts because they feel victimized by the

> Westinghouse and Signode use shareholder value analysis successfully. Where do other companies go wrong?

complexity and restrictive assumptions SVA uses — and because they are frustrated when accounting systems fail to provide the balance sheet and cost information the analysis requires.

Other managers are skeptical of SVA because they see how easily it can be manipulated. Indeed, one user's remark that SVA lets him "get any project I want approved" lends credence to this concern.

Some critics of SVA point to the fact that managers seldom agree on issues that influence the results — like what the discount rate, planning period, and projected cash flows should be. And most of the value SVA measures lies in the residual, or terminal, value at the end of the planning period, which is the projection furthest in the future and therefore the least certain.

Still other managers complain that a preoccupation with calculating values and subjecting them to exhaustive sensitivity testing suppresses strategic thinking. Or they say SVA is unsuitable for analyzing innovative strategies that open markets whose possibilities are not known—like the next generation of television receivers.

These criticisms reflect a basic shortcoming not in the technique itself but in its application. Companies often fail to link the numbers used in SVA to the company's best strategic thinking, and their strategic thinking often lacks rigor and imagination. Given that SVA and strategy formulation are performed by people in different parts of the organization and that managers are susceptible to human shortcomings like overoptimism and narrow thinking, these problems in applying SVA are understandable. Understandable, but not acceptable. That's why managers must find ways around the usual pitfalls if they want to duplicate the successes some companies have achieved with SVA.

Shareholder Value and Competitive Advantage

To understand why SVA often goes awry and how important strategic thinking is to it, a manager must understand the relationship between competitive advantage, value creation, and business strategy. Every manager knows something about those things individually. Competitive advantage means outperforming competitors along dimensions like cost, technological capability, and acquisition of raw materials or providing superior value to customers. Value creation is the increase in shareholder value, which requires that the company earn more than its cost of capital. But not every manager understands how competitive advantage and shareholder value interact. A sound strategy generates both: for a strategy to win in the marketplace, it must create sustainable advantage; only when a strategy wins in the marketplace can it generate sustained shareholder value.

But while SVA and strategy analysis (the analysis of competitive advantage) are ostensibly about the same thing—identifying the best strategy alternative—they are neither synonymous nor equivalent. They use different conceptions of value, focus on different constituencies, pertain to different markets, use different levels of analysis, address different decision variables, and emphasize different measures. In short, they view the purpose of strategy from fundamentally different vantage points.

According to strategy analysis, the purpose of strategy is to establish superior value in the eyes of the customer or to achieve the lowest delivered cost; according to SVA, strategy should maximize returns to shareholders. Strategy analysis focuses on customers and competitors; SVA focuses on shareholders. (For further comparison, see the exhibit, "The Difference Between Strategy Analysis and Shareholder Value Analysis.")

These differences mean it is possible to achieve one kind of value at the expense of the other. One industrial materials company, for example, enhanced its competitive position but hurt shareholder value in the process. It decided to make big improvements in its postsales service, giving customers more value, but it kept prices at competitive levels. The company made some modest gains in market share in the first year, but the cost of the program wiped out any additional profits. And soon after, several competitors responded with similar programs. When the market finally settled down, the company held the market share its postsales service program had gained, but it had spent so much money defending itself against competitors—investing in additional sales force and supporting promotional materials—that its profits actually fell. Customers benefited, but shareholders did not.

Other companies, like Schlitz Brewing, have done the opposite—boosted share price at the expense of the company's competitive position. In the early 1970s, Schlitz reduced brewery labor per barrel, switched to low-cost hops, and shortened the brewing cycle by 50%. Its costs were the lowest in the industry. To the great pleasure of shareholders, profits soared, and the market applauded. By 1974, the stock price had risen to $69.

Consumers were slow to react to the degradation of product quality, but by 1976, complaints were continual and market share was slipping. That year, Schlitz destroyed ten million bottles of beer that failed QC tests. In 1978, Schlitz management tried to get its quality back on track, but consumers had such a low opinion of the product that the company couldn't recover. By 1981, Schlitz's market position had fallen to number seven from number two in 1974, and its stock price had dropped to a mere $5.

In the long run, customer value and shareholder value converge. But what consolation is that if both settle at depressed levels because of earlier misjudgments? SVA should involve the same tough-minded probing of competitive, marketplace realities that characterizes good strategy analysis. Shareholder value is not the same thing as sustainable competitive advantage. For SVA to be meaningful, it should consider a strategy's potential to produce both.

Undervaluation, Optimism, and Oversight

Why is SVA sometimes an untrustworthy measure of a strategy's potential in the marketplace? Partly because the technique makes it hard to value certain things like growth options and partly because people are people—sometimes too optimistic, too narrowly focused, or too complacent. More particularly, SVA can mislead managers in a couple of ways: by undervaluing a strategy alternative, raising the probability that they'll reject a sound strategy (like the statistician's Type I error), or by overvaluing a strategy alternative, causing them to choose a poor one (a Type II error). And of course, SVA cannot show managers the potential value of the best alternative if it is one they haven't even considered.

Undervaluing a Strategy. SVA is notorious for undervaluing two types of investment strategies that are important for building and sustaining competitive advantage: investing in future options and investing to hold customers. Sometimes a company makes an initial investment in an emerging market or technology because it wants the option of making further investments if the market or technology proves to be rewarding. The first investment doesn't commit management to proceed further, but failure to make it often precludes the company from entering the market later. Investing also gives the company an opportunity to learn, so any further investments are likely to be wise. This is one reason why large chemical companies buy small biotechnology startups—to gain knowledge about an unfamiliar technology and become better informed about future opportunities. Similarly, retailers often make small-scale acquisitions in a new country or an unfamiliar region to learn the local purchasing and competitive practices before making a big, expensive push into the market.

Options are intangible assets that can account for a large portion of a company's value, especially in growth markets. Unfortunately, discounted cash flow procedures don't directly recognize that value and understate the attractiveness of new growth areas. In practice, some managers seem to know the value of options and will act on their judgment despite SVA's recommendations to the contrary. Financial markets also seem to recognize the importance of future growth options, which explains why growth stocks sell with high price/earnings multiples.

Unnecessarily high risk hurdles exacerbate the problem of undervaluation. One European electronics manufacturer in an industry that was rapidly consolidating in anticipation of 1992 found it was losing out to competitors in the race for acquisitions because the parent company had assigned a risk hurdle much higher than the competition's—and unwarranted for the real risk that existed. The parent company used the same risk hurdle for all capital investments regardless of the marketplace and technology risks associated with each investment. Consequently, the electronics company was unable to demonstrate to the parent the financial merits of its acquisition proposal and is now in danger of becoming a competitive laggard.

SVA also falls short in measuring the value of keeping customers. Putting a figure on the damage to competitive advantage from not investing is harder than documenting the savings from making an investment. This shortcoming is why some managers eschew formal financial analysis.

The Difference Between Strategy Analysis and Shareholder Value Analysis

	Strategy Analysis	Shareholder Value Analysis
Purpose of strategy	Establish superior value in eyes of customer and/or gain lowest delivered cost	Maximize returns to shareholders
Reference group	Customers and competitors	Shareholders or proxies
Decision variables	Inputs (resources, skills) and intermediate outcomes (market share, relative costs)	Revenues, costs, investments, and capital structure
Level of analysis	Product-market segments and business units	Company and business unit (investment centers)
Basis of measurement	Customer perceptions of benefits, comparisons with competitors, cost analysis, and management judgment	Share prices, market/book ratios, and net present value of cash flows

In 1984, Cone Drive Operations, a manufacturer of heavy-duty gears, faced several problems: profit pressure was severe, inventory costs were climbing, and customers were unhappy because deliveries were routinely late. Cone's management believed that a $2 million computer-integrated manufacturing system would solve these problems, but its cash flow analysis showed the system to be an unwise investment. Because the company had only $26 million in volume, it was hard to justify the $2 million investment in terms of cost savings alone. The financial analysis failed to reflect the intangibles like better quality, faster time to market, quicker order processing, and higher customer satisfaction. Management decided to make the investment anyway, which in retrospect was the right move. New busi-

Sales projections may be high – but can you achieve them if competitors retaliate?

ness and nonlabor savings paid back the investment in just one year, and more important, Cone maintained its existing customer base.

Other problems with SVA are primarily human. SVA relies on forecasts of many kinds to translate the hopes, fears, and expectations associated with a strategy into a financial value. Projections of cash inflows rest on forecasts of sales volumes, product mix, and unit prices; outflows depend on forecasts of each cost element and of working capital and required investments.

Overvaluing a Strategy. Making good forecasts is notoriously difficult – and eminently important. Once someone attaches numbers to judgments about what is likely to happen, people tend to endow those numbers with the concreteness of hard facts. No matter how much or how little care went into deriving them, the numbers associated with a strategy alternative quickly take on a reality all their own, and managers easily lose sight of the underlying assumptions they represent.

Forecasts are often afflicted with unwarranted optimism – which is quite a different thing from the enthusiastic belief in a strategy's ability to mobilize the energy of an organization. When optimism reigns, managers can't imagine competitors making countermoves or customers resisting the new offering, so projections of cash inflows are too high. Or managers overlook the possibility of delays and extra costs, so outflow projections are too low.

For example, an industrial products company planned to regain its leadership position in a market

niche by radically revamping its product line. It added a number of new product features and enhanced the performance of all the items in the line. When the company analyzed the strategic move, it forecast a huge sales increase. Sales did rise the first year, by 15%. But soon competitors retaliated with new, improved products of their own – a response the company, in its optimistic enthusiasm, failed to anticipate. Sales fell below previous levels and far below management's expectations.

Cash flows tend to be biased upward for several reasons. For one thing, facts and opinions that are accessible tend to dominate evaluations of strategy alternatives. Evidence of a past success carries more weight than qualitative assessments of future threats. Also, decision makers tend to anchor on the outcome they believe in most, and the more they focus on it, the more real it becomes. Consequently, they spend less time thinking about the uncertainties and risks that might change that outcome.

Upward bias also creeps in when managers assume that the baseline is synonymous with the status quo. Companies tend to pay little attention to how competitive behavior, prices, and returns would change if they maintained the existing strategy. They also make simplistic assumptions about prices and market shares based on how these things have behaved in the past. But prices can move widely when, for instance, excess capacity is suddenly available or low-cost capacity displaces high-cost facilities.

Another reason cash flows are biased upward is that people are inclined to withhold information to protect their own interests. Forecasts based on certain cost reductions will probably be too high if, for instance, a manager is unsure she can achieve the reductions but keeps that uncertainty to herself.

It is usually operating managers who put an optimistic spin on their forecasts, but financial experts have been known to make similar mistakes. In one large electronics company, the CFO's office customarily developed cash flow, profitability, and value analyses using rough estimates of the sales and costs associated with new products that divisions were considering launching. In one instance, the CFO, without consulting anyone else in the company, analyzed the products and presented to the CEO the one he thought had the most promise. The CEO recommended speeding up the project and, if necessary, committing more resources to it.

Later, marketing and manufacturing examined the data the CEO had received and found big problems. The sales estimates were grossly exaggerated. At best, the product would reach the market two years behind the estimates. The product would put the company in direct competition with players the

EXECLONE LABS
GROWING MANAGEMENT TALENT TODAY FOR THE AMERICA OF TOMORROW.

company was trying to avoid. The costs of the new manufacturing facilities were too low. And it was unclear whether the company had enough in-house technical skill to develop the product fully.

The CFO revised the data and the cash flow projections. This time, the results were very different. The product would likely diminish – not add to – shareholder value.

Overlooking Strategies. Another kind of problem with SVA arises when managers fail to put forward all the best strategy alternatives. After all, SVA is only a tool. It can analyze options, but it cannot create them. There are several explanations for the common error of not considering all the good alternatives. Sometimes managers who have already committed to a strategy – because it suits their needs or fits their assumptions – fabricate a straw-man alternative to make their strategy choice look good. And sometimes the option to continue business as usual promises to deliver acceptable value, so managers have little incentive to look further. In other instances, executives just don't push themselves to think of novel approaches to the existing strategy.

Senior management in a large manufacturing company lacked creativity when it undertook a review of one business whose sales and profits had been declining for several years. The business held about 15% of a market dominated by three big competitors. As part of the analysis to see whether the business could be turned around, the management team identified a set of distinct strategy alternatives, including business as usual, investment in product development, and divestment. It carefully articulated what each strat-

egy would entail, estimated revenues and costs for each, and then determined how much value each would create. The team concluded that selling the business created far more value than any other strategy alternative.

The company sold the business to a foreign enterprise, which immediately began a strategy the original owner had not even considered. The intent of the strategy was to achieve significant cost reduction while maintaining customer service levels. New management drastically reduced the size of the sales force but maintained the same coverage with considerably less call frequency, eliminated the advertising and promotion budgets almost entirely, avoided price competition, and dramatically sliced corporate overhead. In less than a year, the new owner had a handsome profit stream.

Sometimes the strategy alternatives being evaluated are implausible – not that they start out that way. What often happens is that forecasts are entered into a spreadsheet, and people then fiddle with the numbers. The analyst changes one variable at a time, seeing what happens when market growth is 1% higher, when gross margin is 2% better, when working capital is cut by $3 million. After several hours of experimenting and testing, the variables become completely disconnected from the original strategy projections. The forecasts are inconsistent, and it becomes unclear what strategy the numbers are supposed to represent.

Scrutinize, Criticize, and Question

For SVA to work, it must be tightly linked to strategy analysis, and that strategy analysis must be rigorous enough to prevent the problems associated with undervaluing strategies, overvaluing strategies, and failing to consider all the options. Managers must fully consider the competitive context of cash flows and ensure that cash flow projections are directly tied to competitive analysis projections. They must question whether the cash outflows contribute to competitive advantage and to what extent cash inflows are dependent on realizing those advantages. Specifically, they should broaden the range of strategy alternatives, challenge the inherent soundness of each alternative, and test the sensitivity of each alternative to changes in cash inflows and outflows.

Including more options is the most straightforward way to improve the strategy analysis process. Easy to say and to understand, it is nonetheless difficult to put into practice. The pressure for managers to reach conclusions early and to move quickly to numbers is powerful. Even when managers think they have a clear winner, they should continue to explore other potential strategies. And they should try to uncover all the weaknesses and possibilities before attaching numbers to strategy alternatives. One well-known CEO has been known to challenge his managers to think more broadly by asking, "What would you achieve if you had twice the funding you want?" This is a strong signal that incremental change won't satisfy him, especially if the business is not already a dominant force in the market.

Finding solid evidence that a strategy will outperform the competition is another useful step. Before committing any numbers to paper or to spreadsheets, managers should ask penetrating questions about the requirements for success, and they should view all evidence critically. This is where strategy evaluation often founders.

One industrial products company's approach to strategy analysis is instructive. It uses a set of questions to test the competitive advantages of new products. The intent is to encourage management to think more carefully about the organizational and competitive context and to make better judgments about a proposed product's sustainable competitive advantage. Pointed questions—What is the opportunity? How is success defined? What customer-based advantages can the company develop? How can it sustain these advantages?—keep managers from overlooking weaknesses.

Strategy analysis is also greatly improved if management scrutinizes the validity of the underlying assumptions. All strategy alternatives are premised on assumptions about competitors, customers, suppliers, government, industry, technology, and economic conditions. Those assumptions often prove to be quite wrong. This was the case for U.S. companies that did not anticipate how quickly their Japanese competitors would adapt to the massive currency exchange-rate changes in recent years, as well as for IBM, which overestimated customer response to its first personal computer. Continually questioning and challenging those assumptions is the simple—and hard—prescription.

The industrial products company, for example, scrutinized the assumptions behind a proposed new product by asking: Could the R&D group deliver the product with specific features within given cost guidelines? How quickly could the company move the product from R&D into the marketplace? Can it provide sufficient aftersales service to clearly distinguish the product from competitors' offerings? Will customers see added value in the product and be willing to pay for it? In answering these questions, candor is essential. Managers can encourage candor by insisting on evidence to support assertions and by questioning whether answers are plausible.

Management should analyze the vulnerability of strategy alternatives to environmental and internal uncertainties. While all strategies carry risk, some are more sensitive to it than others. An aggressive strategy to build capacity raises the breakeven

---

> **Before you put cash flow forecasts on a spreadsheet, find proof that they're realistic.**

---

point, for instance, and makes the company more vulnerable to disappointing sales than a strategy to manage for current earnings or to lease additional capacity. Companies can assess vulnerabilities by asking two questions: What will happen to key results if important assertions are proven wrong, critical tasks are not accomplished, or program schedules slip badly? How likely are these events to happen?

The industrial products company was considering launching a new product that was especially sensitive to customer acceptance. If the product wasn't well received and didn't gain a 20% penetration rate by the end of the first year, the likelihood of earning any profit in the first two years was slim. And any slips in the product development schedule would mean the loss of its lead over competitors. If both things happened—market penetration fell short of expectations and product development fell behind—the impact would be disastrous.

Of course, a strategy is not valuable unless it is well implemented, so companies must anticipate any problems that might arise during implementation. Many organizations recognize only too late their inability to translate a good idea on paper into rich results. IBM, unable to exploit the alleged synergies that would accrue from its acquisition of ROLM, is one of a myriad of examples showing the importance of implementation. So is GM, whose much-publicized difficulties in bringing its new, small automobiles (the Saturn project) to fruition demonstrate the damage that results from understating implementation problems. IBM discovered that integrating people across two organizations with distinctly different cultures can undermine the best intentions for cooperation. GM found how difficult it is to forecast the time needed to build a new system of supplier relationships with less than a third the usual number of component suppliers.

Managers should ask, Does the organization have the necessary skills and resources to implement the strategy alternative successfully? If not, Is there enough time and money to develop them? In analyzing its new product, the industrial products company questioned whether it had the necessary technical skills and sales force to market the product to its sophisticated customers. It also studied whether managers at various levels would support the strategic move.

Managers shouldn't completely rely on even carefully formulated assumptions but should subject them to sensitivity analysis. How much would the cash flow forecasts have to change to make the strategy decision unattractive? This is not the kind of fiddling that produces implausible strategies. Here the

sensitivity analysis is done only after the strategy has been valued with the most defensible forecasts of inputs and results. By varying key parameters, managers can see which ones have the greatest leverage and where the strategy alternatives are most vulnerable. If the strategy alternative is more attractive than any other under a range of realistic cash inflows and outflows, then it probably deserves funding.

Used correctly, shareholder value analysis is much more like an examination of the strategic fundamentals than a number-crunching exercise. Without a basis in the hard organizational and competitive realities, value-based numbers have no meaning. SVA is useful only when it is the last step in a rigorous evaluation of how strategic alternatives are likely to fare in the marketplace. When accompanied by sharp, critical strategic thinking, SVA gives reliable signals about a strategy's potential to create both shareholder value and sustainable competitive advantage.

Reprint 90204

"The stock market, which closed today at a new high of 2,590, has mysteriously continued to rise after closing, and just passed 3,002."

*People are the key to managing complex
strategies and organizations.*

Matrix Management:
Not a Structure, a Frame of Mind

by Christopher A. Bartlett and Sumantra Ghoshal

Top-level managers in many of today's leading corporations are losing control of their companies. The problem is not that they have misjudged the demands created by an increasingly complex environment and an accelerating rate of environmental change, nor even that they have failed to develop strategies appropriate to the new challenges. The problem is that their companies are organizationally incapable of carrying out the sophisticated strategies they have developed. Over the past 20 years, strategic thinking has far outdistanced organizational capabilities.

All through the 1980s, companies everywhere were redefining their strategies and reconfiguring their operations in response to such developments as the globalization of markets, the intensification of competition, the acceleration of product life cycles, and the growing complexity of relationships with

DRAWING BY MAXINE BOLL

suppliers, customers, employees, governments, even competitors. But as companies struggled with these changing environmental realities, many fell into one of two traps—one strategic, one structural.

The strategic trap was to implement simple, static solutions to complex and dynamic problems. The bait was often a consultant's siren song promising to simplify or at least minimize complexity and discontinuity. Despite the new demands of overlapping industry boundaries and greatly altered value-added chains, managers were promised success if they would "stick to their knitting"; in a swiftly changing international political economy, they were urged to rein in dispersed overseas operations and focus on the "triad markets"; and in an increasingly intricate and sophisticated competitive environment, they were encouraged to choose between alternative "generic strategies"—low cost or differentiation.

Yet the strategic reality for most companies was that both their business and their environment really *were* more complex, while the proposed solutions were often simple, even simplistic. The traditional telephone company that stuck to its knitting was trampled by competitors who redefined their strategies in response to new technologies linking telecommunications, computers, and office equipment into a single integrated system. The packaged-goods company that concentrated on the triad markets quickly discovered that Europe, Japan, and the United States were the epicenters of global competitive activity, with higher risks and slimmer profits than more protected and less competitive markets like Australia, Turkey, and Brazil. The consumer electronics company that adopted an either-or generic strategy found itself facing competitors able to develop cost and differentiation capabilities at the same time.

In recent years, as more and more managers recognized oversimplification as a strategic trap, they began to accept the need to manage complexity rather than seek to minimize it. This realization, however, led many into an equally threatening organizational trap when they concluded that the best response to increasingly complex strategic requirements was increasingly complex organizational structures.

The obvious organizational solution to strategies that required multiple, simultaneous management capabilities was the matrix structure that became so fashionable in the late 1970s and the early 1980s. Its parallel reporting relationships acknowledged the diverse, conflicting needs of functional, product, and geographic management groups and provided a formal mechanism for resolving them. Its multiple information channels allowed the organization to capture and analyze external complexity. And its

overlapping responsibilities were designed to combat parochialism and build flexibility into the company's response to change.

In practice, however, the matrix proved all but unmanageable—especially in an international context. Dual reporting led to conflict and confusion; the proliferation of channels created informational logjams as a proliferation of committees and reports

The CEO as strategic guru is a thing of the past. CEOs must now focus on finding and motivating talent.

bogged down the organization; and overlapping responsibilities produced turf battles and a loss of accountability. Separated by barriers of distance, language, time, and culture, managers found it virtually impossible to clarify the confusion and resolve the conflicts.

In hindsight, the strategic and structural traps seem simple enough to avoid, so one has to wonder why so many experienced general managers have fallen into them. Much of the answer lies in the way we have traditionally thought about the general manager's role. For decades, we have seen the general manager as chief strategic guru and principal organizational architect. But as the competitive climate grows less stable and less predictable, it is harder for one person alone to succeed in that great visionary role. Similarly, as formal, hierarchical structure gives way to networks of personal relationships that work through informal, horizontal communication channels, the image of top management in an isolated corner office moving boxes and lines on an organization chart becomes increasingly anachronistic.

Paradoxically, as strategies and organizations become more complex and sophisticated, top-level general managers are beginning to replace their historical concentration on the grand issues of strategy and structure with a focus on the details of managing people and processes. The critical strategic requirement is not to devise the most ingenious and well

Christopher A. Bartlett is a professor of general management at the Harvard Business School, where he is also chairman of the International Senior Management program. Sumantra Ghoshal is an associate professor who teaches business policy at the European Institute of Business Administration (INSEAD) in Fontainebleau, France. This article is based on a research project reported in detail in their recent book, Managing Across Borders: The Transnational Solution *(Harvard Business School Press, 1989).*

coordinated plan but to build the most viable and flexible strategic process; the key organizational task is not to design the most elegant structure but to capture individual capabilities and motivate the entire organization to respond cooperatively to a complicated and dynamic environment.

Building an Organization

While business thinkers have written a great deal about strategic innovation, they have paid far less attention to the accompanying organizational challenges. Yet many companies remain caught in the structural-complexity trap that paralyzes their ability to respond quickly or flexibly to the new strategic imperatives.

For those companies that adopted matrix structures, the problem was not in the way they defined the goal. They correctly recognized the need for a multidimensional organization to respond to growing external complexity. The problem was that they defined their organizational objectives in purely structural terms. Yet formal structure describes only the organization's basic anatomy. Companies must also concern themselves with organizational physiology – the systems and relationships that allow the lifeblood of information to flow through the organization. And they need to develop a healthy organizational psychology – the shared norms, values, and beliefs that shape the way individual managers think and act.

The companies that fell into the organizational trap assumed that changing their formal structure (anatomy) would force changes in interpersonal relationships and decision processes (physiology), which in turn would reshape the individual attitudes and actions of managers (psychology).

But as many companies have discovered, reconfiguring the formal structure is a blunt and sometimes brutal instrument of change. A new structure creates new and presumably more useful managerial ties, but these can take months and often years to evolve into effective knowledge-generating and decision-making relationships. And since the new job requirements will frustrate, alienate, or simply overwhelm so many managers, changes in individual attitudes and behavior will likely take even longer.

As companies struggle to create organizational capabilities that reflect rather than diminish environmental complexity, good managers gradually stop searching for the ideal structural template to impose on the company from the top down. Instead, they focus on the challenge of building up an appropriate set of employee attitudes and skills and linking them together with carefully developed processes and relationships. In other words, they begin to focus on building the organization rather than simply on installing a new structure.

Indeed, the companies that are most successful at developing multidimensional organizations begin at the far end of the anatomy-physiology-psychology sequence. Their first objective is to alter the organizational psychology – the broad corporate beliefs and norms that shape managers' perceptions and actions. Then, by enriching and clarifying communication and decision processes, companies reinforce these psychological changes with improvements in organizational physiology. Only later do they consolidate and confirm their progress by realigning organizational anatomy through changes in the formal structure.

No company we know of has discovered a quick or easy way to change its organizational psychology to reshape the understanding, identification, and commitment of its employees. But we found three principal characteristics common to those that managed the task most effectively:

1. The development and communication of a clear and consistent corporate vision.

2. The effective management of human resource tools to broaden individual perspectives and develop identification with corporate goals.

3. The integration of individual thinking and activities into the broad corporate agenda by means of a process we call co-option.

Building a Shared Vision

Perhaps the main reason managers in large, complex companies cling to parochial attitudes is that their frame of reference is bounded by their specific responsibilities. The surest way to break down such insularity is to develop and communicate a clear sense of corporate purpose that extends into every corner of the company and gives context and meaning to each manager's particular roles and responsibilities. We are not talking about a slogan, however catchy and pointed. We are talking about a company vision, which must be crafted and articulated with clarity, continuity, and consistency: clarity of expression that makes company objectives understandable and meaningful; continuity of purpose that underscores their enduring importance; and consistency of application across business units and geographical boundaries that ensures uniformity throughout the organization.

Clarity. There are three keys to clarity in a corporate vision: simplicity, relevance, and reinforcement. NEC's integration of computers and communications—C&C—is probably the best single example of how simplicity can make a vision more powerful. Top management has applied the C&C concept so effectively that it describes the company's business focus, defines its distinctive source of competitive advantage over large companies like IBM and AT&T, and summarizes its strategic and organizational imperatives.

The second key, relevance, means linking broad objectives to concrete agendas. When Wisse Dekker became CEO at Philips, his principal strategic concern was the problem of competing with Japan. He stated this challenge in martial terms—the U.S. had abandoned the battlefield; Philips was now Europe's last defense against insurgent Japanese electronics companies. By focusing the company's attention not only on Philips's corporate survival but also on the protection of national and regional interests, Dekker heightened the sense of urgency and commitment in a way that legitimized cost-cutting efforts, drove an extensive rationalization of plant operations, and inspired a new level of sales achievements.

The third key to clarity is top management's continual reinforcement, elaboration, and interpretation of the core vision to keep it from becoming obsolete or abstract. Founder Konosuke Matsushita developed a grand, 250-year vision for his company, but he also managed to give it immediate relevance. He summed up its overall message in the "Seven Spirits of Matsushita," to which he referred constantly in his policy statements. Each January he wove the company's one-year operational objectives into his overarching concept to produce an annual theme that he then captured in a slogan. For all the loftiness of his concept of corporate purpose, he gave his managers immediate, concrete guidance in implementing Matsushita's goals.

Continuity. Despite shifts in leadership and continual adjustments in short-term business priorities, companies must remain committed to the same core set of strategic objectives and organizational values. Without such continuity, unifying vision might as well be expressed in terms of quarterly goals.

It was General Electric's lack of this kind of continuity that led to the erosion of its once formidable position in electrical appliances in many countries. Over a period of 20 years and under successive CEOs, the company's international consumer-product strategy never stayed the same for long. From building locally responsive and self-sufficient "mini-GEs" in each market, the company turned to a policy of developing low-cost offshore sources, which even-

tually evolved into a de facto strategy of international outsourcing. Finally, following its acquisition of RCA, GE's consumer electronics strategy made another about-face and focused on building centralized scale to defend domestic share. Meanwhile, the product strategy within this shifting business emphasis was itself unstable. The Brazilian subsidiary, for example, built its TV business in the 1960s until it was told to stop; in the early 1970s, it emphasized large appliances until it was denied funding; then it focused on housewares until the parent company sold off that business. In two decades, GE utterly dissipated its dominant franchise in Brazil's electrical products market.

Unilever, by contrast, made an enduring commitment to its Brazilian subsidiary, despite volatile swings in Brazil's business climate. Company chairman Floris Maljers emphasized the importance of

> **In a mere 20 years, GE squandered its dominant place in Brazil's electrical products market.**

looking past the latest political crisis or economic downturn to the long-term business potential. "In those parts of the world," he remarked, "you take your management cues from the way they dance. The samba method of management is two steps forward then one step back." Unilever built—two steps forward and one step back—a profitable $300 million business in a rapidly growing economy with 130 million consumers, while its wallflower competitors never ventured out onto the floor.

Consistency. The third task for top management in communicating strategic purpose is to ensure that everyone in the company shares the same vision. The cost of inconsistency can be horrendous. It always produces confusion and, in extreme cases, can lead to total chaos, with different units of the organization pursuing agendas that are mutually debilitating.

Philips is a good example of a company that, for a time, lost its consistency of corporate purpose. As a legacy of its wartime decision to give some overseas units legal autonomy, management had long experienced difficulty persuading North American Philips (NAP) to play a supportive role in the parent company's global strategies. The problem came to a head with the introduction of Philips's technologically first-rate videocassette recording system, the V2000. Despite considerable pressure from world headquarters in the Netherlands, NAP refused to launch the system, arguing that Sony's Beta system and Matsushita's VHS format were too well established and had cost, feature, and system-support advantages Philips couldn't match. Relying on its legal independence and managerial autonomy, NAP management decided instead to source products from its Japanese competitors and market them under its Magnavox brand name. As a result, Philips was unable to build the efficiency and credibility it needed to challenge Japanese dominance of the VCR business.

Most inconsistencies involve differences between what managers of different operating units see as the company's key objectives. Sometimes, however, different corporate leaders transmit different views of overall priorities and purpose. When this stems from poor communication, it can be fixed. When it's a result of fundamental disagreement, the problem is serious indeed, as illustrated by ITT's problems in developing its strategically vital System 12 switching equipment. Continuing differences between the head of the European organization and the company's chief technology officer over the location and philosophy of the development effort led to confusion and conflict throughout the company. The result was disastrous. ITT had difficulty transferring vital technology across its own unit boundaries and so was irreparably late introducing this key product to a rapidly changing global market. These problems eventually led the company to sell off its core telecommunications business to a competitor.

But formulating and communicating a vision—no matter how clear, enduring, and consistent—cannot succeed unless individual employees understand and accept the company's stated goals and objectives. Problems at this level are more often related to receptivity than to communication. The development of individual understanding and acceptance is a challenge for a company's human resource practices.

Developing Human Resources

While top managers universally recognize their responsibility for developing and allocating a company's scarce assets and resources, their focus on finance and technology often overshadows the task of developing the scarcest resource of all—capable managers. But if there is one key to regaining control of companies that operate in fast-changing environments, it is the ability of top management to turn the perceptions, capabilities, and relationships of individual managers into the building blocks of the organization.

One pervasive problem in companies whose leaders lack this ability—or fail to exercise it—is getting

managers to see how their specific responsibilities relate to the broad corporate vision. Growing external complexity and strategic sophistication have accelerated the growth of a cadre of specialists who are physically and organizationally isolated from each other, and the task of dealing with their consequent parochialism should not be delegated to the

> Global coordination failed at ITT, where each national company was an independent fiefdom.

clerical staff that administers salary structures and benefit programs. Top managers inside and outside the human resource function must be leaders in the recruitment, development, and assignment of the company's vital human talent.

Recruitment and Selection. The first step in successfully managing complexity is to tap the full range of available talent. It is a serious mistake to permit historical imbalances in the nationality or functional background of the management group to constrain hiring or subsequent promotion. In today's global marketplace, domestically oriented recruiting limits a company's ability to capitalize on its worldwide pool of management skill and biases its decision-making processes.

After decades of routinely appointing managers from its domestic operations to key positions in overseas subsidiaries, Procter & Gamble realized that the practice not only worked against sensitivity to local cultures—a lesson driven home by several marketing failures in Japan—but also greatly underutilized its pool of high-potential non-American managers. (Fortunately, our studies turned up few companies as shortsighted as one that made overseas assignments on the basis of *poor* performance, since foreign markets were assumed to be "not as tough as the domestic environment.")

Not only must companies enlarge the pool of people available for key positions, they must also develop new criteria for choosing those most likely to succeed. Because past success is no longer a sufficient qualification for increasingly subtle, sensitive, and unpredictable senior-level tasks, top management must become involved in a more discriminating selection process. At Matsushita, top management selects candidates for international assignment on the basis of a comprehensive set of personal characteristics, expressed for simplicity in the acronym SMILE: specialty (the needed skill, capability, or knowledge); management ability (particularly motivational ability); international flexibility (willingness to learn and ability to adapt); language facility; and endeavor (vitality, perseverance in the face of difficulty). These attributes are remarkably similar to those targeted by NEC and Philips, where top executives also are involved in the senior-level selection process.

Training and Development. Once the appropriate top-level candidates have been identified, the next challenge is to develop their potential. The most successful development efforts have three aims that take them well beyond the skill-building objectives of classic training programs: to inculcate a common vision and shared values; to broaden management perspectives and capabilities; and to develop contacts and shape management relationships.

To build common vision and values, white-collar employees at Matsushita spend a good part of their first six months in what the company calls "cultural and spiritual training." They study the company credo, the "Seven Spirits of Matsushita," and the philosophy of Konosuke Matsushita. Then they learn how to translate these internalized lessons into daily behavior and even operational decisions. Culture-building exercises as intensive as Matsushita's are sometimes dismissed as the kind of Japanese mumbo jumbo that would not work in other societies, but in fact, Philips has a similar entry-level training practice (called "organization cohesion training"), as does Unilever (called, straightforwardly, "indoctrination").

The second objective – broadening management perspectives – is essentially a matter of teaching people how to manage complexity instead of merely to make room for it. To reverse a long and unwieldy tradition of running its operations with two- and three-headed management teams of separate technical, commercial, and sometimes administrative specialists, Philips asked its training and development group to de-specialize top management trainees. By supplementing its traditional menu of specialist courses and functional programs with more intensive general management training, Philips was able to begin replacing the ubiquitous teams with single business heads who also appreciated and respected specialist points of view.

The final aim – developing contacts and relationships – is much more than an incidental by-product of good management development, as the comments of a senior personnel manager at Unilever suggest: "By bringing managers from different countries and businesses together at Four Acres [Unilever's international management training college], we build contacts and create bonds that we could never achieve by other means. The company spends as much on training as it does on R&D not only because

of the direct effect it has on upgrading skills and knowledge but also because it plays a central role in indoctrinating managers into a Unilever club where personal relationships and informal contacts are much more powerful than the formal systems and structures."

Career-Path Management. Although recruitment and training are critically important, the most effective companies recognize that the best way to develop new perspectives and thwart parochialism in their managers is through personal experience. By moving selected managers across functions, businesses, and geographic units, a company encourages cross-fertilization of ideas as well as the flexibility and breadth of experience that enable managers to grapple with complexity and come out on top.

Unilever has long been committed to the development of its human resources as a means of attaining durable competitive advantage. As early as the 1930s, the company was recruiting and developing local employees to replace the parent-company managers who had been running most of its overseas subsidiaries. In a practice that came to be known as "-ization," the company committed itself to the Indianization of its Indian company, the Australization of its Australian company, and so on.

Although delighted with the new talent that began working its way up through the organization, management soon realized that by reducing the transfer

> Unilever has so Unileverized its managers that they can spot one another anywhere in the world.

of parent-company managers abroad, it had diluted the powerful glue that bound diverse organizational groups together and linked dispersed operations. The answer lay in formalizing a second phase of the -ization process. While continuing with Indianization, for example, Unilever added programs aimed at the Unileverization of its Indian managers.

In addition to bringing 300 to 400 managers to Four Acres each year, Unilever typically has 100 to 150 of its most promising overseas managers on short- and long-term job assignments at corporate headquarters. This policy not only brings fresh, close-to-the-market perspectives into corporate decision making but also gives the visiting managers a strong sense of Unilever's strategic vision and organizational values. In the words of one of the expatriates in the corporate offices, "The experience initiates you into the Unilever Club and the clear norms, values, and behaviors that distinguish our people – so much so that we really believe we can spot another Unilever manager anywhere in the world."

Furthermore, the company carefully transfers most of these high-potential individuals through a variety of different functional, product, and geographic positions, often rotating every two or three years. Most important, top management tracks about 1,000 of these people – some 5% of Unilever's total management group – who, as they move through the company, forge an informal network of contacts and relationships that is central to Unilever's decision-making and information-exchange processes.

Widening the perspectives and relationships of key managers as Unilever has done is a good way of developing identification with the broader corporate mission. But a broad sense of identity is not enough. To maintain control of its global strategies, Unilever must secure a strong and lasting individual commitment to corporate visions and objectives. In effect, it must co-opt individual energies and ambitions into the service of corporate goals.

Co-Opting Management Efforts

As organizational complexity grows, managers and management groups tend to become so specialized and isolated and to focus so intently on their own immediate operating responsibilities that they are apt to respond parochially to intrusions on their organizational turf, even when the overall corporate interest is at stake. A classic example, described earlier, was the decision by North American Philips's consumer electronics group to reject the parent company's VCR system.

At about the same time, Philips, like many other companies, began experimenting with ways to convert managers' intellectual understanding of the corporate vision – in Philips's case, an almost evangelical determination to defend Western electronics against the Japanese – into a binding personal commitment. Philips concluded that it could co-opt individuals and organizational groups into the broader vision by inviting them to contribute to the corporate agenda and then giving them direct responsibility for implementation.

In the face of intensifying Japanese competition, Philips knew it had to improve coordination in its consumer electronics among its fiercely independent national organizations. In strengthening the central product divisions, however, Philips did not want to deplete the enterprise or commitment of its capable national management teams.

The company met these conflicting needs with two cross-border initiatives. First, it created a top-level World Policy Council for its video business that included key managers from strategic markets – Germany, France, the United Kingdom, the United States, and Japan. Philips knew that its national companies' long history of independence made local managers reluctant to take orders from Dutch headquarters in Eindhoven – often for good reason, since much of the company's best market knowledge and technological expertise resided in its offshore units. Through the council, Philips co-opted their support for company decisions about product policy and manufacturing location.

Second, and more powerful, Philips allocated global responsibilities to units that had previously been purely national in focus. Eindhoven gave NAP the leading role in the development of Philips's projection television and asked it to coordinate development and manufacture of all Philips television sets for North America and Asia. The change in the attitude of NAP managers was dramatic.

A senior manager in NAP's consumer electronics business summed up the feelings of U.S. managers: "At last, we are moving out of the dependency relationship with Eindhoven that was so frustrating to us." Co-option had transformed the defensive, territorial attitude of NAP managers into a more collaborative mind-set. They were making important contributions to global corporate strategy instead of looking for ways to subvert it.

In 1987, with much of its TV set production established in Mexico, the president of NAP's consumer electronics group told the press, "It is the commonality of design that makes it possible for us to move production globally. We have splendid cooperation with Philips in Eindhoven." It was a statement no NAP manager would have made a few years earlier, and it perfectly captured how effectively Philips had co-opted previously isolated, even adversarial, managers into the corporate agenda.

The Matrix in the Manager's Mind

Since the end of World War II, corporate strategy has survived several generations of painful transformation and has grown appropriately agile and athletic. Unfortunately, organizational development has not kept pace, and managerial attitudes lag even further behind. As a result, corporations now commonly design strategies that seem impossible to implement, for the simple reason that no one can effectively implement third-generation strategies through second-generation organizations run by first-generation managers.

Today the most successful companies are those where top executives recognize the need to manage the new environmental and competitive demands by focusing less on the quest for an ideal structure and more on developing the abilities, behavior, and performance of individual managers. Change succeeds only when those assigned to the new transnational and interdependent tasks understand the overall goals and are dedicated to achieving them.

One senior executive put it this way: "The challenge is not so much to build a matrix structure as it is to create a matrix in the minds of our managers." The inbuilt conflict in a matrix structure pulls managers in several directions at once. Developing a matrix of flexible perspectives and relationships within each manager's mind, however, achieves an entirely different result. It lets individuals make the judgments and negotiate the trade-offs that drive the organization toward a shared strategic objective.

Reprint 90401

"We're immortals and all that, but quite a few of us are locked into some very stupid, dead-end jobs."

Crafting strategy

Henry Mintzberg

Imagine someone planning strategy. What likely springs to mind is an image of orderly thinking: a senior manager, or a group of them, sitting in an office formulating courses of action that everyone else will implement on schedule. The keynote is reason – rational control, the systematic analysis of competitors and markets, of company strengths and weaknesses, the combination of these analyses producing clear, explicit, full-blown strategies.

Now imagine someone *crafting* strategy. A wholly different image likely results, as different from planning as craft is from mechanization. Craft evokes traditional skill, dedication, perfection through the mastery of detail. What springs to mind is not so much thinking and reason as involvement, a feeling of intimacy and harmony with the materials at hand, developed through long experience and commitment. Formulation and implementation merge into a fluid process of learning through which creative strategies evolve.

My thesis is simple: the crafting image better captures the process by which effective strategies come to be. The planning image, long popular in the literature, distorts these processes and thereby misguides organizations that embrace it unreservedly.

In developing this thesis, I shall draw on the experiences of a single craftsman, a potter, and compare them with the results of a research project that tracked the strategies of a number of corporations across several decades. Because the two contexts are so obviously different, my metaphor, like my assertion, may seem farfetched at first. Yet if we think of a craftsman as an organization of one, we can see that he or she must also resolve one of the great challenges the corporate strategist faces: knowing the organization's capabilities well enough to think deeply enough about its strategic direction. By considering strategy making from the perspective of one person, free of all the paraphernalia of what has been called the strategy industry, we can learn something about the formation of strategy in the corporation. For much as our potter has to manage her craft, so too managers have to craft their strategy.

At work, the potter sits before a lump of clay on the wheel. Her mind is on the clay, but she is also aware of sitting between her past experiences and her future prospects. She knows exactly what has and has not worked for her in the past. She has an intimate knowledge of her work, her capabilities, and her markets. As a craftsman, she senses rather than analyzes these things; her knowledge is "tacit." All these things are working in her mind as her hands are working the clay. The product that emerges on the wheel is likely to be in the tradition of her past work, but she may break away and embark on a new direction. Even so, the past is no less present, projecting itself into the future.

In my metaphor, managers are craftsmen and strategy is their clay. Like the potter, they sit between a past of corporate capabilities and a future of market opportunities. And if they are truly craftsmen, they bring to their work an equally intimate knowledge of the materials at hand. That is the essence of crafting strategy.

Henry Mintzberg is Bronfman Professor of Management at McGill University. He has written three other HBR articles, including the McKinsey Award winner "The Manager's Job: Folklore and Fact" (July-August 1975), and is currently at work on a two-volume study of strategy formation.

Drawings by Anatoly.

In the pages that follow, we will explore this metaphor by looking at how strategies get made as opposed to how they are supposed to get made. Throughout, I will be drawing on the two sets of experiences I've mentioned. One, described in the insert, is a research project on patterns in strategy formation that has been going on at McGill University under my direction since 1971. The second is the stream of work of a successful potter, my wife, who began her craft in 1967.

Strategies are both plans for the future and patterns from the past.

Ask almost anyone what strategy is, and they will define it as a plan of some sort, an explicit guide to future behavior. Then ask them what strategy a competitor or a government or even they themselves have actually pursued. Chances are they will describe consistency in *past* behavior – a pattern in action over time. Strategy, it turns out, is one of those words that people define in one way and often use in another, without realizing the difference.

The reason for this is simple. Strategy's formal definition and its Greek military origins notwithstanding, we need the word as much to explain past actions as to describe intended behavior. After all, if strategies can be planned and intended, they can also be pursued and realized (or not realized, as the case may be). And pattern in action, or what we call realized strategy, explains that pursuit. Moreover, just as a plan need not produce a pattern (some strategies that are intended are simply not realized), so too a pattern need

not result from a plan. An organization can have a pattern (or realized strategy) without knowing it, let alone making it explicit.

Patterns, like beauty, are in the mind of the beholder, of course. But anyone reviewing a chronological lineup of our craftsman's work would have little trouble discerning clear patterns, at least in certain periods. Until 1974, for example, she made small, decorative ceramic animals and objects of various kinds. Then this "knickknack strategy" stopped abruptly, and eventually new patterns formed around waferlike sculptures and ceramic bowls, highly textured and unglazed.

Finding equivalent patterns in action for organizations isn't that much more difficult. Indeed, for such large companies as Volkswagenwerk and Air Canada, in our research, it proved simpler! (As well it should. A craftsman, after all, can change what she does in a studio a lot more easily than a Volkswagenwerk can retool its assembly lines.) Mapping the product models at Volkswagenwerk from the late 1940s to the late 1970s, for example, uncovers a clear pattern of concentration on the Beetle, followed in the late 1960s by a frantic search for replacements through acquisitions and internally developed new models, to a strategic reorientation around more stylish, water-cooled, front-wheel-drive vehicles in the mid-1970s.

But what about intended strategies, those formal plans and pronouncements we think of when we use the term *strategy*? Ironically, here we run into all kinds of problems. Even with a single craftsman, how can we know what her intended strategies really were? If we could go back, would we find expressions of intention? And if we could, would we be able to trust them? We often fool ourselves, as well as others, by denying our subconscious motives. And remember that intentions are cheap, at least when compared with realizations.

Reading the organization's mind

If you believe all this has more to do with the Freudian recesses of a craftsman's mind than with the practical realities of producing automobiles, then think again. For who knows what the intended strategies of a Volkswagenwerk really mean, let alone what they are? Can we simply assume in this collective context that the company's intended strategies are represented by its formal plans or by other statements emanating from the executive suite? Might these be just vain hopes or rationalizations or ploys to fool the competition? And even if expressed intentions exist, to what extent do others in the organization share them? How do we read the collective mind? Who is the strategist anyway?

The traditional view of strategic management resolves these problems quite simply, by what organizational theorists call attribution. You see it all the time in the business press. When General Motors acts, it's because Roger Smith has made a strategy. Given realization, there must have been intention, and that is automatically attributed to the chief.

In a short magazine article, this assumption is understandable. Journalists don't have a lot of time to uncover the origins of strategy, and GM is a large, complicated organization. But just consider all the complexity and confusion that gets tucked under this assumption—all the meetings and debates, the many people, the dead ends, the folding and unfolding of ideas. Now imagine trying to build a formal strategy-making system around that assumption. Is it any wonder that formal strategic planning is often such a resounding failure?

To unravel some of the confusion—and move away from the artificial complexity we have piled around the strategy-making process—we need to get back to some basic concepts. The most basic of all is the intimate connection between thought and action. That is the key to craft, and so also to the crafting of strategy.

Strategies need not be deliberate— they can also emerge.

Virtually everything that has been written about strategy making depicts it as a deliberate process. First we think, then we act. We formulate, then we implement. The progression seems so perfectly sensible. Why would anybody want to proceed differently?

Our potter is in the studio, rolling the clay to make a waferlike sculpture. The clay sticks to the rolling pin, and a round form appears. Why not make a cylindrical vase? One idea leads to another, until a new pattern forms. Action has driven thinking: a strategy has emerged.

Out in the field, a salesman visits a customer. The product isn't quite right, and together they work out some modifications. The salesman returns to his company and puts the changes through; after two or three more rounds, they finally get it right. A new product emerges, which eventually opens up a new market. The company has changed strategic course.

In fact, most salespeople are less fortunate than this one or than our craftsman. In an organization of one, the implementor is the formulator, so innovations can be incorporated into strategy quickly and easily. In a large organization, the innovator may be ten levels removed from the leader who is supposed to dictate strategy and may also have to sell the idea to dozens of peers doing the same job.

Some salespeople, of course, can proceed on their own, modifying products to suit their customers and convincing skunkworks in the factory to produce them. In effect, they pursue their own strategies. Maybe no one else notices or cares. Sometimes, however, their innovations do get noticed, perhaps years later, when the company's prevalent strategies have broken down and its leaders are groping for something new. Then the salesperson's strategy may be allowed to pervade the system, to become organizational.

Is this story farfetched? Certainly not. We've all heard stories like it. But since we tend to see only what we believe, if we believe that strategies have to be planned, we're unlikely to see the real meaning such stories hold.

Consider how the National Film Board of Canada (NFB) came to adopt a feature-film strategy. The NFB is a federal government agency, famous for its creativity and expert in the production of short documentaries. Some years back, it funded a filmmaker on a project that unexpectedly ran long. To distribute his film, the NFB turned to theaters and so inadvertently gained experience in marketing feature-length films. Other filmmakers caught onto the idea, and eventually the NFB found itself pursuing a feature-film strategy—a pattern of producing such films.

My point is simple, deceptively simple: strategies can *form* as well as be *formulated*. A realized strategy can emerge in response to an evolving situation, or it can be brought about deliberately, through a process of formulation followed by implementation. But when these planned intentions do not produce the desired actions, organizations are left with unrealized strategies.

Today we hear a great deal about unrealized strategies, almost always in concert with the claim that implementation has failed. Management has been lax, controls have been loose, people haven't been com-

mitted. Excuses abound. At times, indeed, they may be valid. But often these explanations prove too easy. So some people look beyond implementation to formulation. The strategists haven't been smart enough.

While it is certainly true that many intended strategies are ill conceived, I believe that the problem often lies one step beyond, in the distinction we make between formulation and implementation, the common assumption that thought must be independent of (and precede) action. Sure, people could be smarter—but not only by conceiving more clever strategies. Sometimes they can be smarter by allowing their strategies to develop gradually, through the organization's actions and experiences. Smart strategists appreciate that they cannot always be smart enough to think through everything in advance.

Hands & minds

No craftsman thinks some days and works others. The craftsman's mind is going constantly, in tandem with her hands. Yet large organizations try to separate the work of minds and hands. In so doing, they often sever the vital feedback link between the two. The salesperson who finds a customer with an unmet need may possess the most strategic bit of information in the entire organization. But that information is useless if he or she cannot create a strategy in response to it or else convey the information to someone who can—because the channels are blocked or because the formulators have simply finished formulating. The notion that strategy is something that should

happen way up there, far removed from the details of running an organization on a daily basis, is one of the great fallacies of conventional strategic management. And it explains a good many of the most dramatic failures in business and public policy today.

We at McGill call strategies like the NFB's that appear without clear intentions—or in spite of them—emergent strategies. Actions simply converge into patterns. They may become deliberate, of course, if the pattern is recognized and then legitimated by senior management. But that's after the fact.

All this may sound rather strange, I know. Strategies that emerge? Managers who acknowledge strategies already formed? Over the years, our research group at McGill has met with a good deal of resistance from people upset by what they perceive to be our passive definition of a word so bound up with proactive behavior and free will. After all, strategy means control—the ancient Greeks used it to describe the art of the army general.

Strategic learning

But we have persisted in this usage for one reason: learning. Purely deliberate strategy precludes learning once the strategy is formulated; emergent strategy fosters it. People take actions one by one and respond to them, so that patterns eventually form.

Our craftsman tries to make a freestanding sculptural form. It doesn't work, so she rounds it a bit here, flattens it a bit there. The result looks better, but still isn't quite right. She makes another and another and another. Eventually, after days or months or years, she finally has what she wants. She is off on a new strategy.

In practice, of course, all strategy making walks on two feet, one deliberate, the other emergent. For just as purely deliberate strategy making precludes learning, so purely emergent strategy making precludes control. Pushed to the limit, neither approach makes much sense. Learning must be coupled with control. That is why the McGill research group uses the word *strategy* for both emergent and deliberate behavior.

Likewise, there is no such thing as a purely deliberate strategy or a purely emergent one. No organization—not even the ones commanded by those ancient Greek generals—knows enough to work everything out in advance, to ignore learning en route. And no one—not even a solitary potter—can be flexible enough to leave everything to happenstance, to give up all control. Craft requires control just as it requires responsiveness to the material at hand. Thus deliberate and emergent strategy form the end points of a continuum along which the strategies that are crafted in the real world may be found. Some strategies may approach either end, but many more fall at intermediate points.

Effective strategies develop in all kinds of strange ways.

Effective strategies can show up in the strangest places and develop through the most unexpected means. There is no one best way to make strategy.

The form for a cat collapses on the wheel, and our potter sees a bull taking shape. Clay sticks to a rolling pin, and a line of cylinders results. Wafers come into being because of a shortage of clay and limited kiln space in a studio in France. Thus errors become opportunities, and limitations stimulate creativity. The natural propensity to experiment, even boredom, likewise stimulate strategic change.

Organizations that craft their strategies have similar experiences. Recall the National Film Board with its inadvertently long film. Or consider its experiences with experimental films, which made special use of animation and sound. For 20 years, the NFB produced a bare but steady trickle of such films. In fact, every film but one in that trickle was produced by a single person, Norman McLaren, the NFB's most celebrated filmmaker. McLaren pursued a *personal strategy* of experimentation, deliberate for him perhaps (though who can know whether he had the whole stream in mind or simply planned one film at a time?) but not for the organization. Then 20 years later, others followed his lead and the trickle widened, his personal strategy becoming more broadly organizational.

Conversely, in 1952, when television came to Canada, a *consensus strategy* quickly emerged at the NFB. Senior management was not keen on producing films for the new medium. But while the arguments raged, one filmmaker quietly went off and made a single series for TV. That precedent set, one by one his colleagues leapt in, and within months the NFB—and its management—found themselves committed for several years to a new strategy with an intensity unmatched before or since. This consensus strategy arose spontaneously, as a result of many independent decisions made by the filmmakers about the films they wished to make. Can we call this strategy deliberate? For the filmmakers perhaps; for senior management certainly not. But for the organization? It all depends on your perspective, on how you choose to read the organization's mind.

While the NFB may seem like an extreme case, it highlights behavior that can be found, albeit in muted form, in all organizations. Those who doubt this might read Richard Pascale's account of how Honda stumbled into its enormous success in the American motorcycle market. Brilliant as its strategy may have looked after the fact, Honda's managers

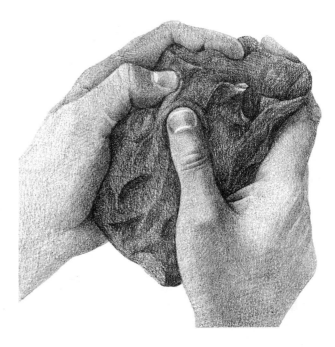

made almost every conceivable mistake until the market finally hit them over the head with the right formula. The Honda managers on site in America, driving their products themselves (and thus inadvertently picking up market reaction), did only one thing right: they learned, firsthand.[1]

Grass-roots strategy making

These strategies all reflect, in whole or part, what we like to call a grass-roots approach to strategic management. Strategies grow like weeds in a garden. They take root in all kinds of places, wherever people have the capacity to learn (because they are in touch with the situation) and the resources to support that capacity. These strategies become organizational when they become collective, that is, when they proliferate to guide the behavior of the organization at large.

Of course, this view is overstated. But it is no less extreme than the conventional view of strategic management, which might be labeled the hothouse approach. Neither is right. Reality falls between the two. Some of the most effective strategies we uncovered in our research combined deliberation and control with flexibility and organizational learning.

Consider first what we call the *umbrella strategy*. Here senior management sets out broad guidelines (say, to produce only high-margin products at the cutting edge of technology or to favor products using bonding technology) and leaves the specifics (such as what these products will be) to others lower down in the organization. This strategy is not only deliberate (in its clear, organizations pursue strategies to set direction, to lay out courses of action, and to elicit cooperation from their members around common, established guidelines. By any definition, strategy imposes stability on an organization. No stability means no strategy (no course to the future, no pattern from the past). Indeed, the very fact of having a strategy, and especially of making it explicit (as the conventional literature implores managers to do), creates resistance to strategic change!

What the conventional view fails to come to grips with, then, is how and when to promote change. A fundamental dilemma of strategy making is the need to reconcile the forces for stability and for change – to focus efforts and gain operating efficiencies on the one hand, yet adapt and maintain currency with a changing external environment on the other.

Quantum leaps

Our own research and that of colleagues suggest that organizations resolve these opposing forces by attending first to one and then to the other. Clear periods of stability and change can usually be distinguished in any organization: while it is true that particular strategies may always be changing marginally, it seems equally true that major shifts in strategic orientation occur only rarely.

In our study of Steinberg Inc., a large Quebec supermarket chain headquartered in Montreal, we found only two important reorientations in the 60 years from its founding to the mid-1970s: a shift to self-service in 1933 and the introduction of shopping centers and public financing in 1953. At Volkswagenwerk, we saw only one between the late 1940s and the 1970s, the tumultuous shift from the traditional Beetle to the Audi-type design mentioned earlier. And at Air Canada, we found none over the airline's first four decades, following its initial positioning.

Our colleagues at McGill, Danny Miller and Peter Friesen, found this pattern of change so common in their studies of large numbers of companies (especially the high-performance ones) that they built a theory around it, which they labeled the quantum theory of strategic change.[3] Their basic point is that organizations adopt two distinctly different modes of behavior at different times.

Most of the time they pursue a given strategic orientation. Change may seem continuous, but it occurs in the context of that orientation (perfecting a given retailing formula, for example) and usually

guidelines) and emergent (in its specifics), but it is also deliberately emergent in that the process is consciously managed to allow strategies to emerge en route. IBM used the umbrella strategy in the early 1960s with the impending 360 series, when its senior management approved a set of broad criteria for the design of a family of computers later developed in detail throughout the organization.[2]

Deliberately emergent, too, is what we call the *process strategy*. Here management controls the process of strategy formation – concerning itself with the design of the structure, its staffing, procedures, and so on – while leaving the actual content to others.

Both process and umbrella strategies seem to be especially prevalent in businesses that require great expertise and creativity – a 3M, a Hewlett-Packard, a National Film Board. Such organizations can be effective only if their implementors are allowed to be formulators because it is people way down in the hierarchy who are in touch with the situation at hand and have the requisite technical expertise. In a sense, these are organizations peopled with craftsmen, all of whom must be strategists.

Strategic reorientations happen in brief, quantum leaps.

The conventional view of strategic management, especially in the planning literature, claims that change must be continuous: the organization should be adapting all the time. Yet this view proves to be ironic because the very concept of strategy is rooted in stability, not change. As this same literature makes

1 Richard T. Pascale, "Perspective on Strategy: The Real Story Behind Honda's Success," *California Management Review*, May-June 1984, p. 47.

2 James Brian Quinn, IBM (A) case, in James Brian Quinn, Henry Mintzberg, and Robert M. James,

The Strategy Process: Concepts, Contexts, Cases (Englewood Cliffs, N.J.: Prentice-Hall, forthcoming).

3 See Danny Miller and Peter H. Friesen, *Organizations: A Quantum View* (Englewood Cliffs, N.J.: Prentice-Hall, 1984).

amounts to doing more of the same, perhaps better as well. Most organizations favor these periods of stability because they achieve success not by changing strategies but by exploiting the ones they have. They, like craftsmen, seek continuous improvement by using their distinctive competencies in established courses.

While this goes on, however, the world continues to change, sometimes slowly, occasionally in dramatic shifts. Thus gradually or suddenly, the organization's strategic orientation moves out of sync with its environment. Then what Miller and Friesen call a strategic revolution must take place. That long period of evolutionary change is suddenly punctuated by a brief bout of revolutionary turmoil in which the organization quickly alters many of its established patterns. In effect, it tries to leap to a new stability quickly to reestablish an integrated posture among a new set of strategies, structures, and culture.

But what about all those emergent strategies, growing like weeds around the organization? What the quantum theory suggests is that the really novel ones are generally held in check in some corner of the organization until a strategic revolution becomes necessary. Then as an alternative to having to develop new strategies from scratch or having to import generic strategies from competitors, the organization can turn to its own emerging patterns to find its new orientation. As the old, established strategy disintegrates, the seeds of the new one begin to spread.

This quantum theory of change seems to apply particularly well to large, established, mass-production companies. Because they are especially reliant on standardized procedures, their resistance to strategic reorientation tends to be especially fierce. So we find long periods of stability broken by short disruptive periods of revolutionary change.

Volkswagenwerk is a case in point. Long enamored of the Beetle and armed with a tightly integrated set of strategies, the company ignored fundamental changes in its markets throughout the late 1950s and 1960s. The bureaucratic momentum of its mass-production organization combined with the psychological momentum of its leader, who institutionalized the strategies in the first place. When change finally did come, it was tumultuous: the company groped its way through a hodgepodge of products before it settled on a new set of vehicles championed by a new leader. Strategic reorientations really are cultural revolutions.

Cycles of change

In more creative organizations, we see a somewhat different pattern of change and stability, one that's more balanced. Companies in the business of producing novel outputs apparently need to fly off in all directions from time to time to sustain their creativity. Yet they also need to settle down after such periods to find some order in the resulting chaos.

The National Film Board's tendency to move in and out of focus through remarkably balanced periods of convergence and divergence is a case in point. Concentrated production of films to aid the war effort in the 1940s gave way to great divergence after the war as the organization sought a new raison d'être. Then the advent of television brought back a very sharp focus in the early 1950s, as noted earlier. But in the late 1950s, this dissipated almost as quickly as it began, giving rise to another creative period of exploration. Then the social changes in the early 1960s evoked a new period of convergence around experimental films and social issues.

We use the label "adhocracy" for organizations, like the National Film Board, that produce individual, or custom-made, products (or designs) in an innovative way, on a project basis.[4] Our craftsman is an adhocracy of sorts too, since each of her ceramic sculptures is unique. And her pattern of strategic change was much like that of the NFB's, with evident cycles of convergence and divergence: a focus on knick-knacks from 1967 to 1972; then a period of exploration to about 1976, which resulted in a refocus on ceramic sculptures; that continued to about 1981, to be followed by a period of searching for new directions. More recently, a focus on ceramic murals seems to be emerging.

Whether through quantum revolutions or cycles of convergence and divergence, however, organizations seem to need to separate in time the basic forces for change and stability, reconciling them by attending to each in turn. Many strategic failures can be attributed either to mixing the two or to an obsession with one of these forces at the expense of the other.

The problems are evident in the work of many craftsmen. On the one hand, there are those who seize on the perfection of a single theme and never change. Eventually the creativity disappears from their work and the world passes them by—much as it did Volkswagenwerk until the company was shocked into

its strategic revolution. And then there are those who are always changing, who flit from one idea to another and never settle down. Because no theme or strategy ever emerges in their work, they cannot exploit or even develop any distinctive competence. And because their work lacks definition, identity crises are likely to develop, with neither the craftsmen nor their clientele knowing what to make of it. Miller and Friesen found this behavior in conventional business too; they label it "the impulsive firm running blind."[5] How often have we seen it in companies that go on acquisition sprees?

To manage strategy is to craft thought and action, control and learning, stability and change.

The popular view sees the strategist as a planner or as a visionary, someone sitting on a pedestal dictating brilliant strategies for everyone else to implement. While recognizing the importance of thinking ahead and especially of the need for creative vision in this pedantic world, I wish to propose an additional view of the strategist—as a pattern recognizer, a learner

if you will—who manages a process in which strategies (and visions) can emerge as well as be deliberately conceived. I also wish to redefine that strategist, to extend that someone into the collective entity made up of the many actors whose interplay speaks an organization's mind. This strategist *finds* strategies no less than creates them, often in patterns that form inadvertently in its own behavior.

What, then, does it mean to craft strategy? Let us return to the words associated with craft: dedication, experience, involvement with the material, the personal touch, mastery of detail, a sense of harmony and integration. Managers who craft strategy do not spend much time in executive suites reading MIS reports or industry analyses. They are involved, responsive to their materials, learning about their organizations and industries through personal touch. They are also sensitive to experience, recognizing that while individual vision may be important, other factors must help determine strategy as well.

Manage stability. Managing strategy is mostly managing stability, not change. Indeed, most of the time senior managers should not be formulating strategy at all; they should be getting on with making their organizations as effective as possible in pursuing the strategies they already have. Like distinguished craftsmen, organizations become distinguished because they master the details.

To manage strategy, then, at least in the first instance, is not so much to promote change as to know *when* to do so. Advocates of strategic planning often urge managers to plan for perpetual instability in the environment (for example, by rolling over five-year plans annually). But this obsession with change is dysfunctional. Organizations that reassess their strategies continuously are like individuals who reassess their jobs or their marriages continuously—in both cases, people will drive themselves crazy or else reduce themselves to inaction. The formal planning process repeats itself so often and so mechanically that it desensitizes the organization to real change, programs it more and more deeply into set patterns, and thereby encourages it to make only minor adaptations.

So-called strategic planning must be recognized for what it is: a means, not to create strategy, but to program a strategy already created—to work out its implications formally. It is essentially analytic in nature, based on decomposition, while strategy creation is essentially a process of synthesis. That is why

4 See my article
"Organization Design: Fashion or Fit?"
HBR January-February 1981, p. 103;
also see my book *Structure in Fives:*
Designing Effective Organizations
(Englewood Cliffs, N.J.: Prentice-Hall, 1983).
The term *adhocracy* was coined by

Warren G. Bennis and Philip E. Slater in
The Temporary Society
(New York: Harper & Row, 1964).

5 Danny Miller and Peter H. Friesen,
"Archetypes of Strategy Formulation,"
Management Science, May 1978, p. 921.

trying to create strategies through formal planning most often leads to extrapolating existing ones or copying those of competitors.

This is not to say that planners have no role to play in strategy formation. In addition to programming strategies created by other means, they can feed ad hoc analyses into the strategy-making process at the front end to be sure that the hard data are taken into consideration. They can also stimulate others to think strategically. And of course people called planners can be strategists too, so long as they are creative thinkers who are in touch with what is relevant. But that has nothing to do with the technology of formal planning.

Detect discontinuity. Environments do not change on any regular or orderly basis. And they seldom undergo continuous dramatic change, claims about our "age of discontinuity" and environmental "turbulence" notwithstanding. (Go tell people who lived through the Great Depression or survivors of the siege of Leningrad during World War II that ours are turbulent times.) Much of the time, change is minor and even temporary and requires no strategic response. Once in a while there is a truly significant discontinuity or, even less often, a gestalt shift in the environment, where everything important seems to change at once. But these events, while critical, are also easy to recognize.

The real challenge in crafting strategy lies in detecting the subtle discontinuities that may undermine a business in the future. And for that, there is no technique, no program, just a sharp mind in touch with the situation. Such discontinuities are unexpected and irregular, essentially unprecedented. They can be dealt with only by minds that are attuned to existing patterns yet able to perceive important breaks in them. Unfortunately, this form of strategic thinking tends to atrophy during the long periods of stability that most organizations experience (just as it did at Volkswagenwerk during the 1950s and 1960s). So the trick is to manage within a given strategic orientation most of the time yet be able to pick out the occasional discontinuity that really matters.

The Steinberg chain was built and run for more than half a century by a man named Sam Steinberg. For 20 years, the company concentrated on perfecting a self-service retailing formula introduced in 1933. Installing fluorescent lighting and figuring out how to package meat in cellophane wrapping were the "strategic" issues of the day. Then in 1952, with the arrival of the first shopping center in Montreal, Steinberg realized he had to redefine his business almost overnight. He knew he needed to control those shopping centers and that control would require public financing and other major changes. So he reoriented his business. The ability to make that kind of switch in thinking is the essence of strategic management. And it has more to do with vision and involvement than it does with analytic technique.

Know the business. Sam Steinberg was the epitome of the entrepreneur, a man intimately involved with all the details of his business, who spent Saturday mornings visiting his stores. As he told us in discussing his company's competitive advantage:

"Nobody knew the grocery business like we did. Everything has to do with your knowledge. I knew merchandise, I knew cost, I knew selling, I knew customers. I knew everything, and I passed on all my knowledge; I kept teaching my people. That's the advantage we had. Our competitors couldn't touch us."

Note the kind of knowledge involved: not intellectual knowledge, not analytical reports or abstracted facts and figures (though these can certainly help), but personal knowledge, intimate understanding, equivalent to the craftsman's feel for the clay. Facts are available to anyone; this kind of knowledge is not. Wisdom is the word that captures it best. But wisdom is a word that has been lost in the bureaucracies we have built for ourselves, systems designed to distance leaders from operating details. Show me managers who think they can rely on formal planning to create their strategies, and I'll show you managers who lack intimate knowledge of their businesses or the creativity to do something with it.

Craftsmen have to train themselves to see, to pick up things other people miss. The same holds true for managers of strategy. It is those with a kind of peripheral vision who are best able to detect and take advantage of events as they unfold.

Manage patterns. Whether in an executive suite in Manhattan or a pottery studio in Montreal, a key to managing strategy is the ability to detect emerging patterns and help them take shape. The job of the manager is not just to preconceive specific strategies but also to recognize their emergence elsewhere in the organization and intervene when appropriate.

Like weeds that appear unexpectedly in a garden, some emergent strategies may need to be uprooted immediately. But management cannot be too quick to cut off the unexpected, for tomorrow's vision may grow out of today's aberration. (Europeans, after all, enjoy salads made from the leaves of the dandelion, America's most notorious weed.) Thus some patterns are worth watching until their effects have more clearly manifested themselves. Then those that prove useful can be made deliberate and be incorporated into the formal strategy, even if that means shifting the strategic umbrella to cover them.

To manage in this context, then, is to create the climate within which a wide variety of strategies can grow. In more complex organizations, this may mean building flexible structures, hiring creative people, defining broad umbrella strategies, and watching for the patterns that emerge.

Reconcile change and continuity. Finally, managers considering radical departures need to keep the quantum theory of change in mind. As Ecclesiastes reminds us, there is a time to sow and a time to reap. Some new patterns must be held in check until the organization is ready for a strategic revolution, or at least a period of divergence. Managers who are obsessed with either change or stability are bound eventually to harm their organizations. As pattern recognizer, the manager has to be able to sense when to exploit an established crop of strategies and when to encourage new strains to displace the old.

While strategy is a word that is usually associated with the future, its link to the past is no less central. As Kierkegaard once observed, life is lived forward but understood backward. Managers may have to live strategy in the future, but they must understand it through the past.

Like potters at the wheel, organizations must make sense of the past if they hope to manage the future. Only by coming to understand the patterns that form in their own behavior do they get to know their capabilities and their potential. Thus crafting strategy, like managing craft, requires a natural synthesis of the future, present, and past.

Tracking strategy

In 1971, I became intrigued by an unusual definition of strategy as a pattern in a stream of decisions (later changed to actions). I initiated a research project at McGill University, and over the next 13 years a team of us tracked the strategies of 11 organizations over several decades of their history. (Students at various levels also carried out about 20 other less comprehensive studies.) The organizations we studied were: Air Canada (1937-1976), Arcop, an architectural firm (1953-1978), Asbestos Corporation (1912-1975), Canadelle, a manufacturer of women's undergarments (1939-1976), McGill University (1829-1980), the National Film Board of Canada (1939-1976), Saturday Night Magazine (1928-1971), the Sherbrooke Record, a small daily newspaper (1946-1976), Steinberg Inc., a large supermarket chain (1917-1974), the U.S. military's strategy in Vietnam (1949-1973), and Volkswagenwerk (1934-1974).

As a first step, we developed chronological lists and graphs of the most important actions taken by each organization—such as store openings and closings, new flight destinations, and new product introductions. Second, we inferred patterns in these actions and labeled them as strategies.

Third, we represented graphically all the strategies we inferred in an organization so that we could line them up to see whether there were distinct periods in their development—for example, periods of stability, flux, or global change. Fourth, we used interviews and in-depth reports to study what appeared to be the key points of change in each organization's strategic history.

Finally, armed with all this strategic history, the research team studied each set of findings to develop conclusions about the process of strategy formation. Three themes guided us: the interplay of environment, leadership, and organization; the pattern of strategic change; and the processes by which strategies form. This article presents those conclusions.

Author's note: Readers interested in learning more about the results of the tracking strategy project have a wide range of studies to draw from. Works published to date can be found in Robert Lamb and Paul Shivastava, eds., *Advances in Strategic Management*, Vol. 4 (Greenwich, Conn.: Jai Press, 1986), pp. 3-41; *Management Science*, May 1978, p. 934; *Administrative Science Quarterly*, June 1985, p. 160; J. Grant, ed., *Strategic Management Frontiers* (Greenwich, Conn.: Jai Press, forthcoming); *Canadian Journal of Administrative Sciences*, June 1984, p. 1; *Academy of Management Journal*, September 1982, p. 465; Robert Lamb, ed., *Competitive Strategic Management* (Englewood Cliffs, N.J.: Prentice-Hall, 1984).

Reprint 87407

Robert H. Hayes

Strategic planning— forward in reverse?

Are corporate planners going about things the wrong way 'round?

With all the time and resources that American manufacturing companies spend on strategic planning, why has their competitive position been deteriorating? Certainly not because the idea of doing such planning is itself misguided. Nor because the managers involved are not up to the task. Drawing on his long experience with the nuts and bolts of operations deep inside American and foreign companies, the author proposes a different answer. Perhaps the problem lies in how managers typically approach the work of planning: first by selecting objectives or ends, then by defining the strategies or ways of accomplishing them, and lastly by developing the necessary resources or means. A hard look at what the new industrial competition requires might suggest, instead, an approach to planning based on a means-ways-ends sequence.

Mr. Hayes is the William Barclay Harding Professor of Management of Technology at the Harvard Business School. He is the author or coauthor of three McKinsey Award-winning articles in HBR and, with Steven C. Wheelwright, of Restoring Our Competitive Edge *(Wiley, 1984), which was selected by the Association of American Publishers as the best book on business, management, and economics published in 1984.*

Since I began to study American industry almost 30 years ago, there has been a revolution in the science and practice of management and, especially, in the attraction of bright, professionally trained managers to the work of strategic planning. Yet as corporate staffs have flourished and as the notion of strategy has come to dominate business education and practice, our factories have steadily lost ground to those in other countries where strategy receives far less emphasis and the "professionalization" of management is far less advanced.

Over the years, I have prowled through hundreds of American factories and talked at length with innumerable line managers. Of late, I have been increasingly troubled by a recurring theme in the explanations they give for their companies' competitive difficulties. Again and again they argue that many of those difficulties—particularly in their manufacturing organizations—stem from their companies' strategic planning processes. Their complaint, however, is not about the *mis*functioning of strategic planning but about the harmful aspects of its *proper* functioning.

In explaining why they continue to use old, often obsolete equipment and systems in their factories, some of these managers assert that their corporate strategic plans call for major investments elsewhere: in acquisitions, new lines of business, new plants in new locations, or simply the subsidization of other parts of their organizations. Their job, they say, is to "manage for cash," not to upgrade the capabilities of their existing plants. Others complain that their companies' strategic plans force on them new products and equipment that require capabilities their organizations do not have (or, worse, no longer have). Still others report that they must assimilate acquired companies that "do not fit" or must grow faster than is prudent or even possible. With money being thrown at them faster than they can absorb it, much of it is poorly spent.

These comments do not come from ineffective managers who are looking for excuses. Nor are their companies unsophisticated in the art of strategic planning. Most of them have been at it for a long time and are widely regarded as experts. How, then, are we to make sense of the fact that, although the United States has poured more resources – both in total and on a per company basis – into strategic planning over the past 20 years than has any other country in the world, a growing number of our industries and companies today find themselves more vulnerable strategically than when they started? Not only do they fall short of goals, but they also lag behind competitors, largely of foreign origin, that place much less emphasis on strategic planning.[1]

Consider, for example, the experience of one company that, for a dozen years, emphasized the expansion of its market and the achievement of "low-cost-producer" status while allowing its R&D budget to fall to just over half its previous level (in constant dollars). The company has now come to realize that the high-volume, low-cost end of its business has moved irretrievably offshore and that its only hope for survival lies in rapid product innovation. There is, however, little innovative spark left in the organization, and neither increases in the R&D budget nor additions of new people appear to have had much impact. In desperation, the company is contemplating a merger with another company that has a better record of product innovation, but it is finding stiff resistance to its advances because of its reputation as a "researchers' graveyard."

Or consider the experience of another company that has a reputation for having modern production facilities and for being in the forefront of product technology in its fast-changing industry. As soon as it tests out the process for making a new product, management builds a new factory dedicated to that product. Unfortunately, once in place, this new facility tends to ossify because management also believes that the product life cycle in its industry is so short that continual investment in process improvement is uneconomic. As a result, the company has recently found itself losing market position to competitors that have pushed ahead in process technology. Although loath to cede business to those who came later, it has so far been unable to muster the ability (or, some say, the commitment) to keep up with its challengers' processing capabilities. Worse, management is realizing that the next generation of new products will require many of the manufacturing skills that it has neglected and its competitors have forced themselves to master.

How can these well-run companies that impose on themselves the rigorous discipline – and employ the sophisticated techniques – of modern strategic planning end up worse off than when they started? Is this a statistical accident or is there something about the process itself that is bad for corporate health? In this article, I will argue that, under certain circumstances, the methodology of formal strategic planning and, even worse, the organizational attitudes and relationships that it often cultivates can impair a company's ability to compete. Moreover, the circumstances under which this occurs is true for much of U.S. industry today.

To understand the damaging effects of that methodology, we must take a hard look at the logic that shapes it. The traditional strategic planning process rests on an "ends-ways-means" model: establish corporate objectives (ends); given those objectives, develop a strategy (ways) for attaining them; then marshal the resources (means) necessary to implement this strategy.

There are two familiar lines of argument for keeping these three elements of the planning process (ends, ways, means) in their current order. First, ends should precede ways because managers must know what their objectives are before deciding how to go about attaining them. A generation of MBA students has had pounded into their heads the story of Lewis Carroll's logician, the Cheshire Cat in *Alice in Wonderland*. When Alice comes upon the Cat and asks, "Would you tell me, please, which way I ought to go from here?" the Cat responds, "That depends… on where you want to get to." Alice answers, "I really don't much care where," and the Cat tells her, "Then it doesn't matter which way you go!"

The second argument has a different basis: to maximize efficiency, the choice of strategy should precede the assembling of the resources for carrying it out. Because each strategy is likely to require a different mix of resources, developing resources before choosing one of them exposes a company to the risk that it will be short of some resources and have too much of others.

What is wrong with this model? Let me raise questions about four of its aspects: (1) the ends that companies usually select, (2) the ways they try to attain those ends, (3) the means through which they carry out those ways, and (4) the logic that strings these elements together in the ends-ways-means order.

1 A number of studies suggest there is either no relationship between planning and various measures of organizational performance or a negative one. See, for example, P.H. Grinyer and D. Norburn, "Planning for Existing Markets: Perceptions of Executives and Financial Performance," *Journal of the Royal Statistical Society (A)* 138, pt.1 (1975), p.70; Ernest A. Kallman and H. Jack Shapiro, "The Motor Freight Industry – A Case Against Planning," *Long Range Planning,* February 1978, p. 81; Ronald J. Kudla, "The Effects of Strategic Planning on Common Stock Returns," *Academy of Management Journal,* March 1980, p. 5; Milton Leontiades and Ahmet Tezel, "Planning Perceptions and Planning Results," *Strategic Management Journal,* January-March 1980, p. 65; Leslie W. Rue and Robert M. Fulmer, "Is Long-Range Planning Profitable?" *Academy of Management Proceedings* (1973), p. 66.

Choosing ends

Most companies select goals that are too short term. It is almost impossible for a company to create a truly sustainable competitive advantage—one that is highly difficult for its competitors to copy—in just five to ten years (the time frame that most companies use). Goals that can be achieved within five years are usually either too easy or based on buying and selling something. Anything that a company can buy or sell, however, is probably available for purchase or sale by its competitors as well.

A series of short-term goals also encourages episodic thinking. When attention focuses on meeting immediate objectives, organizations often find the successive hurdles they have set for themselves increasingly difficult to surmount. Finally, the accumulated weight of deferred changes and seemingly innocuous compromises becomes too great, and managers trip badly on a hurdle that seemed no higher than the rest.

In most of the companies that I have observed, the goals are not only short term but also highly quantitative, focusing on rates of growth in profitability, return on investment, and market share. Unfortunately, quantitative goals follow Gresham's Law: they tend to drive out nonquantitative goals. It is easy for an organization tied to quantitative goals to believe (or to act as if it believes) that anything that is not quantitative is not important.

In practice, the danger is that hard numbers will encourage managers to forget that different kinds of goals have different values at different levels in an organization. Goals like return on investment have great meaning and value for senior managers, who understand the need to allocate capital efficiently and who are themselves evaluated on their ability to do so. ROI has almost no meaning for production workers, however, whose only contact with investment decisions is indirect: roofs that leak, old equipment that does not hold tolerances, new equipment that creates more problems than it solves. What does have meaning for these workers is quality (getting the work done correctly), timing (meeting delivery schedules), the working environment, and the satisfaction that comes from doing a good job as part of an appreciative organization. Objectives that have little meaning for large segments of an organization cannot be shared and cannot weld it together. Nor, for that matter, can episodic goals ("last year's emphasis was on quality, but this year's emphasis is on productivity"), which succeed only in diffusing commitment.

What makes the grass grow

Attempts at despotism…represent, as it were, the drunkenness of responsibility. It is when men…are overwhelmed with the difficulties and blunders of humanity, that they fall back upon a wild desire to manage everything themselves…

This belief, that all would go right if we could only get the strings into our own hands, is a fallacy almost without exception…The sin and sorrow of despotism is not that it does not love men, but that it loves them too much and trusts them too little…

When a man begins to think that the grass will not grow at night unless he lies awake to watch it, he generally ends either in an asylum or on the throne of an emperor.

From
G.K. Chesterton,
Robert Browning (1903)

Developing ways

Short-term goals also work to back companies into a mode of thinking that is based on forecasts (What do we think is going to happen?) rather than on visions (What do we want to happen?). Unfortunately, even though the usual five- to ten-year time periods are too short to achieve truly strategic objectives, they are much too long to obtain accurate forecasts.

Consider, for example, the forecasts made more than a decade ago of a stable, slow-moving enterprise: the U.S. economy. In 1970, when a number of eminent economists tried to predict how the economy would fare during "the sizzling seventies," their consensus was that inflation would continue at about 2.5%, productivity growth would average about 3%, and real growth in GNP would approach 4.5%. Instead, inflation averaged 8%, productivity growth only 1.3%, and real GNP a bit over 3%. As a result, the average American in 1980 enjoyed an income nearly 15% less than that predicted ten years before.

In the early 1970s, many U.S. corporations based their strategies on comparable forecasts of economic growth, as well as on their own forecasts of the much less predictable behavior of particular markets and competitors. Should we be surprised that most of their forecasts were totally off the mark, as were the elaborate strategies to which they gave rise? I suspect that the surge in domestic merger and acquisition activity in the late 1970s reflected in part the growing frustration of American managers who realized they could not reach the forecast-driven goals they had set for their companies and themselves through internal activities alone.

Inevitably, quantitative goals and reliance on long-term forecasts, combined with too-short planning horizons, lead corporate strategists to spend most of their time worrying about structural, rather than behavioral, means for achieving their objectives. After all, they reason, specific, measurable results come through "hard," measurable efforts: investments in new plants and equipment, the introduction of new products, the redesign of organization charts, and so on. This leads them to neglect less easily measured factors like performance evaluation and reward systems, work-force policies, information systems, and management selection and development policies. As the recent interest in "corporate culture" suggests, however, real strategic advantage comes from changing the way a company behaves, a task far more difficult and time-consuming than simply making a few structural decisions.

Another problem with today's strategic planning processes is that they reduce a company's flexibility. Like all organizational processes, strategic planning is subject to the first law of bureaucracy: if you give a smart, ambitious person a job to do, no matter how meaningless, he or she will try to make it bigger and more important. Jack Welch learned this lesson soon after he became chairman and CEO at General Electric. According to Welch, "Once written, the strategic document can take on a life of its own, and it may not lend itself to flexibility....An organization can begin to focus on form rather than substance."[2] He also described to a group of Harvard MBA students how GE's strategic plans had become less and less useful as they got bigger and bigger, as more and more hours went into preparing them, and as planners embellished them with increasingly sophisticated graphics and fancy covers.

William Bricker, chairman and CEO of Diamond Shamrock, has much the same reaction: "Why has our vision been narrowed? Why has our flexibility been constricted? To my mind there is one central reason: our strategies have become too rigid....A detailed strategy [is] like a road map...[telling] us every turn we must take to get to our goal....The entrepreneur, on the other hand, views strategic planning not as a road map but as a compass...and is always looking for the new road."[3] This is a provocative analogy: when you are lost on a highway, a road map is very useful; but when you are lost in a swamp whose topography is constantly changing, a road map is of little help. A simple compass—which indicates the general direction to be taken and allows you to use your own ingenuity in overcoming various difficulties—is much more valuable.

Strategic leaps or small steps?

The difficulties that highly visible U.S. industries are now experiencing surprise and puzzle many Americans. Why is the nation that put a man on the moon and invented genetic engineering unable to produce a consumer videocassette recorder (all those sold by U.S. companies are imported, even though a U.S. company produced the first commercial videotape machine 30 years ago) or even a better small car than Toyota? One possible reason, of course, is that we *can* put a man on the moon. The very skills and psychology that enable us to conceive and carry out something like the Apollo project may hamper us when we are in a competitive environment that bases success more on a series of small steps than on a few dramatic breakthroughs.

Consider the graph in *Exhibit I*, where the horizontal axis measures the passage of time and the vertical, competitive effectiveness (lower cost, better quality, more features, faster delivery). In a free market, a company's competitive effectiveness should improve over time—that is, it will move from a position in the lower left of the graph to a position in the upper right. Now, how does a company accomplish this movement?

One approach, shown in *Exhibit II*, is through a series of strategic leaps, a few giant upward steps at critical moments. These leaps may take a variety of forms: a product redesign, a large-scale factory modernization or expansion, a move to another location that promises great improvement in wage rates or labor relations, an acquisition of a supplier of a critical material or component, or adoption of a new manufacturing technology. Between taking these giant steps, managers seek only incidental improvements in competitiveness, as the company digests the last step and contemplates the next.

At the opposite extreme, as shown in *Exhibit III*, a company may try to progress through a series of small steps whose cumulative impact will be just as great. Rather than rely on a series of discontinuities, such a company continuously strives to bolster its competitive position through a variety of incremental improvements.

Which approach is best? Both can get you to the same point, but each places different demands on an organization and exposes it to very different risks.

2 "Managing Change,"
keynote address,
Dedication Convocation,
Fuqua School of Business,
Duke University,
April 21, 1983.

3 "Entrepreneurs Needed,"
Oil and Gas Digest,
November 15, 1982.

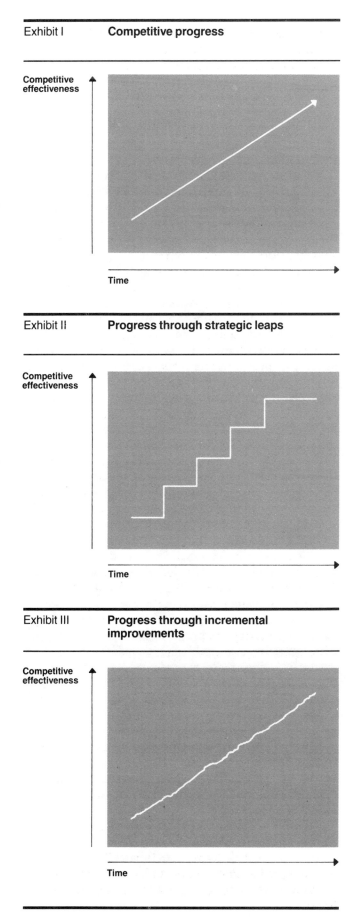

Exhibit I Competitive progress

Competitive
effectiveness

Time

Exhibit II Progress through strategic leaps

Competitive
effectiveness

Time

Exhibit III Progress through incremental improvements

Competitive
effectiveness

Time

Strategic leaps. Each step in *Exhibit II* is highly visible and usually requires a major expenditure of funds. Thus the timing of the change becomes important. A decline in profits, a potential acquisition, a sudden surge of orders that pushes the organization to the limit of its resources—any such development can delay the project or put it on hold. Further, managers at all levels in an organization must get involved in analyzing and approving the decision to take the step. Extensive staff involvement is also essential, as is the expertise of many specialists—financial analysts, strategic planners, legal experts, scientists, outside consultants, and public relations personnel—who often have more allegiance to their own "professions" than to the company itself.

Because each step is so big and so visible, whoever proposes the change takes on an enormous risk in return for the chance to reap huge rewards. Success creates heroes; failure brings severe consequences. The people who rise to the top in such organizations usually fall into one of two camps: they are either "lucky gamblers," who were involved in two or three successful leaps, or "corporate kibitzers," who managed to avoid entanglement in any disasters.

Such companies regard the corporate staff as an elite group and treat assignments of line managers to staff positions as promotions. At lower levels in the organization, however, there is little need for outstanding, highly trained people. The task of people at these levels is simply to operate the structure that top management and its staff of experts have created. It does not seem necessary in such companies to put much time and effort into training and upgrading factory workers or managers because the next strategic leap may make their newly developed skills obsolete. Nor do personnel policies that reward employee longevity seem particularly desirable because they reduce the company's flexibility—its ability, say, to pull up stakes and move to a new location, to sell the business, or to implement a significant reduction in employment as part of an automation program.

In similar fashion, a reliance on strategic leaps makes it unnecessary for workers or lower level managers to have a detailed understanding of how their own operations affect—and are affected by—other parts of the organization. The same logic robs employee suggestion programs of their usefulness, for workers cannot possibly understand how the changes they may propose fit into the company's overall strategy, much less the leap it is contemplating next.

Small steps. If, however, a company follows an incremental approach to improvement, few of the steps it takes are highly visible or risky. Because major capital authorization requests are seldom necessary, there is little need for much staff assistance or outside advice. Rather than put massive resources into the development of elaborate plans in the rarefied atmosphere of a remote headquarters, such a company expects the bulk of its improvements to bubble up, in an entrepreneurial fashion, from lower levels in the organization. Its corporate staff is much smaller and less powerful than that of a strategic leap organization. Its main role is to offer support services. In effect, the organization charts of these companies look more like tables than pyramids.

This incremental approach requires immense low-level expertise – not expertise *of* a low level, but expertise *at* low levels. Developing this kind of expertise takes a long time. Executives need to expend great effort on recruiting people who are both loyal and trainable, and on continuously improving their capabilities once hired – through both formal education programs and job assignments that provide a broad understanding of the company's products, processes, and competitive environment. In turn, top management needs to augment this understanding and keep it up to date by disseminating information about current financial results, market behavior, and competitors' activities.

Having made so extensive an investment in low-level expertise, a company will do its best to retain the people who have it. Long-time employees have another advantage: over time, through their multiple job assignments, they develop relationships with people in different parts of the organization. These relationships make it easier to implement the small changes that require communication and cooperation among several different groups.

Incremental projects generally require so little capital that managers can often fund them out of a plant's annual operating budget. It stands to reason that plant managers will support such efforts if they are intimately familiar with the production systems and people involved and are committed to the plant's long-term success because they expect to stay in their jobs for a long time. Such projects are also more likely to thrive if workers, plant engineers, and lower level managers participate in developing them – through suggestion programs, quality circles, and the like – and if they identify the company's long-term success with their own.

This kind of company does not believe that many of its problems can be solved by top management. The information and expertise needed for dealing with them reside lower down in the organization, and the problems themselves are continuously evolving. Therefore, top management's role is less to spot and solve problems than to create an organization that can spot and solve its own problems.

The tortoise & the hare

Up to this point, I have been describing, rather abstractly, two contrasting "pure" strategies. In practice, of course, few companies choose approaches so extreme; most strategies fall somewhere along the spectrum between them. U.S. companies do, however, tend to adopt approaches toward the strategic leap end; those of our two most powerful international competitors, Germany and Japan, tend to seek incremental improvements within an existing structure and technology. They are the tortoise; we are the hare.

In the fable, as we may recall with some apprehension, the tortoise won the race. Are we to share the hare's fate? To answer that question, let us examine the risks and rewards of each approach.

The central risk of following the incremental approach is that a company will be "leapfrogged" and left behind by a competitor that abandons its traditional technology, location, or corporate strategy and adopts a new and more successful one. The folklore of American business is full of such examples: the replacement of piston engines by jet engines, of vacuum tubes by transistors, of ditto machines by xerography, of New England textile companies by those that moved south. The list goes on and on.

Conversely, the central risk of following the strategic leap approach is that a breakthrough may not always be available exactly when it is needed. After seizing a major competitive advantage, a company may see its lead nibbled away by competitors that gradually adapt themselves to the new technology or strategy and then push it beyond its initial limits. This is the time to make another leap, but what if the company's technicians and strategists reach into their hats and find nothing there?

One obvious response to this predicament is to use an incremental approach, like that of the competition, until a breakthrough does become available. Doing so, however, is not easy for a company that has organized itself around the expectation of repeated breakthroughs. As I have argued, the kind of organization adept at making strategic leaps bears little resemblance to one that takes the incremental approach. Entrepreneurship from below cannot be "ordered" by managers from above – particularly when, as is usually the case, top-down, staff-dominated planning and control systems have caused most of the entrepreneurs to leave.

Unfortunately, the reverse is not true. As our Japanese and German competitors are demonstrating all too well, companies that adopt an incremental approach *can* eventually accommodate themselves to a new technology. As a rule, they are not as fast but, if given the time, they can do it. In other words, the ability to progress through incremental change does not preclude, although it may slow down, a company's ability to master discontinuous change. In fact, an organization that is used to continuous small changes and that has balanced strategic expertise at the top with operating expertise and entrepreneurship at the bottom is probably better prepared for a big leap than is an organization that has gone for several years without any change at all.

Assembling means

The third element (after ends and ways) in the strategic planning paradigm is the selection and assembling of the resources necessary to implement the chosen strategy. Although a strategy will usually require many different types of resources, strategic planning in most corporations devotes most of its attention to just one: financial wherewithal. There are two reasons for this.

First, since managers usually state their ultimate objectives in financial terms, it is natural for them to state required resources in financial terms as well. Second, resources get used most efficiently when management provides only those that are absolutely necessary. Understandably, companies try to maintain their resources in as liquid (that is, financial) a form as possible for as long as possible, for doing so gives them maximum flexibility to convert liquid resources into the desired form at just the moment they are needed.

Such a practice works well if reasonably efficient markets exist for important assets like market position, worker or manager skills, and technological capabilities. Many companies have come to realize, however, that technology, market position, and organizational skills are not as transferable as they had expected. As a result, those that try to buy them often run into the infrastructure problems I described earlier.

Informed businesspeople, who understand well the danger of trying to place a modern steel mill in a less developed country like Bangladesh, have sometimes been willing to try to implant advanced new technologies in organizations that are unprepared to receive them. In most cases, these organizations respond by starving the new technology of understanding and resources—just as the human body tries to reject a heart transplant that is essential to its survival. No matter how brilliant its technological underpinnings, a new product will fail if the company's manufacturing organization is unable to make that product efficiently or if the company's sales force is unable to sell it effectively. Such capabilities cannot be bought from the outside. They must be grown from within, and growing them takes time.

The logic of ends-ways-means

When managers in strategic planning demand that ends should precede ways and both should precede means, they make certain assumptions about the environment and the nature of competition. First, they assume that the world of competition is predictable and that clear paths can be charted across it much like a highway system across a road map. Equally important, they assume that reasonable objectives, arrived at by thoughtful people, can be achieved through purposeful activity and that progress toward those objectives is both measurable and controllable.

The managerial logic of ends-ways-means also attributes a certain stability to the company itself. There is an expectation that the company's values and needs will not change over the planning horizon and that the objectives it sets will seem as desirable up close as they do from afar. Managers can, therefore, concern themselves with "static optimization"—that is, with making a few key decisions and then holding to them. There is a further expectation that, once these objectives and the strategies for achieving them are in place, managers can assemble the necessary resources in the required time frame and convert them into the appropriate form.

Underlying all these assumptions is the belief that responsibility for organizational success rests primarily on the shoulders of top management. This "command-and-control" mentality allocates all major decisions to top management, which imposes them on the organization and monitors them through elaborate planning, budgeting, and control systems. In many ways this logic is similar to that which underlies modern conventional warfare: generals set the strategy, provide the resources, establish the detailed plan of action, and continuously monitor the progress of engagements as they occur.

Does this logic make sense? Earlier I questioned the notion that means should follow ways on the ground that important resources—technology, skills, and effective working relationships—cannot always be purchased when needed. Now I also question whether managers should decide on ends before selecting ways.

Taken to an extreme, these questions could turn into a general attack on logic as applied to business planning. Such attacks are more and more common these days, from *In Search of Excellence*'s claim that "detached, analytical justification for all decisions...has arguably led us seriously astray" to the *Washington Post*'s insistence that "preoccupation with logic has helped to improve and reform the world, but it has also put professionals dangerously out of touch with the gritty everyday world." My point is not to disparage the relevance of all logic to planning but to suggest that there may be alternative logics worth exploring. One of them, in fact, is to turn the ends-ways-means paradigm on its head: means-ways-ends.

How might such a logic work? First, it suggests that a company should begin by investing in the development of its capabilities along a broad front (means). It should train workers and managers in a variety of jobs; educate them about the general competitive situation and the actions of specific competitors; teach them how to identify problems, how to develop solutions for them, and how to persuade others to follow their recommendations. It should acquire and experiment with new technologies and techniques so that workers and managers gain experience with them and come to understand their capabilities and constraints. It should focus R&D activity on fewer lines but spread it more widely throughout the organization. Managers should have cross-functional assignments so that they develop a broad understanding of the company's markets, technologies, and factories.

Second, as these capabilities develop and as technological and market opportunities appear, the company should encourage managers well down in the organization to exploit matches wherever they occur (ways). Top management's job, then, is to facilitate this kind of entrepreneurial activity, provide it with resources from other parts of the company, and, where feasible, encourage cooperative activities. In short, the logic here is, Do not develop plans and then seek capabilities; instead, build capabilities and then encourage the development of plans for exploiting them. Do not try to develop optimal strategies on the assumption of a static environment; instead, seek continuous improvement in a dynamic environment.

The guiding force throughout such disparate activities will not come from a set of directions or controls. To the contrary, it will come from a balance between integration, which arises out of a sense of organizational unity and camaraderie, an instinctive banding together in the face of common enemies, and direction, which arises out of a set of shared values rooted in a long-term vision of the kind of company that its people want it to become—in short, group cohesion and a compass. A compass, remember, is not an end; it only provides a sense of direction, a means to a variety of possible ends.

Under what circumstances might such a means-ways-ends logic be effective? When the competitive world is like a swamp that is shifting in unpredictable ways, particular objectives are likely to lose

their attractiveness over time. Even so, a common vision can keep people moving ahead, moving around unforeseen obstacles and beyond immediate (largely because they are visible) objectives.

Is guerrilla warfare always better?

An organization that takes a means-ways-ends approach to strategic planning assumes everybody is responsible for its prosperity. Its success rests on its ability to exploit opportunities as they arise, on its ingenuity, on its capacity to learn, on its determination and persistence.

There is an obvious analogy here with guerrilla warfare. It would, of course, be wrong to suggest that strategic planning based on a strategic leap approach is always less effective than that based on an incremental approach. Even in guerrilla warfare, someone must decide where to fight and which goals to seek. Someone must select and train leaders and rally soldiers to the cause. On occasion, conventional pitched battles are perfectly appropriate.

Sometimes companies must change their objectives; they may decide to enter a new business or abandon an old one. These decisions seldom bubble up from the bottom. Instead, they flow down from the top. The trick, of course, to managing such discontinuities without alienating the organization or undermining its capabilities is to employ a patient, consensus-seeking decision process in which all parties have an opportunity to be heard. More important, everyone must regard a necessary leap as the exception, not the rule. Once a guerrilla army decides that the only person with any real authority is the supreme leader, its field commanders lose their credibility.

Therefore, I suspect that the Japanese and German companies that are currently studying the American approach to strategic planning do not intend to make it a way of life. They intend simply to graft it onto their existing systems so they can be better prepared for dealing with the discontinuities that sometimes confront them. What they may not appreciate is how seductive such an approach can be for top management. When the balance of power begins to shift, when the "counters" gain ascendency over the "doers," the best doers may seek to become counters. Or they go elsewhere, where they can do it *their* way.

Further, in most mature industries, the development of markets and technology is not discontinuous but moves forward in a steady, almost predictable manner. Even in high-technology industries like semiconductors and computers, for example, progress during the past decade has taken place within technological frameworks that were essentially in place more than 15 years ago. The opportunities for dramatic breakthroughs and strategic "end runs" have diminished as sophisticated multinational companies have identified most of the untapped markets and have uncovered most of the unexploited pools of low-cost labor in the world. They are running out of islands to move to.

Seen in this light, the present struggle between U.S. companies and their foreign competitors can be likened to a battle between a bunch of hares, trained in conventional warfare and equipped with road maps, and an unknown number of tortoises, equipped with compasses and an expertise in guerrilla warfare. Unfortunately, the battle is taking place in a swamp and not on a well-defined highway system.

The logic of ends-ways-means that got the hares into this situation is unlikely to get them out. They will need to explore a new logic, possibly a reverse logic, and be willing to question the basis of formal strategic planning as it is practiced today. Perhaps they should return to the approaches they used to follow—when they spent less time developing strategies but their industrial capabilities were the envy of the world. ▽

Backing into the future

If, in conclusion, I may give for what they are worth the impressions of a brief visit to Washington, I believe that there is much devoted and intelligent work in progress there, and that the fittest ideas and the fittest men are tending to survive. In many parts of the world the old order has passed away. But, of all the experiments to evolve a new order, it is the experiment of young America which most attracts my own deepest sympathy. For they are occupied with the task of trying to make the economic order work tolerably well, while preserving freedom of individual initiative and liberty of thought and criticism.

The older generation of living Americans accomplished the great task of solving the technical problem of how to produce economic goods on a scale adequate to human needs. It is the task of the younger generation to bring to actual realization the potential blessings of having solved the technical side of the problem of poverty. The central control which the latter requires involves an essentially changed method and outlook. The minds and energies which have found their fulfillment in the achievements of American business are not likely to be equally well adapted to the further task. That must be, as it should be, the fulfillment of the next generation.

The new men will often appear to be at war with the ideas and convictions of their seniors. This cannot be helped. But I hope that these seniors will look as sympathetically as they can at a sincere attempt—I cannot view it otherwise—to complete, and not to destroy, what they themselves have created.

From
John Maynard Keynes
New York Times, June 10, 1934

Reprint 85607

At Shell, planning means changing minds, not making plans.

Planning as Learning

by ARIE P. DE GEUS

Some years ago, the planning group at Shell surveyed 30 companies that had been in business for more than 75 years. What impressed us most was their ability to live in harmony with the business environment, to switch from a survival mode when times were turbulent to a self-development mode when the pace of change was slow. And this pattern rang a familiar bell because Shell's history is similarly replete with switches from expansion to self-preservation and back again to growth.

Early in our history, for example, there was a burst of prosperity in the Far East and we dominated the market for kerosene in tins and "oil for the lamps of China." Survival became the keynote, however, when Rockefeller's Standard Oil snatched market share by cutting price. In fact, it was the survival instinct that led in 1907 to the joining of Royal Dutch Petroleum and the Shell Transport and Trading Company—separate businesses until then and competitors in the Far East. This, in turn, paved the way for Shell's expansion into the United States in 1911 with a new product, Sumatran gasoline—also a reaction to Standard Oil's activities.

Outcomes like these don't happen automatically. On the contrary, they depend on the ability of a company's senior managers to absorb what is going on in the business environment and to act on that information with appropriate business moves. In other words, they depend on learning. Or, more precisely, on institutional learning, which is the process whereby management teams change their shared mental models of their company, their markets, and their competitors. For this reason, we think of planning as learning and of corporate planning as institutional learning.

Institutional learning is much more difficult than individual learning. The high level of thinking among individual managers in most companies is admirable. And yet, the level of thinking that goes on in the management teams of most companies is considerably below the individual managers' capacities. In institutional learning situations, the learning level of the team is often the lowest common denominator, especially with teams that think of themselves as machines with mechanistic, specialized parts: the production manager looks at production, the distribution manager looks at distribution, the marketing manager looks at marketing.

Because high-level, effective, and continuous institutional learning and ensuing corporate change are the prerequisites for corporate success, we at Shell* have asked ourselves two questions. How does a company learn and adapt? And, What is planning's role in corporate learning?

My answer to the first question, "how does a company learn and adapt," is that many do not or, at least, not very quickly. A full one-third of the *Fortune* "500" industrials listed in 1970 had vanished by 1983. And W. Stewart Howe has pointed out in his 1986 book *Corporate Strategy* that for every successful turnaround there are two ailing companies that fail to recover. Yet some companies obviously do learn and can adapt. In fact, our survey identified several that were still vigorous at 200, 300, and even 700 years of age. What made the difference? Why are some companies better able to adapt?

Sociologists and psychologists tell us it is pain that makes people and living systems change. And certainly corporations have their share of painful crises, the recent spate of takeovers and takeover threats conspicuously among them. But crisis management—pain management—is a dangerous way to manage for change.

---

*Author's note: I use the collective expression "Shell" for convenience when referring to the companies of the Royal Dutch/Shell Group in general, or when no purpose is served by identifying the particular Shell company or companies.

Arie P. de Geus is head of planning for the Royal Dutch/Shell Group of companies. During more than 30 years with Shell, he has worked throughout the world, most recently as coordinator for Africa and South Asia and as the director of Shell's oil operations in Brazil.

Once in a crisis, everyone in the organization feels the pain. The need for change is clear. The problem is that you usually have little time and few options. The deeper into the crisis you are, the fewer options remain. Crisis management, by necessity, becomes autocratic management. The positive characteristic of a crisis is that the decisions are quick. The other side of that coin is that the implementation is rarely good; many companies fail to survive.

The challenge, therefore, is to recognize and react to environmental change before the pain of a crisis. Not surprisingly, this is what the long-lived companies in our study were so well able to do.

All these companies had a striking capacity to institutionalize change. They never stood still. Moreover, they seemed to recognize that they had internal strengths that could be developed as environmental conditions changed. Thus, Booker McConnell, founded in 1906 as a sugar company, developed shipping on the back of its primary resource. British American Tobacco recognized that marketing cigarettes was no different from marketing perfume. Mitsubishi, founded in 1870 as a marine and trading company, acquired coal mines to secure access to ships' bunkers, built shipyards to repair imported ships, and developed a bank from the exchange business it had begun to finance shippers.

Changes like these grow out of a company's knowledge of itself and its environment. All managers have such knowledge and they develop it further all the time, since every living person – and system – is continuously engaged in learning. In fact, the normal decision process in corporations is a learning process, because people change their own mental models and build up a joint model as they talk. The problem is that the speed of that process is slow – too slow for a world in which the ability to learn faster than competitors may be the only sustainable competitive advantage.

Some five years ago, we had a good example of the time it takes for a message to be heard. One way in which we in Shell trigger institutional learning is through scenarios.[1] A certain set of scenarios gave our planners a clear signal that the oil industry, which had always been highly integrated, was so no longer. That contradicted all our existing models. High integration means that you are more or less in control of all the facets of your industry, so you can start optimizing. Optimization was the driving managerial model in Shell. What these scenarios essentially were saying was that we had to look for other management methods.

The first reaction from the organization was at best polite. There were few questions and no discussion. Some managers reacted critically: the scenarios were "basic theory that everyone already knew"; they had "little relevance to the realities of today's business." The message had been listened to but it had not yet been heard.

After a hiatus of some three months, people began asking lots of questions; a discussion started. The intervening months had provided time for the message to settle and for management's mental models to develop a few new hooks. Absorption, phase one of the learning process, had taken place.

During the next nine months, we moved through the other phases of the learning process. Operating

> ## The ability to learn faster than your competitors may be the only sustainable competitive advantage.

executives at Shell incorporated this new information into their mental models of the business. They drew conclusions from the revised models and tested them against experience. Then, finally, they acted on the basis of the altered model. Hearing, digestion, confirmation, action: each step took time, its own sweet time.

In my experience this time span is typical. It will likely take 12 to 18 months from the moment a signal is received until it is acted on. The issue is not whether a company will learn, therefore, but whether it will learn fast and early. The critical question becomes, "Can we accelerate institutional learning?"

I am more and more persuaded that the answer to this question is yes. But before explaining why, I want to emphasize an important point about learning and the planner's role. The only relevant learning in a company is the learning done by those people who have the power to act (at Shell, the operating company management teams). So the real purpose of effective planning is not to make plans but to change the microcosm, the mental models that these decision makers carry in their heads. And this is what we at Shell and others elsewhere try to do.

In this role as facilitator, catalyst, and accelerator of the corporate learning process, planners are apt to fall into several traps. One is that we sometimes start with a mental model that is unrecognizable to our audience. Another is that we take too many steps at

---

1. Pierre Wack wrote about our system in "Scenarios: Uncharted Waters Ahead," HBR September-October 1985, p. 72 and in "Scenarios: Shooting the Rapids," HBR November-December 1985, p. 139.

once. The third, and most serious, is that too often we communicate our information by teaching. This is a natural trap to fall into because it's what we've been conditioned to all our lives. But teaching, as John Holt points out, is actually one of the least efficient ways to convey knowledge.[2] At best, 40% of what is taught is received; in most situations, it is only about 25%.

It was a shock to learn how inefficient teaching is. Yet some reflection on our own experience drove the point home. After all, we had spent nearly 15 man-years preparing a set of scenarios which we then transmitted in a condensed version in 2½ hours. Could we really have believed that our audience would understand all we were talking about?

Teaching has another disadvantage as well, especially in a business setting. Teachers must be given authority by their students based on the teachers' presumed superior understanding. When a planner presents the results of many man-years of looking at the environment to a management team, she is usually given the benefit of the doubt: the planner probably knows more about the environment than the management team she is talking to. But when the same planner walks into a boardroom to start teaching about the strategy of the company, her authority disappears. When you cannot be granted authority, you can no longer teach.

Fortified with this understanding of planning and its role, we looked for ways to accelerate institutional learning. Curiously enough, we learned in two cases that changing the rules, or suspending them, could be a spur to learning. Rules in a corporation are extremely important. Nobody likes them but everybody obeys them because they are recognized as the glue of the organization. And yet, we have all known extraordinary managers who got their organizations out of a rut by changing the rules. Intuitively they changed the organization and the way it looked at matters, and so, as a consequence, accelerated learning.

Several years ago one of our work groups introduced, out of the blue, a new rule into the corporate rain dance: "Thou shalt plan strategically in the first half of the calendar year." (We already had a so-called business planning cycle that dealt with capital budgets in the second half of the calendar year.)

The work group was wise enough not to be too specific about what it had in mind. Some operating companies called up and asked what was meant by "strategic planning." But the answer they got—that ideas were more important than numbers—was vague. Other companies just started to hold strategic planning meetings in the spring.

In the first year the results of this new game were scanty, mostly a rehash of the previous year's business plans. But in the second year the plans were fresher and each year the quality of thinking that went into strategic planning improved. So we asked ourselves whether, by having changed the rules of the game—because that's what the planning system is, one of the rules of the corporate game—we had accelerated institutional learning. And our answer was yes. We changed the rules and the corporation played by the new rules that evolved in the process.

A similar thing happened when we tried suspending the rules. In 1984 we had a scenario that talked about $15 a barrel oil. (Bear in mind that in 1984 the price of a barrel of oil was $28 and $15 was the end of the world to oil people.) We thought it important that, as early in 1985 as possible, senior managers throughout Shell start learning about a world of $15 oil. But the response to this scenario was essentially, "If you want us to think about this world, first tell us when the price is going to fall, how far it will fall, and how long the drop will last."

A deadlock ensued which we broke by writing a case study with a preface that was really a license to play. "We don't know the future," it said. "But neither do you. And though none of us knows whether the price is going to fall, we can agree that it would be

2. John Holt, *How Children Learn*, rev. ed. (New York: Delacorte, 1983) and John Holt, *How Children Fail*, rev. ed. (New York: Delacorte, 1982).

pretty serious if it did. So we have written a case showing one of many possible ways by which the price of oil could fall." We then described a case in which the price plummeted at the end of 1985 and concluded by saying: "And now it is April 1986 and you are staring at a price of $16 a barrel. Will you please meet and give your views on these three questions: What do you think your government will do? What do you think your competition will do? And what, if anything, will you do?"

Since at that point the price was still $28 and rising, the case was only a game. But that game started off serious work throughout Shell, not on answering the question "What will happen?" but rather exploring the question "What will we do if it happens?" The acceleration of the institutional learning process had been set in motion.

As it turned out, the price of oil was still $27 in early January of 1986. But on February 1 it was $17 and in April it was $10. The fact that Shell had already visited the world of $15 oil helped a great deal in that panicky spring of 1986.

By now, we knew we were on to something: games could significantly accelerate institutional learning. That's not so strange when you think of it. Some of the most difficult and complex tasks in our lives were learned by playing: cycling, tennis, playing an instrument. We did it, we experimented, we played. But how were we going to make it OK to play?

Few managers are able to say, "I don't mind a little mistake. Go ahead, experiment," especially with a crisis looming. We didn't feel we could go to executives who run some of the biggest companies in the world and say, "Come on, let's have a little game." And in any case, board meetings have agendas, are fixed to end at a certain time, and require certain action to be taken. Still, within these constraints, we have found ways to learn by playing.

One characteristic of play, as the Tavistock Institute in London has shown, is the presence of a transitional object. For the person playing, the transitional object is a representation of the real world. A child who is playing with a doll learns a great deal about the real world at a very fast pace.

Successful consultants let themselves be treated as transitional objects. The process begins when the consultant says something like this to a management team: "We know from experience that many good strategies are largely implicit. If you let us interview people at various levels in your organization, we'll see whether we can get your strategy out on paper. Then we'll come back and check whether we've understood it."

Some weeks later the consultant goes back to the team and says: "Well, we've looked at your strategy and we've played it through a number of likely possibilities, and here is what we think will be the outcome. Do you like it?" The management team will almost certainly say no. So the consultant will say: "All right, let's see how we can change it. Let's go back to your original model and see what was built in there that produced this result." This process is likely to go through a number of iterations, during which the team's original model will change considerably. Those changes constitute the learning that is taking place among the team's members.

Like consultants, computer models can be used to play back and forth management's view of its mar-

To speed up learning, change the rules that managers live by.

ket, the environment, or the competition. The starting point, however, must be the mental model that the audience has at the moment. If a planner walks into the room with a model on his computer that he has made up himself, the chances are slim that his audience will recognize this particular microworld. If the target group is a management team, the starting model must be the sum of their individual models. How can this be done?

One way is to involve team members in the development of a new common model and leave their individual models implicit. Alternatively, one can bring the individual models out in the open through interviews and make them explicit. In both approaches, computers can serve as transitional objects in which to store the common models that get built.

To most planners, one all-important aspect of these microworlds is counterintuitive: the probability that they have little relation to the real world. God seems to have told model builders that a model should have predictive qualities and that therefore it should represent the real world. In building microworlds, however, this is totally irrelevant. What we want to capture are the models that exist in the minds of the audience. Almost certainly, these will not represent the real world. None of us has a model that actually captures the real world, because no complex reality can be represented analytically and a model is an analytical way of representing reality. Moreover, for the purpose of learning, it is not the reality that matters but the team's model of reality, which will change as members' understanding of their world improves.

But why go to all this trouble? Why not rely on the natural learning process that occurs whenever a management team meets? For us at Shell, there are three compelling reasons. First, although the models in the human mind are complex, most people can deal with only three or four variables at a time and do so through only one or two time iterations.

Look, for instance, at current discussions about the price of oil. Nine out of ten people draw on a price-elasticity model of the market: the price has come down, therefore demand will go up and supply will eventually fall. Ergo, they will conclude, at some time in the future the price of oil must rise. Now we all know that what goes up must come down. But our minds, in thinking through this complex model, work through too few iterations, and we stop at the point where the price goes up. If we computerize the model of the person who stops thinking at the moment the price rises, however, the model will almost certainly show the price falling after its rise. Yet this knowledge would be counterintuitive to the very person (or persons) who built the model.

The second reason for putting mental models into computers is that in working with dynamic models, people discover that in complex systems (like markets or companies) cause and effect are separated in time and place. To many people such insight is also counter-intuitive. Most of us, particularly if we are engaged in the process of planning, focus on the effect we want to create and then look for the most immediate cause to create that effect. The use of dynamic models helps us discover other trigger points, separated in time and place from the desired effect.

Lastly, by using computer models we learn what constitutes relevant information. For only when we start playing with these microworlds do we find out what information we really need to know.

When people play with models this way, they are actually creating a new language among themselves that expresses the knowledge they have acquired. And here we come to the most important aspect of institutional learning, whether it be achieved through teaching or through play as we have defined it: the institutional learning process is a process of language development. As the implicit knowledge of each learner becomes explicit, his or her mental model becomes a building block of the institutional model. How much and how fast this model changes will depend on the culture and structure of the organization. Teams that have to cope with rigid procedures and information systems will learn more slowly than those with flexible, open communication channels. Autocratic institutions will learn faster or not at all – the ability of one or a few leaders being a risky institutional bet.

Human beings aren't the only ones whose learning ability is directly related to their ability to convey information. As a species, birds have great potential to learn, but there are important differences among them. Titmice, for example, move in flocks and mix

> ## Learning is not a luxury. It's how companies discover their future.

freely, while robins live in well-defined parts of the garden and for the most part communicate antagonistically across the borders of their territories. Virtually all the titmice in the U.K. quickly learned how to pierce the seals of milk bottles left at doorsteps. But robins as a group will never learn to do this (though individual birds may) because their capacity for institutional learning is low; one bird's knowledge does not spread.[3] The same phenomenon occurs in management teams that work by mandate. The best learning takes place in teams that accept that the whole is larger than the sum of the parts, that there is a good that transcends the individual.

What about managers who find themselves in a robin culture? Clearly, their chances of accelerating institutional learning are reduced. Nevertheless, they can take a significant step toward opening up communication and thus the learning process by keeping one fact in mind: institutional learning begins with the calibration of existing mental models.

We are continuing to explore other ways to improve and speed up our institutional learning process. Our exploration into learning through play via a transitional object (a consultant or a computer) looks promising enough at this point to push on in that direction. And while we are navigating in poorly charted waters, we are not out there alone.[4]

Our exploration into this area is not a luxury. We understand that the only competitive advantage the company of the future will have is its managers' ability to learn faster than their competitors. So the companies that succeed will be those that continually nudge their managers towards revising their views of the world. The challenges for the planner are considerable. So are the rewards.

3. Jeff S. Wyles, Joseph G. Kunkel, and Allan C. Wilson, ''Birds, Behavior and Anatomical Evolution,'' *Proceedings of the National Academy of Sciences, USA*, July 1983.
4. Through MIT's Program in Systems Thinking and the New Management Style, a group of senior executives are looking at this and other issues.

Many best ways to make strategy

Michael Goold and Andrew Campbell

"The shoe that fits one person pinches another; there is no recipe for living that suits all cases," observed Carl Jung in *Modern Man in Search of a Soul.* Jung wasn't thinking about strategic management when he wrote that passage. But he could have been.

Managing a multibusiness organization means managing the relationship between executives in the central office and those who run the business units or divisions. And strategy gurus notwithstanding, there is no one best way to do that. Rather, the best way always depends on the nature and needs of the businesses in a company's portfolio, on the styles of the people in the corporate office, on the company's strategy and goals.

Any style can succeed if it plays to strength.

At British Petroleum, headquarters is involved in all the important strategy decisions; it leaves the operating decisions to division managers. And BP flourishes. BTR wears a different shoe. At BTR, strategy issues are determined by managers in close touch with their markets. Top management concentrates on the operating ratios and financial controls. BTR also thrives.

In a study of 16 large, diversified British companies, we identified three successful styles of managing strategy, which we call "strategic planning," "financial control," and "strategic control." (See the

Before joining the Centre for Business Strategy at the London Business School as a senior research fellow, Michael Goold was a vice president of the Boston Consulting Group. Andrew Campbell, also with the Centre for Business Strategy, has worked as a consultant for McKinsey & Company, Inc. and as a loan officer for a British bank. They are the authors of Strategies and Style *(Blackwell, 1987).*

ruled insert, "Strategy & Style," for details of the study.) Each is characterized by a particular way of organizing the relationships between headquarters and the business units. The secret to choosing among them is to find the style that suits the circumstances best. Then keep a sharp eye out for its inevitable drawbacks.

Bolder strategies, slower decisions

In many companies headquarters is deeply involved in strategy. Unit managers formulate proposals, but headquarters reserves the right to have the final say. The rationale is simple. As one senior manager commented to us, "There are two or three decisions each decade that make or break a business. Do you really want to leave the business manager alone to make them?" BP, the BOC Group, Cadbury Schweppes, Lex Service Group, STC, and United Biscuits (UB) are among the companies that do not.

One strength of this "strategic planning" style is that it builds checks and balances into the process of determining each business unit's strategy. Responsibilities typically overlap, so business unit managers and corporate staffers are forced to communicate. This exchange of ideas stretches the thinking and improves strategy proposals by the exposure to a variety of views. Unit managers also have a strong incentive to produce good proposals. They will be challenged by managers from headquarters. Although the corporate leaders will ultimately rely on their own judgment, unit managers know that their views will be carefully examined.

A second strength of this style is that it encourages strategies that are well integrated across business units. The close involvement of central managers, strong staff functions, and overlapping responsibilities make it possible for the units to coordinate their plans. Doing so is especially important when business areas are linked through shared resources, for instance, or common distribution networks. As Dominic Cadbury, chief executive of Cadbury Schweppes, noted: "I'm trying to ensure that we maximize our opportunities for synergy in our core businesses, confectionery and soft drinks. We must make sure we are transferring skills and product knowledge and sharing assets." Or as Sir Kenneth Corfield, former chairman of STC, remarked: "In businesses like electronics, the divisions have to help each other. One may have to forgo things so another can get on better."

Perhaps the greatest strength of the strategic planning style is that it fosters the creation of ambitious business strategies. Strategic planning companies are most effective in helping business units strive to gain advantage over competitors. Once headquarters establishes the direction in which the business should be going, unit managers are free to develop bold plans to achieve whatever goal has been set. "We would never have been able to pursue such an ambitious strategy if we were an independent company," one business unit manager in a strategic planning company told us. And that statement characterizes the thinking of many similarly situated unit managers.

Moreover, because the strategic objectives come from the top, the units can support those objectives without great concern for the short-term financial impact of their actions. They are, in a sense, buffered from capital market pressures. Finally, at its best, the agreement between the corporate office and the business unit creates a shared purpose that helps motivate those who must carry out the plan.

Proof of these strengths is evident in the records of the strategic planning companies, which experience more expansion of their existing businesses than the strategic control or financial control companies (see *Exhibit I*). They also make more investments with long paybacks. As Sir Kenneth Corfield of STC commented, "Sometimes you need to go along with a development for five to seven years before getting any business." As Sir Hector Laing, chairman of UB, explained: "In my experience, it takes about seven years to build a viable business in today's competitive environment."

The strategic planning style is most effective, then, in organizations that are searching for a broad, integrated strategy for developing the business units, where the focus is on long-term competitive advantage. BP, for example, has invested heavily in minerals, coal, nutrition, electronics, and a number of other areas that yield low immediate returns. BOC has plowed resources into strengthening its worldwide position in gases. It has also directed large amounts of capital to its health-care and carbon-graphite electrode businesses. Cadbury's, Lex, STC, and UB have all made important investments in the United States. Each company believes that a U.S. presence is essential to the long-term strength of its core businesses, even though

Strategy & style

We studied 16 leading British companies to determine current practices, to identify important issues as perceived at different levels, and to relate strategic decision-making processes to the companies' results.

To that end, we conducted open-ended interviews with 5 to 20 corporate, divisional, and business managers in each company, including in almost all cases the chief executive. We also gathered internal data, usually from the head of planning, about formal aspects of the company's strategic decision-making process. Finally, we drew on published reports.

The companies we studied are all publicly quoted, with headquarters in the United Kingdom. They cover a range of manufacturing and service sectors (none of the companies was in financial services or retailing). Their common characteristics are size, diversity, and success.

The companies that took part in the study are British Petroleum, Imperial Chemical Industries, General Electric Company, Imperial Group, BTR, Hanson Trust, Courtaulds, STC, BOC, Cadbury Schweppes, United Biscuits, Tarmac, Plessey, Lex Service Group, Vickers, and Ferranti.

it knows that returns may be temporarily low or volatile.

In a given business, strategic planning companies are more likely to choose an ambitious, expansive option than a cautious one. For example, STC, the Plessey Company, and General Electric Company (GEC) have all competed in manufacturing electronic components for defense and telecommunications systems. But only STC (the strategic planning company) made the decision to compete in the international market by building businesses in Europe and the United States and moving into the production of integrated circuits. Plessey chose to specialize rather than expand, while GEC essentially turned its back on the business because the profit returns in the industry were cyclical and low overall.

Good as this management style may sound, however, it is not without drawbacks. Chief among them are the motivation problems that often plague line managers. Because so many people are involved in planning, with each trying to stamp his or her own view on the outcome, the process can be cumbersome, frustrating, and costly. Line managers may become demoralized when their strategy choices are rejected or changed. They may possess little ownership of the decisions being made about the business ostensibly in their charge, and they may resent superiors for being bossy. The comment of a division manager in one

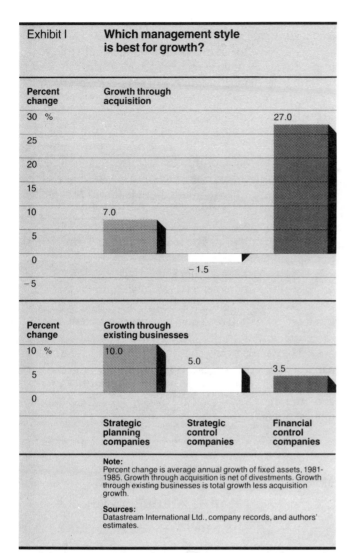

Exhibit I   Which management style is best for growth?

Growth through acquisition

Percent change		
30 %		
25		27.0
20		
15		
10	7.0	
5		
0	−1.5	
−5		

Growth through existing businesses

Percent change		
10 %	10.0	
5	5.0	3.5
0		
	Strategic planning companies	Strategic control companies	Financial control companies

Note:
Percent change is average annual growth of fixed assets, 1981-1985. Growth through acquisition is net of divestments. Growth through existing businesses is total growth less acquisition growth.

Sources:
Datastream International Ltd., company records, and authors' estimates.

strategic planning company is typical: "In this organization, if you ask the CEO for advice, you'll get instruction." In response, business managers often become protective of their decisions and try to avoid situations in which they have to defend their policies and methods.

The loss of autonomy at the business-unit level is particularly troublesome when the distance between headquarters and the market is great. If central managers misunderstand the environment or lose touch with the business, bold investments can become risky ventures that impose harsh consequences on the company. Cadbury, Lex, and STC have all experienced setbacks in their expansion strategies, and each company saw its aggregate earnings decline as a result. BP, BOC, and UB have suffered heavy losses from some of their unsuccessful ventures.

Diminished flexibility is another characteristic weakness of the strategic planning style. The extensive decision-making process inhibits the company's ability to respond quickly to changing market needs or environmental conditions. Business units do not easily jump into emerging markets or close unprofitable operations.

Companies that use this style support losing strategies for too long. Headquarters can be slow to change its mind because it is invested in a particular plan or doesn't fully understand the factors involved. We encountered businesses or divisions that have performed poorly for five or even ten years and yet are still asking headquarters for one more chance to get the long-term strategy right. This problem is particularly acute in highly diversified corporations, because it's so hard to fully understand each business. For this reason, successful strategic planning companies tend to focus on a few core businesses, divesting those that don't fit into their main areas.

Better financials, less innovation

The "financial control" style is almost a reverse image of the strategic planning style (see the ruled insert, "The Styles Matrix"). Responsibility for strategy development rests squarely on the shoulders of business unit managers. Headquarters does not formally review strategic plans. Instead, it exerts influence through short-term budgetary control. The objective is to get the business units to put forward tough but achievable profit targets that will provide both a high return on capital and year-to-year growth.

The greatest value of the financial control style is the motivation it gives managers to improve financial performance immediately. Targets are clear and unequivocal. Investment paybacks are short. Performance is monitored carefully. Variances against plan invoke penetrating questions from the top and speedy action from the bottom. Companies set up this way don't buffer managers from financial pressures. Rather, they impose a more demanding and penetrating discipline than the capital market itself. All of this leads to strong profit performance, at least in the short term.

The results of our study support this assertion. As *Exhibit II* shows, the financial control companies—BTR, Ferranti, GEC, Hanson Trust, Tarmac—have, on average, higher profitability ratios (return on sales, return on capital) than the other companies. They are also better at rationalizing poor performing businesses quickly and turning around new acquisitions.

Other strong points of the financial control style are less obvious. First, it has a way of shaking managers loose from ineffective strategies. By setting demanding targets and strictly enforcing them, corporate management constantly challenges plans that are

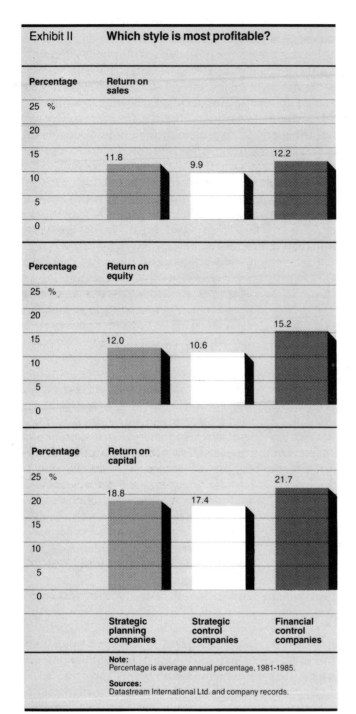

Exhibit II **Which style is most profitable?**

Percentage — Return on sales

Percentage — Return on equity

Percentage — Return on capital

Strategic planning companies | Strategic control companies | Financial control companies

Note:
Percentage is average annual percentage, 1981-1985.

Sources:
Datastream International Ltd. and company records.

producing poor results. Corporate doesn't go so far as to suggest alternatives, but it provides the impetus for business managers to break away from strategies that aren't working.

Second, the financial control style is good for developing executives. Assigning profit responsibility to the lowest possible level gives potential high fliers general management experience early in their careers. Those who succeed have years of experience and results to call on by the time they reach the top. Those less suited to general management tasks are

identified early and weeded out before they do damage to the company.

Survivors in the financial control system know they have been tested against the toughest benchmarks of performance. This knowledge gives them a great sense of achievement and self-confidence to push their businesses forward as they see fit. This "winner's psychology" creates decisive, ambitious leadership. As Graeme Odgers, former group managing director at Tarmac, commented, "Pure logic would argue that managers will set a low budget, to make life easy. But if they do, we make them feel that they've let the team down, that they're not ambitious enough to be part of the group. For the most part, our problem lies in the other direction. The managers have so much faith in themselves that they think they can do anything."

This winner's psychology improves the quality of the dialogue between headquarters and the business general managers. Business managers with a track record of delivering will argue their views more forcefully and with less concern about pleasing the boss. They understand that their progress in the company depends on the results they achieve, not on their eloquence in meetings. "It's their business, their budget—and their heads that are on the block," explained one manager.

To maximize profits, let unit managers set the course.

One final strength of the financial control style is its effectiveness with highly diversified portfolios. Corporate executives need not have an intimate knowledge of each unit's competitors and marketplace. Because the business units develop their own strategies, headquarters can manage through the relevant ratios by comparing performance among different businesses. "We peer at the businesses through the numbers," explained a manager at GEC.

One shortcoming of this system is its bias against strategies and investments with long lead times and paybacks. At a minimum, this makes financial control companies vulnerable to aggressive, committed competitors that can tolerate a long-term view. In essence, that's what happened to BTR, which gave up a strong position in the belting business because it was reluctant to invest aggressively in new technology. Rather than follow the trend to plastic belting (which captured more than 50% of the market), BTR chose to develop a niche position in steel cord belting and thus forfeited its market share to competitors.

The styles matrix

The strategic planning, strategic control, and financial control styles form part of a continuum of ways headquarters can influence business units. The continuum has two dimensions: (1) planning influence, which expresses the degree to which strategy is centralized, and (2) control influence, which shows the importance companies attach to short-term financial targets.

Companies that fall in the bottom left-hand corner can be labeled holding companies. In such organizations the center has little influence over the subsidiaries. Our research found that successful companies moved away from the holding company style to one of the three alternatives.

The top right-hand corner of the matrix is blank because this style appears to be infeasible. Some companies in our research tried to combine a high degree of planning influence with tight short-term controls, but they have moved away from it. Either business-unit managers became demotivated by a seemingly oppressive corporate center or headquarters failed to maintain sufficient objectivity to keep the controls tight.

Strategic management styles

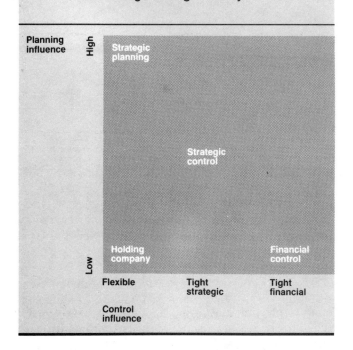

vents healthy business development. When we asked managers from Hanson and BTR how they respond to Japanese competitors, they replied almost in unison, "They are good competitors to avoid."

The failure to back aggressive strategies means that growth in financial control companies comes more from acquisition than from internal development (see *Exhibit I*). Despite the highly successful record of companies like Hanson and BTR, there are limits to how far acquisition-based growth can be taken. Given Hanson's current size, for instance, few potential targets would make much impact on the company's overall financial performance.

Another drawback to this system is the difficulty decentralized strategy has in exploiting potential synergies between business units. In theory, of course, this problem can be solved by redefining the business units so that two linked businesses are viewed as one. But in fact, it's much more common for financial control companies to tear businesses apart in the quest to weed out low-profit activities. Moreover, few units in financial control companies try to build coordinated global positions. More often, they focus on segments or niches and avoid integrated strategies across a broad business area.

Finally, rigorous control systems limit the flexibility of financial control organizations. Blind adherence to last year's budget targets can preclude adaptive strategies and advantageous moves. Particularly in businesses where circumstances change rapidly, controls can become a straitjacket, and opportunities can be missed.

More balance, less clarity

Companies that follow a "strategic control" style aim to capture the advantages of the other two while avoiding their weaknesses. In practice, however, the tensions involved in balancing control and decentralization make this style of management the hardest to execute because it creates ambiguity.

At best, a strategic control system accommodates both the need to build a business and the need to maximize financial performance. Responsibility for strategy rests with the business and division managers. But strategies must be approved by headquarters. For this purpose, there is an elaborate planning process. Corporate executives use the planning reviews to test logic, to pinpoint weak arguments, and to encourage businesses to raise the quality of their strategic thinking. They also judge whether or not the appropriate balance is being struck between investing to build a business and pushing for short-term financial per-

Similarly, Hanson Trust passed up a proposal from one business unit to produce a promising generation of new products because corporate decision makers found the seven- to eight-year payback too hard to deal with. (Indeed, they sold the business shortly thereafter.) Pushed to extremes, therefore, the financial control style can lead to milking businesses for purely short-term gains and to excessive risk aversion that preformance, often with the use of portfolio planning systems.

Financial targets are set in a separate budgeting process. The strategic plan and the budget sometimes pull in opposite directions, and one or the other may have to give. One manager commented, "It's normal for risky investments to drop out of the plan as it gets turned into the budget." It is this tension between the plan and the budget that helps to maintain a balance between new development ideas and cash generation.

A balanced approach is the toughest to pull off.

Once headquarters has approved a plan and a budget, it attempts to monitor businesses against strategic milestones, such as market share, as well as budgeted performance. The tension between strategic milestones and financial ratios, along with that between the planning and budgeting systems, creates uncertainty and ambiguity. Every business in the portfolio wants to be viewed as a growth prospect. Yet some must be cash cows. As a result, objectives can become confused and the planning process can be a political platform.

The performance of the strategic control companies we studied – Courtaulds, Imperial Chemical Industries (ICI), Imperial Group, Plessey, Vickers – shows the results of this balanced approach. As *Exhibits I* and *III* display, these companies had, in general, less internal growth than strategic planning companies, but they achieved substantial improvement in their profitability ratios. Long-term development is traded for short-term financial gains.

Some business units do, of course, pursue long-term strategies aimed at building major positions. The pharmaceutical division of ICI and the international paints division of Courtaulds made systematic, long-term investments and are among the greatest success stories in British industry. For the most part, however, the strategic control companies are focused on cleaning up the portfolio. Large investments and acquisitions, so important to the business-building strategies of strategic planning companies, are rare, ICI's recent acquisition of Stauffer being an exception. These companies have investigated many acquisitions, but few have come to fruition.

Further, although headquarters cares about financial results, it is less ruthless than with financial control in driving to raise performance. As with strategic planning companies, "strategic" arguments

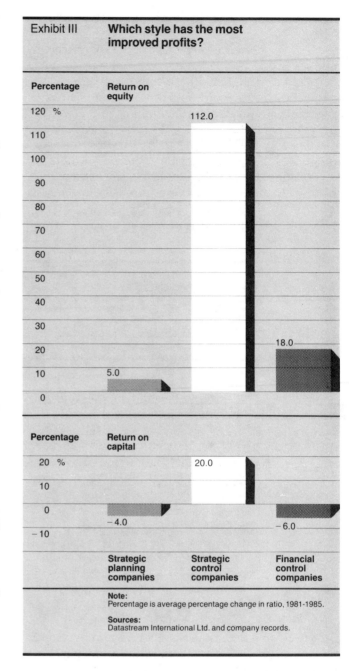

Exhibit III   Which style has the most improved profits?

Percentage	Return on equity		
	Strategic planning companies	Strategic control companies	Financial control companies
	5.0	112.0	18.0

Percentage	Return on capital		
	Strategic planning companies	Strategic control companies	Financial control companies
	−4.0	20.0	−6.0

Note:
Percentage is average percentage change in ratio, 1981-1985.

Sources:
Datastream International Ltd. and company records.

(or excuses) have allowed less profitable businesses to operate at unsatisfactory levels of return for too long. For example, Imperial Group took more than five years to bite the bullet and dispose of the Howard Johnson chain, which severely depressed corporate earnings during the early 1980s.

One of the benefits of the style is that business unit managers are motivated by the freedom and responsibility they are given. The chairman of a Vickers division explained: "Giving freedom like this is a bit nerve-racking at times because you feel you're not in control. But if you always ask questions and monitor things at the center, the unit managers act as though they're not really responsible for the decisions.

If something goes wrong it's as much your fault as theirs."

Another advantage of the style is that it can cope with diversity. Because headquarters decentralizes strategy and tailors the controls to the needs of the business, it can manage a broad range of businesses in different circumstances. But doing so is not easy. And managed badly, diversity can lead to superficial planning. One manager echoed many others when he complained that in his company there are "a whole series of rakings-over at different levels—all of them too shallow." In these circumstances managers lower down are likely to lose the benefits of freedom and responsibility and become demotivated.

What trade-offs are right for your company?

The main disadvantage of the style is that the strategic and financial objectives, the long- and short-term goals, make accountability less clear-cut and create ambiguity. Business unit managers can be uncertain whether they should be putting forward aggressive growth plans or tight performance plans. They can be too cautious about high-growth businesses and too soft on mature lines.

This ambiguity is compounded by the difficulty of establishing strategic goals. If strategic goals are not easily measured, excuses for poor performance can't be tested and managers become confused about how they will be evaluated. The only real measures of performance then become financial. At its worst, the style becomes an ineffective form of financial control in which time is spent on planning without any tangible benefits and in which achieving planned objectives takes second place to impressing the boss.

The right fit

As we've seen, there are at least three ways to divide responsibility between corporate executives and business unit managers. We believe these different styles exist because of certain tensions implicit in the role of corporate management. Virtually all executives want strong leadership from the center, coordinated strategies that build in a variety of viewpoints, careful analysis of decisions, long-term thinking, and flexibility. But they also want autonomy for unit managers, clear accountability, the freedom to respond entrepreneurially to opportunities, superior short-term results, and tight controls.

The two sets of wishes are contradictory. Central leadership, if it has any teeth, inhibits business autonomy. Coordinated strategies detract from personal accountability. Thorough reviews preclude quick entrepreneurial responses. Long-term plans compromise short-term performance. Flexibility is at odds with precise adherence to planned objectives.

Successful corporations make trade-offs between these choices and draw on the combination that best fits the businesses in their portfolios. Is it worth sacrificing tight control and individual responsibility to build up core businesses? Do the benefits of clear goals and devolved responsibility outweigh the dangers of risk aversion and short-term thinking? Can managers cope with the ambiguity needed to achieve a balanced approach across a diverse portfolio? The answers depend on the very things top management knows best—the characteristics of its businesses and the people who make them work. ▽

Reprint 87604

Uses and misuses of strategic planning

Daniel H. Gray

There's nothing wrong with formal strategic planning— if you do it right

It has become fashionable to attack formal strategic planning as a source of corporate America's competitive ills. Recent management best-sellers and the business press are vocal in criticizing companies for adhering to excessively rational planning systems that are time-consuming to complete, divorced from reality, and worst of all, conducive to a dangerous, short-term financial orientation in top managers.

Yet for all these criticisms, this commentator points out that most corporate executives and business unit managers continue to practice—and value—strategic planning. The concept itself isn't the problem, according to the executives surveyed and interviewed. Rather, planning systems often break down because of faulty preparation and implementation. Well-managed companies can overcome these problems, says the author, by involving line managers in the planning process, defining business units correctly, outlining action steps in detail, and integrating the strategic plan with other organizational controls.

Mr. Gray is president and chief executive officer of Gray-Judson, Inc., a consulting firm based in Boston that specializes in strategic management.

Some writers on management today claim that strategic planning is on the wane—or at least on the defensive. Is yet another management fad about to fade away? Are we seeing still another example that shows the folly of trying to manage in "too rational" a way? Consider all those companies that have spent so much money on strategic planning yet still have problems. And look at all those impressive plans that fall apart during implementation.

Though it seems as if strategic planning is on the way out in some companies because of faulty diagnosis of its defects, I would say, on the basis of my research and experience, that reports of its demise are exaggerated and premature.

Strategic planning as many textbooks describe it may not be around much longer but not for the reasons most critics give. If formal strategic planning vanishes in a few years, it will be because wherever it is undertaken it either gets better or it gets worse, depending on how well it's done: if you do it poorly, either you drop out or you rattle around in its mechanics; if you do it well, you evolve beyond strategic planning to strategic management.

Strategic planning is usually seen, on adoption, as a separate discipline or a management function. It involves the allocation of resources to programmed activities calculated to achieve a set of business goals in a dynamic, competitive environment. Strategic management, on the other hand, treats strategic thinking as a pervasive aspect of running a business and regards strategic planning as an instrument around which all other control systems—budgeting, information, compensation, organization—can be integrated. This interdependency usually comes to light when a business has trouble implementing the results of a freestanding strategic planning process.

These distinctions and definitions emerged from a year-long research project that focused on where things most often go wrong in "good" strategic planning systems and what has been learned about shoring up these weak spots. In this research my colleagues and I have contacted a broad sample of business unit heads, corporate planning directors, and chief executive officers engaged in strategic planning in American multibusiness corporations. We used a questionnaire to pinpoint where things have gone wrong and conducted 14 executive seminars to search for remedies (see *Exhibit I* and *Exhibit II*). To date there have been 300 respondents to the questionnaire and 216 participants in the day-and-a-half seminars.

At this point we can report the following findings:

☐   First, most companies in our sample remain firmly committed to strategic planning, even though 87% report feelings of disappointment and frustration with their systems.

☐   Second, 59% attribute their discontent mainly to difficulties encountered in the implementation of plans.

☐   Third, when multibusiness executives compare their experiences, 67% trace their implementation problems to the design of their systems and the way they manage them.

While implementation failures have for some been the cause of frustration and withdrawal, such experiences have helped others learn to run their planning systems better. Consider the "Gamma Corporation," a provider of upscale women's garments, jewelry, luggage, and cosmetics whose growth curve had flattened out. To recover, it acquired a related but embryonic service business with apparel and cosmetic appendages. The service business became a new Gamma profit center, while its appendages were assimilated into kindred profit centers of the parent. The corporate requirement that the new service business match the profit and cost control performance of the established business made rapid sales growth an imperative.

The hotshot, upscale marketer who was given the entrepreneurial opportunity to make something of the service unit tried to accomplish this through dress pattern and cosmetic giveaways. When sister profit centers blocked this move, he missed his targets and quit. The Gamma strategy to rejuvenate a low-growth company with a vigorous new synergistic service acquisition was the company's maiden voyage into strategic planning. The verdict at corporate headquarters was that the plan "fell apart through poor implementation."

After an extensive audit of this implementation failure, Gamma executives perceived that their strategy had been deeply flawed well before implementation: the company had made only a financial evaluation of the acquisition candidate. The new retail service unit was a poorly designed strategy center. It

| Exhibit I | **Topics and responses in the evaluation of strategic planning systems in U.S. multibusiness companies** |

Topic	Response
Source of greatest frustration or disappointment	Implementation difficulties
Other areas of major concern	Skills of line managers Adequacy of information
Rating of current planning system on a scale of 1 to 10, from worst to best	56 % in 6-7-8 range Mode: 7 Mean: 5.5
Nature of planning output	General direction or thrust for strategic action
Locus of planning responsibility	Line managers: 78 %
Relation to budget process	Planning first, budgeting afterward: 55 %
Sources of market information	In-house: 80 %
Number of strategic business units (SBUs)	Range from 6 to 48
Basis of unit definition	Product lines: 57 %
Relation of SBUs to profit centers	Coincide: 51 %
How unit goals and objectives are set	Top–down: 33 % Bottom–up: 67 %
Who owns an SBU's cash flow	Corporation: 83 %
Unit strategy development process	Interdepartmental group give-and-take: 34 %
Linkage of planning to other controls	More to budgets than anything else: 42 %
Impact of strategic planning on organizational structure	Structure often adapted to support strategy: 70 %
Relationship of executive bonuses to strategic performance	Financial results only: 60 % Financial and strategic mix: 22 %
Authority of groups or divisions over SBU planning	Not significant: 68 % Controlling: 32 %
Corporate resource allocation process when resource requests exceed resources available	Perceived as unfair: 49 % Perceived as fair: 37 %

was lodged in the same organization with mature wholesale product businesses. Its best strategic options were preempted by an inappropriate financial strategy. There was no portfolio strategy to reconcile the new unit with others. The new unit head was not allowed to behave entrepreneurially. The company had no detailed action plan to mesh the new and old business strategies.

The Gamma Corporation and many other companies have stuck to their strategic plans in spite of their frustrations. Their persistence is rooted in the needs that led them to adopt strategic planning in the first place. They have come to realize that steering a business by financial controls alone is not enough. However vital the bottom line, balance sheet feedback is too lumpy, too stripped of connotative information, and often too late. Financial plans must be augmented and supplemented by strategic plans if managers are to make more timely and accurate midcourse corrections in response to external change. The competitive penalty for inability to adapt along the way is too great for most companies to do without strategic planning.

Another reason that companies persist in planning despite disappointment is evident in the way many respondents to our questionnaire rated their planning systems. On a scale of 1 to 10 (1 meaning worst and 10 meaning best), the modal rating (7) accounted for 27% of all responses. This rating was assigned to any system considered to be excellent for clarification of where one wants to go but not very good in execution. This finding suggests a view of planning as a two-part process – a strategy development part and a strategy execution part. One can then look with approval on strategy development and with disapproval on strategy execution. This allows strategy developers to view themselves as the victims of the poor work of implementers lower down in the organization and to overlook the crucial role that strategy development plays in determining whether a plan can be implemented.

Common problems & workable solutions

When chief executives, corporate planning directors, and business unit heads in our sample got together to discuss common problems, we observed that they tended to have second thoughts about how good their planning systems are, what is wrong with them, and where and how to put things right. (For a sample of what they said, see the ruled insert.) Two-thirds of what these managers called implementation difficulties were, on closer scrutiny, attributed to these six preimplementation factors:

1   Poor preparation of line managers.

2   Faulty definition of business units.

3   Vaguely formulated goals.

4   Inadequate information bases for action planning.

5   Badly handled reviews of business unit plans.

6   Inadequate linkage of strategic planning with other control systems.

Exhibit II	**Executive seminar participants**				
Management level			**Industry type**		
Corporate executives	91	42 %	Service businesses	89	41 %
Corporate planning directors and staff	85	39	Manufacturing businesses	111	52
Business unit managers	40	19	Government agencies	16	7
Total	216	100 %	Total	216	100 %

The uncovering of these design and management errors can lead to new insights about how to avoid many implementation problems. In this article, we examine several of them. There are undoubtedly more to be uncovered in the ongoing search for the most effective principles of strategic planning. (See *Exhibit III* for some suggestions.)

Involve line managers

It does little good to allocate planning responsibility to line managers if they receive no preparation or poor preparation for this key role.

At a major aerospace and automotive supplier, for example, managers complained that a sophisticated planning system had failed to "come alive" and that formal business unit plans were lying "unused in bottom drawers." Recently, four years into their system and just after making a major acquisition, the company convened more than 40 heads of strategic business units (SBUs) to teach them the skills that strategic planning requires. Picture a week-long conference in posh surroundings: visiting management gurus doing star turns; reprints of landmark cases describing classic acquisition assimilation problems; workshops where messages from the participants to the corporate hierarchy could be hammered out; and, at the end of the week, a flying visit from the CEO to talk about his vision of the future. Total cost: more than $250,000. Result: last-minute watering-down of the messages, a 60-day fade-out of the experience, and no significant change in behavior.

It is now widely accepted that strategic planning is a line management function in which staff specialists play a supporting role. Yet many companies have done little to prepare line managers for this kind of leadership. When they are left to grope for the operational meaning of concepts like "strategic mindset," "issue formulation," "conflict management," and

Exhibit III	Some principles for strategic planning

Strategic planning is a line management function for which training in strategic analysis and participative skills is usually necessary.

Strategic business units need to be defined so that one executive can control the key variables essential to the execution of his or her strategic business plan.

A unit's concept of the business it is in must above all be formulated from the outside in so that it can most effectively engage the dynamics of its strategic environment.

Action plans for achieving business objectives are the key to implementing and monitoring strategy. They require extensive lower-level participation and special leadership skills. Action plans are complete when underlying assumptions, allocation of responsibilities, time and resource requirements, risks, and likely responses have been made explicit.

Participative strategy development, a prerequisite for successful strategy execution, often requires cultural change at the upper levels of corporations and their business units.

The strategic planning system and other control systems designed to guide managerial and organizational behavior must be integrated in a consistent whole if business strategies are to be executed well.

Productivity improvement programs are best treated as aspects of strategic business plans since productivity takes on significantly different meanings as the strategic balance between marketing and production shifts.

Well-managed organizations must be both centralized and decentralized – centralized so that strategies and control systems can be integrated and decentralized so that units in each strategic environment can act and be treated with appropriate differentiation.

Over time, good strategic planning, once considered a separate activity, becomes a mindset, a style and a set of techniques for running a business – not something more to do but a better way of doing what has always had to be done.

"portfolio role," they feel ill at ease. Strategic planning seems more like a burden imposed from above than a better way of running their units. Not surprisingly, some of these line managers adopt a modest, mechanical approach to their planning duties. Then staff planners may creep back in to lend a hand and help fill the void.

Line managers in charge of business units say they want coaching in the skills required to guide strategy debates. They want to know how to draw department heads out of their specialized frames of reference and into a general management view of trade-offs between functions. They want to know what questions will be asked and what challenges to expect when they send their business plans up for approval.

Some companies have tried to help their unit heads by offering them quick-fix management development courses – often with disappointing results. A great deal of management development training is still carried on with generic or hypothetical case materials and with packages of received wisdom presented to groups of peers. Such training may be valuable, but it usually does not replicate the real conditions facing the line management strategist.

A better practice is to focus on real problems in managers' own companies so as to see the trouble in its current strategic context. This opportunity to learn how to be more flexible and adaptive (and to learn about learning) should be offered not as a gift but as part of a transaction – this assistance in exchange for that change in behavior. It should be offered to groups representing the various functions and levels whose cooperation is needed to solve tough problems.

An example of a company that successfully involved line managers in planning is a manufacturer of electronic components in the Sunbelt. Facing an urgent need to offset price declines with cost reductions, the company assembled a 25-person training squad of managers ranging from the level of superintendent to that of divisional chief operating officer. With the help of a process facilitator and with engineering, marketing, and personnel staff on call, the training squad was charged to explore the rationale, the feasibility and cost, the potential savings, and the cultural consequences of four options – asset reduction, productivity gain sharing, plant rationalization, and operator training – and then to recommend a remedial action program. Four of the twelve lowest ranking members of the team would be chosen for promotion and training roles in their own or other plants. In the end, the squad's plan was accepted, three men were promoted, and divisional operating costs dropped 17% in the ensuing six months.

Define the business unit

Even when its boundaries are strategically correct, a business unit is vulnerable to an outmoded conceptualization of the business it is in. Consider the difference between being a brewer of beer and being a seller of beer in English pubs. Under either category, the assets, products, markets, people, and functions are the same; but there is a world of difference in the kind of strategy developed, the direction of people's energies, the priorities of action, the indicators to be monitored, and the places where profit is taken. In one case, beer production is all-important; in the other, beer is fourth or fifth in importance in the customer's purchase decision. In an aging, oligopolistic industry with excess capacity, Courage Breweries' shift from a supply-side mindset to a consumer life-style mindset helped break open a stalemated industry's market share equilibrium and improve profits.

How a strategy center or an SBU conceives of its business can have a significant bearing on its strategic behavior and its competitive clout. Management's attitude toward a business is as important as its boundaries. For example, a manufacturer of rubber and plastic control devices and assemblies saw its business flatten out under a definition of itself as a company that supplies "these specific products to these specific industries." While continuing to make large batches of flow valves and gaskets for automobile and appliance makers, the manufacturer began to diagnose and treat the precision-molding process control problems of manufacturers in general. To its single-tier, high-volume, production-driven product line the company added an R&D and marketing-driven premium-price line.

If a multibusiness fails to define its strategy centers or its strategic business units correctly, the best planning techniques available can't undo the damage. When strategic planning is newly installed, it is often assumed that the organizational units already in place should handle the planning. These units, however, may owe their boundaries to many factors that make them inappropriate to use as a basis for planning: geography, administrative convenience, the terms of old acquisition deals, product lines, traditional profit centers, a belief in healthy internal competition, or old ideas about centralization and decentralization.

Frequently these familiar rationales for unit boundaries make for poor strategy centers. That they could be wrong may not occur to executives who take organizational structure as a given before planning begins. But strategic planning teaches its more successful practitioners that the main purpose of organization (including both structure and process) is to support the development and execution of strategy. Thus organization should come after strategic planning.

The following principles should guide the definition of business units:

☐   Include within the jurisdiction of the strategy center all variables the unit head needs for executing the strategy. For example, it may not be wise to require a manager charged with opening up new markets for a cluster of products to buy manufacturing and distribution services from sister profit centers.

☐   Leave the unit head free to take profits where strategy dictates. Hence nothing smaller than a strategy center should be a profit center.

☐   Let external rather than internal forces shape unit boundaries. If competitive forces require a larger unit than normal spans of control would dictate, go with the larger unit.

☐   When separate units are strategically appropriate for external reasons but must, for economies of scale, share central facilities and services, let them share, but keep them as separate units. A Texas chemical company, for example, decided against combining the planning processes of its generic and specialized businesses. Although they share a common infrastructure, their customers and competitors are so different that the managers of these businesses could never agree on a common strategy.

We've come to praise strategic planning, not to bury it.

Quotes from postseminar self-evaluation sheets

"We expected too much of strategic planning and were disappointed. Now we know that planning is part of a larger process, and mastering *that* is fulfilling our expectations."

– Corporate planning officer, insurance company

"I can't conceive of doing business without a strategy and a plan. Every company has to do it. Either you get to be good at it, or you do it poorly and suffer the consequences."

– Chief executive officer, diversified manufacturer

"What we had was a kind of strategic rain dance – war cries, smoke signals, sacrificial offerings. We're much more thorough and disciplined now – more analytical and more demanding of ourselves."

– President, retail division, clothing business

"We actually used to tell ourselves our planning system was OK, even though we admitted it fell apart in implementation. That was our way of telling ourselves that the trouble was not at the top."

– Head of a strategic business unit in a 17-unit corporation

"The way to get into a planning bind is to go at everything piecemeal....First the organization chart – that's done....Then the plan – that's done. ...Then the budget – that's done....The bonus system – that's done....All that hard work and then nothing fits."

– Executive vice president, health care holding company

"When you have two rival plans – a strategic business plan and a financial plan – either you dovetail them or before long the strategic plan and the will to do it are dead."

– Financial director, department store chain

While the application of these principles of unit definition is crucial to good strategy development and execution, they can conflict with one another. As a practical matter, therefore, these principles cannot serve as absolutes. In the end, boundary setting is an executive judgment call but not a purely subjective one. The final judgment can be either adaptive, in which case the boundaries line up with the realities of the prevailing strategic game, or willful, in which case the company accepts the risks of trying to change the way the external game is played.

Failure to address the unit definition question at all or to address it without giving due weight to the external environment can lead to serious problems. Looking first at the environment, however, is by itself no guarantee of success. A rule often used in unit boundary setting is one product, one manager. This is meant to ensure direct accountability and single-minded strategic concentration on the fate of the product. The penalty for this approach, however, can be the loss of opportunities for discretionary profit taking, synergistic manipulation of related products, marketing cooperation, and economies of scale. The result is often the creation of too many business units too narrow to compete effectively.

Move beyond general goals

Implementation is bound to go awry if strategy formulation goes no further than defining general thrusts and end-point goals. Consider a public utility that adopted a strategy of "energy conservation, high earnings, diversification, and excellence." These four goals were so general that the person in charge of managing each one could unwittingly be at cross-purposes with the others. Field personnel cuts made to improve earnings eliminated the very people needed to run a new diversification venture aimed at saving energy through home and factory audits and retrofits. At the same time, the pursuit of engineering "excellence" led to the purchase of materials that were too durable to mesh with the utility's plan for capacity replacement.

Approximately seven out of ten companies in our sample do not carry the formulation of strategy much beyond some general statement of thrust such as market penetration or internal efficiency and some generalized goal such as excellence. Having only generalizations to work with makes implementation very difficult. Targets don't mean much if no one maps out the pathways leading to them. After this kind of half-baked strategy is handed over for execution, subordinates who have not been in on the formulation of the strategy are left to deal with its cross-impacts and trade-offs when they bump into them. If told only that the name of the strategic game is high quality and prompt delivery, various people in an organization—designers, inspectors, schedulers, piece workers, and salespeople—may each reconcile these two factors differently. Subordinates' efforts are often parochial and improvisational; the way they carry out an undefined strategy is often unsatisfactory—if they elect to complete it at all.

Make more detailed action plans

The cure for half-baked strategy is action detailing, but this task often baffles and irritates many executives. Only one in three of the companies in our study has a process or a forum for the interfunctional debate and testing of unit strategies. Their procedures for action detailing and other kinds of reality testing are often nonexistent or merely rudimentary. Action detailing of a sort is carried on in some places as a part of operational planning, but it usually follows strategic planning and takes the strategy as given. Planning in detail should be used as a further test of a strategy's feasibility.

One way to combine operational and strategic planning is to begin an advocacy process as soon as agreement on strategic thrusts has been reached. An interfunctional task force is set up for each thrust—with strong representation from middle management. Each team can identify and analyze the options for reaching a particular objective and then rough out the major action steps necessary to accomplish the option that it will advocate to the unit strategy team.

The team's job is to explain and defend what it considers the best way of bringing this option to life. Each team must deal with time frame, risk analysis, allocation of responsibility, resource requirements, organization obstacles, and monitoring devices. In mapping out and testing strategic options, managers begin to think explicitly about assumptions, alternatives, contingencies, and what competitive reactions to expect. Failure to come to grips with these details can undermine the execution of the strategy.

When senior executives are invited to try their hands at action detailing, they often find it an uncomfortable exercise. They tend to offer as action steps what are really no more than wishes or desired results—such as "upgrading front-line supervision," "introducing services that appeal to the customer," or "eliminating wasteful practices." Good action detailing, however, requires the participation of middle and lower management and the work force. Top management knows the direction; those below know the terrain. Not only is lower level participation essential to working out practical steps, but it is also highly desirable. Through such participation, managers generate the kind of understanding, ownership, commitment, and motivation necessary for successful implementation. The alternative, which is to try to push strategic planning out into the organization and down through the ranks by exhortation and other forms of one-way "communication," has only minimal effect.

Companies trapped in half thought-out planning may lack the information and motivation necessary to good strategy execution. These companies may avoid the front-end costs of participation, discussion, and explicit detailing, but they pay the cost of not seeing their options, not reaching their goals, and spending days bogged down in implementation.

Manage the face-off

Even when all the steps in the strategy development process are taken according to the principles of best practice, strategic plans can be ruined and the whole system undermined at the final review stage. The issue is how good the design and management of the planning cycle is when the business units' proposed plans hit the corporate screen. We call this crucial encounter managing the face-off.

The face-off is a moment of inevitable, healthy conflict. Not only do all the units' resource requests frequently exceed what headquarters is prepared to provide, but their aggregate performance promises are often less than the corporation as a whole requires. Since performance requirements come from an analysis of capital markets while performance promises arise from strategies for dealing with each business unit's particular environment, this conflict is not surprising.

What should happen at the face-off is reconciliation, which often involves queuing, downsizing, redirection, and recycling. What actually does happen is often rather primitive: exhortation, backdoor dealing, across-the-board cuts, moving the goalposts, and mandated performance promises. In other words, the units' plans are force-fit in various ways into the corporate plan. At this stage of the game, companies normally focus their attention more on the numbers in the business plan than on the strategies. For example, one general manager responsible for an aging product described scaling down his profit projections after a rival company had captured a 4% market share in five months with a generic commodity substitute. This manager's boss, however, ordered the higher profit figures restored and asked him how he expected to win the marketing wars with "negative thinking." Unfortunately, this example is typical. Numbers are often altered at the face-off so as to close the gap without any discussion of the need to revise the risk assessments, competitive reactions, probability estimates, and other problems lying beneath the numbers.

Even if all the units have done their strategic planning very well up to the time of final review, think of the consequences for the next round of planning if they tack new financial projections arbitrarily onto strategies whose predicted effects in a particular competitive environment have already been calculated to be lower. The obligatory promise that headquarters extracts from a subunit may close the gap

for a while, but it will undercut and degrade the next round of planning and budgeting. The force-fit at the face-off is an invitation to play games and a clear signal that scrupulous planning is considered a waste of valuable time.

Only a small minority of the companies we studied (13%) say they have a satisfactory process for managing the face-off. A little over one-third report some attempt at "rigorous trade-off analysis among business units." Among corporate controls, strategic planning is often the new kid on the block. Some executives see strategic planning as challenging financial controls and think of the face-off as the place where financial management supercedes strategic management. In these companies, financial strategy is not reconciled with other strategies but preempts them as the final arbiters of corporate resource allocation.

Integrate plans & controls

A strategic planning system can't achieve its full potential until it is integrated with other control systems such as budgets, information systems, and reward systems. The badly designed, poorly managed face-off is a manifestation of a deeper problem – the "compartmentalization syndrome," which treats various control systems as freestanding and strategically neutral.

While most executives who have adopted strategic planning see it as an indispensable tool, they tend to treat it at first as just another addition to an array of control devices. Before long they may discover that one control is at odds with another. Then the notion of linking these different controls arises, and that is as close as most companies in our study have come to a concept of integrated control. The three linkage problems they frequently identified have to do with plans and budgets, plans and information systems, and plans and reward systems.

Plans and budgets. The conflict between strategic plans and budgets is the most commonly perceived area of dissonance. Managers tend to view the annual planning and budgeting sequence as logically connected but not integrated in fact. While the best strategic planning starts from an environmental analysis and then works in the unit's ability to respond, budgeting usually proceeds by making incremental adjustments to the previous year's internal departmental budgets. This practice allows the momentum of last year's (possibly obsolete) business strategy and this year's functional strategies to determine the funding of this year's business unit plan.

The absence of strategic action planning often thwarts those who want to integrate plans and budgets. Not until a company has formulated explicit action steps can it cast fixed capital, working capital, operating expense, and revenue and head-count implications in the form of strategy-based budgets. Most CEOs yearn for such budgets so that they can see how their strategies, not just their departments, are doing. But the same CEOs often report that they are told such budgets are not possible without disrupting the whole accounting system.

Plans and information systems.

Many strategic planners in the units and at the top of multi-business corporations express concern about the adequacy of their planning information bases and decision support systems. They worry about linking poor information bases with sophisticated computers. Even accurate, timely, and accessible information will not help the planner if it leads to an inappropriate strategy.

For example, a manufacturer of components for automobiles, appliances, medical equipment, and the like once developed a sophisticated data base for manpower planning that it can no longer use. The company's well-stocked management information system displays on demand how many machinists–white and black, male and female, high school educated and not–live within 30 minutes' commuting distance of its plant in New Jersey. The trouble is, the competition has changed, so that the company cannot be globally cost competitive unless it bases its production in Europe or Asia.

Like many businesses, this company based its strategy on data that had accumulated in response to questions raised by its financial managers and its technical and professional specialists, whose expertise was too narrow. The information system drove the strategy instead of the other way around. Strategy is what makes a fact relevant or irrelevant, and a relevant fact significant or insignificant.

Corporate CEOs and their business unit heads are the ones who must raise the issues, ask the questions, and formulate the business definitions, missions, objectives, and strategies that will drive their decision support systems. With today's information technology, it is possible to move in the right or the wrong strategic direction with great speed.

Plans and reward systems.

When companies design reward systems as separate, freestanding controls, they may overlook the fact that such controls are not strategically neutral. For example, a strategy for competitive survival required a Tennessee manufacturer of temperature control devices to put expensive new assets in place to bring out a new version of a fading product. Its management had less than a year to realize the six-figure bonuses they would receive under a three-year average ROI payout formula. The head-on collision of a strategy that increased the asset base at the expense of reducing executive bonuses delayed the strategy's implementation for five months.

Many companies have witnessed the quiet destruction of a two- or a three-year strategy while their executives protected their first-year profit-sharing bonuses. It is folly to appeal to managers' self-interest with rewards for behavior other than the kind the strategic business plan calls for, and it is naive to expect them to override the powerful incentives that reward systems evoke.

The primacy of strategic planning

No organizational arrangement, control system, or productivity program is strategically neutral. Strategic planning becomes the device for consistently lining up such factors.

Among companies exploring the problem of integrated control systems, the idea is taking shape that strategic planning can serve as the core control instrument of a business enterprise, with other controls adjusted and adapted to facilitate the execution of strategy. Why this emphasis on strategic planning? Because of all control devices, it is the one that is driven by the business environment. Strategic planning comes before the final results are known, determines whether profit will be taken now or later, and decides which facts are relevant. While financial controls are obviously indispensable, the feedback they give is often too aggregated, too homogenized, and too late–not to mention too conservative of past business practices.

With strategic planning, the concept of integrated, or fused, controls goes further than the reconciliation of budgets, rewards, and decision support systems. As the unifying role of strategy in running a business becomes clear, we see that getting control over the productivity of a business is not strategically neutral either. It is apparent that in embryonic and growth industries productivity should refer to such things as market response time and market penetration, even if the price of these achievements is some internal inefficiency or postponed profit.

A leading paint manufacturer once lost volume by holding a price umbrella over its competitors and then seeking to restore falling margins through a productivity drive in every department of every plant. The company learned that the price cuts it made to restore volume and raise plant utilization above the break-even point did eight times as much for productivity as a $3 million waste elimination campaign had done earlier.

Seen as part of strategy, productivity is not exclusively concerned with physical input and output ratios or even with current net revenue. Productivity is keyed to the intended outcome of a business plan. Sometimes the intended outcome is profit today, in which case productivity may mean moving down the experience curve. Sometimes the goal is profit tomorrow, in which case productivity may mean pre-empting rivals and buying shares for future payback. Traditional corporate productivity czars presiding over programs that treat all business units alike can kill growth units before they ever get to the mature stage, when low-cost strategies are appropriate.

Finally, effective strategic planning that reflects the importance of integrated controls also takes organizational structure into account. For example, their strategic planning experience is enabling some executives to rethink the age-old problem of whether to centralize or decentralize management. Everyone knows that centralization inhibits the motivation of decision makers on the periphery of large organizations. In a multibusiness setup, centralization can lead to passive or reactive unit leadership. It is also widely understood that decentralization frequently leads to highly energetic policies and behaviors that may be suboptimal from the corporate viewpoint. Many companies trying to escape this apparent dilemma have swung back and forth between centralization and decentralization.

Now there appears to be a way out: multibusiness strategic planning clearly calls for both centralization and decentralization. No strategic corporate portfolio management and resource allocation rationale can exist without bringing the family of unit heads together at the center. Similarly, differentiated unit strategies cannot be executed in varying business environments without a process for local advocacy and local discretion in execution. In short, the planning process demands both integration and differentiation. These terms may be more useful and revealing than centralization and decentralization because they leave strategic planners free to decide what needs to be integrated at the center as well as what needs to be differentiated on the periphery and free to set up whatever organizational arrangements best facilitate strategy development, reconciliation, execution, and adaptation.

From this line of reasoning it is a short step to the conclusion that strategic planning, at its leading edge, is really just an aspect of strategic management. From this perspective it no longer makes sense to question people about the merits of their planning systems. What matters is whether their mindsets, their plans, their practices, and their overall controls are coordinated and fit together harmoniously. In the most effective companies I've observed, strategic planning is no longer an added managerial duty. It is a way of thinking about a business and how to run it. ⊟

Reprint 86105

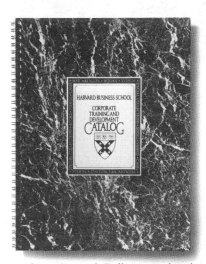